Building a Multi-Use
BARN

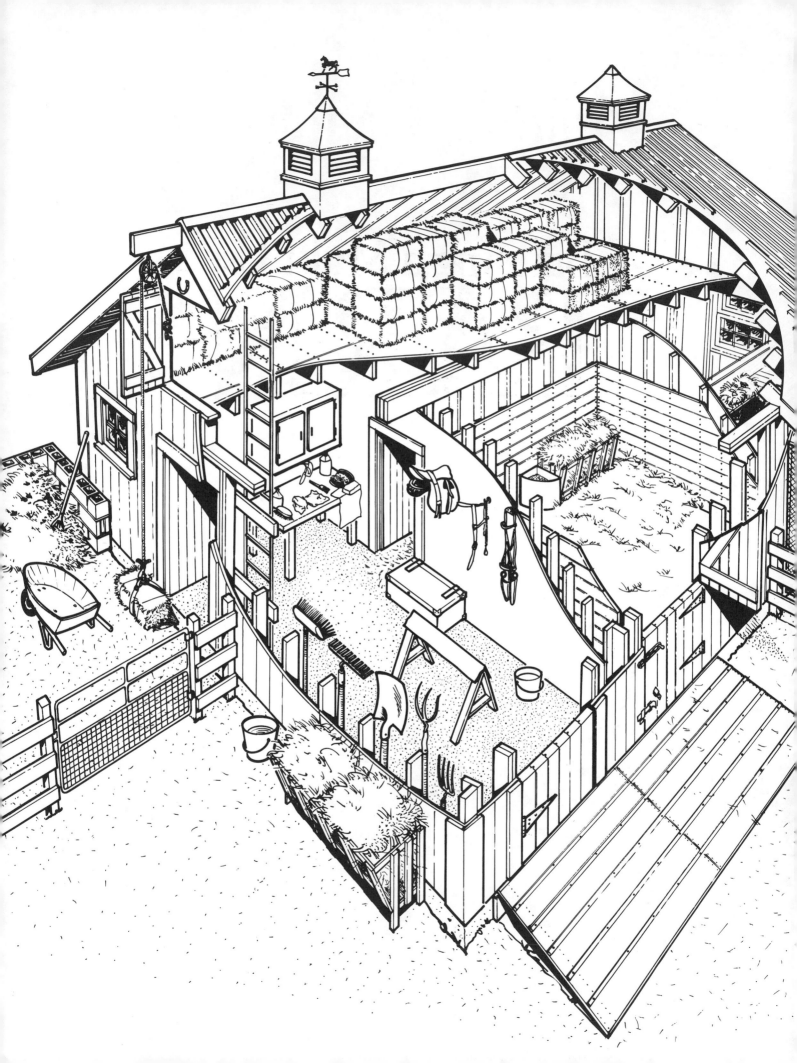

Building a Multi-Use
BARN

FOR GARAGE, ANIMALS, WORKSHOP, STUDIO

JOHN D. WAGNER

WILLIAMSON PUBLISHING COMPANY

CHARLOTTE, VERMONT 05445

ACKNOWLEDGMENTS

This book simply could not have been written without the help and support of Leita Hancock, Clayton DeKorne, Sal Alfano, my editor Bill Jaspersohn, and our illustrator Tim Healey. I'd also like to thank John Puleio, Duffy Gallagher, Susan and Jack Williamson, and my family: Mom, Dad, Carole, Paul, Mark, Chris, Mary Pat, Greg, and the B. Thanks to you all.

Illustrations by **Tim Healey**
Photographs by **Bill Jaspersohn**
Design by **Joseph Lee**
Printing by **Capital City Press**
Indexing by **Paul Kish**
Photographs on pages 7 and 116, courtesy of Laurel Brownell.

Manufactured in the United States
WILLIAMSON PUBLISHING
P.O. Box 185
Charlotte, VT 05445
Telephone: (800) 234-8791
10 9 8 7

Library of Congress Cataloging-in-Publication Data

Wagner, John, 1957–
    Building a multi-use barn for garage, animals, workshop or studio / John Wagner.
    p. cm.
    Includes index.
    ISBN 0-913589-76-4
    1. Barns—Design and construction— Amateurs' manuals. I. Title. TH4930.W34 1994
    690'.8922–dc20   93-43291 CIP

Notice: The information contained in this book is true, complete, and accurate to the best of our knowledge. All recommendations are made without any guarantees on the part of the author or WILLIAMSON PUBLISHING. The author and publisher disclaim all liability incurred in connection with the use of this information.

Building a Multi-Use Barn

Contents

Introduction

The word *barn* derives from combining the word *barley* with the Old English *ern*, which meant *place of*. For centuries the word was *bern;* it's been *barn* since the Late Middle Ages. Over the centuries a barn's uses have expanded way beyond barley storage. Today, a barn can also be a place of tools and seedlings, cars and carpentry, hay and animals, play and puttering.

This book offers a design and approach for building a structurally sound "place" for a wide range of purposes and activities, from a simple workspace to a structure you can finish off for year-round living or any combination therein. As you read, you'll find that each chapter offers basic building strategies for every aspect of a sound structure. But within each chapter you'll find options—different paths to take if you are finishing your barn for one kind of purpose or another. Essentially, then, this book presents the complete basics for building a well-proportioned, all-purpose shell, as well as options for finishing that shell to serve a variety of needs.

Some of you will simply erect the shell, consider the barn done, and regard the sections on finishing the interior spaces as pleasure reading. Others of you who want a more finished structure will read and follow those later sections of the book as well. In all, this book is designed to give each of you appropriate guidelines, whether you intend to raise a few goats on a slab floor and store your gardening tools on rough shelves or are building the carpenter's shop of your

A 24 x 30-foot barn has many uses—as you'll discover once you build your own.

dreams, complete with an upstairs apartment for guests or year-round living.

Whatever your intentions, consider this book a foundation, a beginning. It's a *good* foundation, believe me. But though it contains time-saving tips of the trades and loads of information on structure, building techniques, and products, it should be just one of many books in the builder's library you assemble during the planning stages of your barn. In the same way that you consult different sources, or seek different opinions when you engage in any other process that will take as much time and expense as building a barn, you should seek other sources and examine other building techniques suggested by other builders before committing to one plan of attack. What kind of other sources? There is an old joke about a man who goes to the doctor for a checkup. The doctor says, "You're a very sick man!" The man, who feels great, says, "I'd like a second opinion," "O.k.," says the doctor, "You're ugly, too!" In medicine and barn-building random opinions won't do. You must seek *informed* opinions from solid sources. In the back of this book I've listed some good books and publications that might be helpful to you.

Don't let books be your only source of information, though. Consult other builders; drop by a site where an interesting project is underway. Ask questions of builders. Tell them how you plan on carrying out a certain procedure and see if they have suggestions. Every builder has tips or time-saving techniques to share. Though many books and magazines contain lots of worthwhile information, I have never talked to a good builder without learning something new.

Don't be intimidated. Though some builders or lumberyard help may seem reserved or gruff, once you get them talking about construction, you probably won't be able to stop them. And they're usually loaded with information: lessons learned the hard way, a funny story about building something backwards, or just good, solid advice.

I remember my first day working a concrete job out west years ago, when all I heard was how nasty the concrete foreman was. His name was Weiner and he was indeed a tough guy, from Rifle, Colorado. A real cowboy, he chewed and spit tobacco *while* he smoked cigarettes, and sometimes had two lit at once. I was really intimidated by his bark and how he drove the crew. But on my third day, I looked up and saw him watching me finishing a slab of concrete. "Don't turn your trowel edge up so much, you bring up rocks," he said. After that, he was very forthcoming with information, such as how to test concrete to see if it's cured enough to finish, how to build "log-cabin" forms, how to use a cutting torch, and lots more. He just wanted me to prove my interest before he showed me his. I think you'll find most builders are like that. Show them you want to learn and they'll teach you anything.

Also, don't be afraid to contact manufacturers and ask technical questions about their products or installation techniques. You'd be surprised what resources are available to you, often just by dialing an 800 number.

A source of intimidation for new builders is not knowing the vocabulary of the trade. If right now someone asked you if you used Schedule 40 PVC for your DWV system, or if you used clear VG all heart Western Red Cedar on your siding, you might stammer a bit and say, "Yeah, I think we're planning that for dinner tomorrow night." But after reading this book, you may respond, "No, I went with ABS in the DWV system, and for the siding rough-sawn barn board was cheaper by the board foot." You'll pick up the lingo as you go, but to help you I've defined terms throughout the book and included a very complete index.

No matter what part of the construction process you undertake after reading this book—dreaming, planning, or actually building—you are about to engage in one of the oldest, most satisfying activities known to humankind. After your barn is up, you'll have the additional satisfaction of looking at it and saying to yourself, "Wow, *I* built that place."

Good luck.

ENGLISH TO METRIC CONVERSIONS

inches	×	25.4	= millimeters
feet	×	.3048	= meters
miles	×	1.6093	= kilometers
square inches	×	6.4515	= square centimeters
square feet	×	.0929	= square meters
acres	×	.4047	= hectares
acres	×	.00405	= square kilometers
cubic inches	×	16.3872	= cubic centimeters
cubic feet	×	.02832	= cubic meters
cubic yards	×	.76452	= cubic meters
cubic inches	×	.01639	= liters
U. S. gallons	×	3.7854	= liters
ounces	×	28.35	= grams
pounds	×	.4536	= kilograms
ton (2000 lbs.)	×	.9072	= metric tons (1000 kg.)
lbs. per sq. in. (PSI)	×	.0703	= kg.'s per sq. cm.

METRIC TO ENGLISH CONVERSIONS

millimeters	×	.03937	= inches
meters	×	3.2809	= feet
kilometers	×	.62138	= miles
square centimeters	×	.155	= square inches
square meters	×	10.7641	= square feet
hectares	×	2.471	= acres
square kilometers	×	247.1098	= acres
cubic centimeters	×	.06103	= cubic inches
cubic meters	×	35.314	= cubic feet
cubic meters	×	1.308	= cubic yards
liters	×	61.023	= cubic inches
liters	×	.26418	= U.S. gallons
grams	×	.03527	= ounces
kilograms	×	2.2046	= pounds
metric tons (1000 kg.)	×	1.1023	= tons (2000 lbs.)
kg.'s per sq. cm.	×	14.2231	= lbs. per sq. in. (PSI)

DECIMAL EQUIVALENTS OF AN INCH

$1/32$ = .03125	$9/32$ = .28125	$17/32$ = .53125	$25/32$ = .78125
$1/6$ = .0625	$5/16$ = .3125	$9/16$ = .5625	$13/16$ = .8125
$3/32$ = .09375	$11/32$ = .34375	$19/32$ = .59375	$27/32$ = .84375
$1/8$ = .125	$3/8$ = .375	$5/8$ = .625	$7/8$ = .875
$5/32$ = .15625	$13/32$ = .40625	$21/32$ = .65625	$29/32$ = .90625
$3/16$ = .1875	$7/16$ = .4375	$11/16$ = .6875	$15/16$ = .9375
$7/32$ = .21875	$15/32$ = .46875	$23/32$ = .71875	$31/32$ = .96875
$1/4$ = .25	$1/2$ = .5	$3/4$ = .75	1 = 1.000

OTHER USEFUL INFORMATION

Area of a triangle = $1/2$ base × perpendicular height.

Area of a circle = π × radius squared *or* diameter squared × .7854.

Area of a square = length × width.

Length of one side of a square × 1.128 = the diameter of an equal circle.

The capacity of a pipe = diameter squared (in inches) × the length (in inches) × .0034. Doubling the diameter of a pipe or cylinder increases its capacity 4 times.

1 Design and Purpose

Whether you plan to use your barn to keep animals, make a workshop, or just add storage space for the stuff that's been accumulating in your yard, one general-purpose design can fit many of these varied uses. In this book we'll assume a single set of dimensions for an all-purpose barn and use that size for all our calculations and planning. Of course, you can modify the dimensions for your particular requirements by making the barn longer or wider and then accounting for your expansion in the plans the book presents.

HOW BIG SHOULD IT BE?

After years of studying structures and how they accommodate the varied uses of an "outbuilding," I've come to conclude that a good, functional utility barn ought to measure about 30 feet long by 24 feet wide. For the purposes of this book, those are the dimensions we'll be working with.

To help you visualize that space, take a tape measure and go to where you'd like to build the barn (or find any area large enough to conduct this exercise) and drive four stakes into the ground to create a box 24 feet wide by 30 feet

If building a barn for animals, you should know the square footage requirements for the number and kind you want to raise.

long. Connect the stakes with kite string, making sure the string forms a perfect 90-degree angle at each corner. Even at this visualizing stage try to avoid a racked rectangle—one whose corners aren't 90 degrees. You want as pure a picture of your barn's dimensions as you can make.

Understand that this string box will not be the *exact* interior dimension of the barn you'll build because you have to subtract the thickness of the walls on all four sides. But even if you frame the actual structure with hefty 2x6s, you'll only be losing a foot or so lengthwise and the

FIGURE 1–1

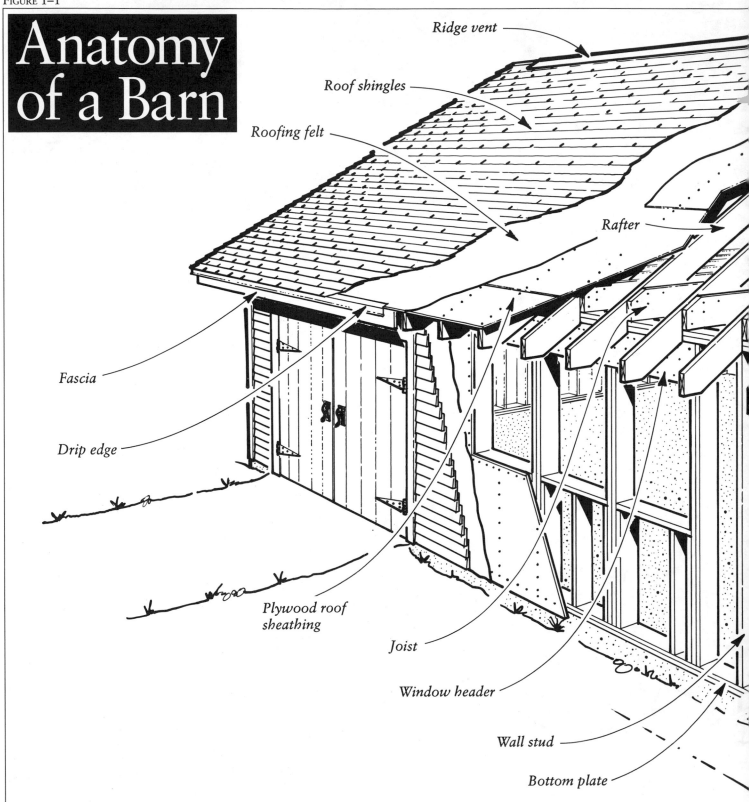

Anatomy of a Barn

Ridge vent

Roof shingles

Roofing felt

Rafter

Fascia

Drip edge

Plywood roof sheathing

Joist

Window header

Wall stud

Bottom plate

same distance widthwise (a standard 2x6 board is actually 5 ½ inches wide, so two 6-inch-thick walls will take 11 inches from each dimension, length and width). But the strings *do* represent the outer edge of the walls you'll erect.

When siting your barn, it's best to align it on a north-south axis. The south and east sides—where your barn will receive the most sunlight and resulting *solar gain* (heat gained through sun pouring in its windows)—should have, ideally, the most windows and your pedestrian access door. On the west side, you may want to add

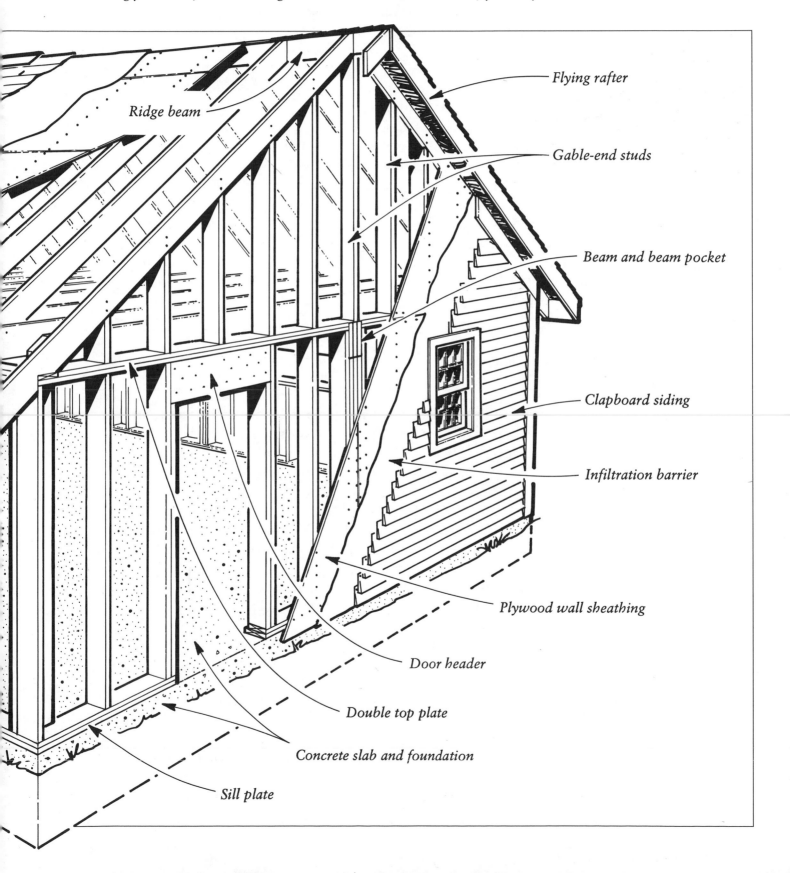

Flying rafter

Gable-end studs

Beam and beam pocket

Clapboard siding

Infiltration barrier

Plywood wall sheathing

Ridge beam

Door header

Double top plate

Concrete slab and foundation

Sill plate

more windows and a garage door. The north side should be sealed as much as possible to the weather, with perhaps only a window or two. (More on siting in the next chapter.)

As a second part of this string-layout exercise, let's determine what you'll have room for in your barn. Using your string, divide your rectangle in half with a "wall" across the width of what would be your barn's midpoint (the 15-foot mark on the longer, 30-foot wall. Given our structural requirements, we'll need a post in the center of this midwall to support a beam that carries some of the load created by the joists and flooring on the second floor. Otherwise, the span (24 feet one way, or 30 feet the other way) would be too far for the size joists and carrying beam we plan to use. Think of it this way: if there were no beam in the middle of the barn to support the joists (those boards laid edgewise to support upstairs flooring), we'd have to use joists that were sized so large—they'd have to span such a vast space—it would be hard to manage them because of their weight and size, plus they'd cost us a fortune.

If you want a large, unobstructed open space for your first floor, you don't have to split your barn in half with a wall. Instead, you can just install the post (typically round, made of steel, and called a lolly column) or create a clear span by running a steel girder or a length of engineered lumber (composite wood framing engineered for great strength) to serve as your carrying beam. (More on the load-bearing aspects of the midwall in chapter 4.)

For now, the string box you've staked should give you a good idea of how big your structure will be. After dividing the barn in half across its width to indicate where your post and perhaps a wall will be, you have spaces on either side of the first floor that are each about 14 feet 6 inches by 23 feet.

On the second floor, there's no need for a load-bearing post or wall, since the rafters which form the roof structure will support themselves (they lean against the ridge beam at the roof's peak, or ridge, and sit on the first-floor wall's top plate). So, your second-floor space can be as big as 29 x 23 feet, unless you divide it inter-

nally for rooms or workspaces. Since our barn will be framed with a gable roof whose rafters sit on the top of the first-floor walls (the roof will slope inward right off the second floor platform), the second floor's vertical space will be somewhat limited the closer you move toward the east and west walls.

WORKING SPACE

On the main level, our 30 x 24 foot-barn gives us a total working space of about 667 square feet. Divide the barn in half and you have two rooms, each with 333.5 square feet of space.

If you plan to raise animals on the main level, check with a good source (a university agricultural extension service, for example, or a text on raising farm animals). Find out the minimum number of square feet required for the number and kind of animals you want to raise.

Let's say you want to commit half your barn to storage and the other half to raising horses. A brood mare needs a tie stall that's minimally 5 x 12 feet, or 60 square feet. If you commit this space to the horse, you have 273.5 square feet remaining. If your brood mare has a foal, which requires a tie stall of $4\frac{1}{2}$ x 9 feet, or 40.5 square feet, you have 233 feet remaining.

Or let's say you're interested in raising turkeys and chickens. Breeder turkeys can require up to 6 square feet each, and chickens (layers) require between 2 and 3 square feet each. Additionally, for whatever animals you plan on housing, you have to account for bedding, hay, water troughs, and all the other paraphernalia animals require. If you consider space for feed, water, tools, animal stalls, and your own work and traffic patterns, you'll find yourself filling half the barn rather quickly.

If you intend to use the entire main level of the barn for animals, the spatial stresses diminish, but if you are considering raising lots of animals, and you also need storage space for your farm and gardening equipment, you may want to consider putting up a bigger barn.

No matter how you use its space, a barn is a

USE A COMPASS WHEN CONSTRUCTING YOUR STRING GRID SO THAT YOU ORIENT YOUR BARN IN A SOUTHERLY DIRECTION.

wonderful, handy thing. Half of it can be committed to a garage, for instance, and the other half to a spacious workshop or gardening materials storehouse. And don't forget all the things you've been yearning to store all these years, the stuff clogging up your back hall and attic (and yard and basement and closets)! A barn is a great place for storing sleds, bikes, skis, firewood, odd-shaped lumber that you just can't discard, and, heaven knows, any other thing. In fact, if you build a barn, I guarantee that a year or two from now you'll wonder how you ever got along without one.

A well-designed barn allows for a variety of end uses, from a spacious workshop to a comfortable home for animals.

PERMITS

No matter what barn design you settle on, you must obtain the required building and zoning permits to build it. Most towns have building and zoning codes. Regarding zoning: before you commit time to the detailed design and planning for your barn, check with your local zoning board to make sure the structure you plan to build is allowed and find out generally what is and isn't permitted in your location. You may have to submit a plan to your town's zoning commission and walk the plan through an approval process. In that case, a detailed plan of your barn, drawn at ¼-inch scale, is useful for presentation at hearings (figures 1–3 and 1–4). In addition, you can use this ¼-inch scale drawing to estimate the materials and beam sizes you'll need, as well as foresee possible layout

and construction problems.

When drawing your plans, be aware that some towns have *setback* or variance rules (which may vary with the use of your building), so be sure to show how your barn will be positioned relative to other buildings on the property, and how far it is set back from your property line and from the road. If you intend to raise animals, zoning boards can quickly become concerned about the proximity of your farm animals to local houses, where you plan to store feed and supplies, and how you intend to dispose of animal waste.

Though zoning approval can be a fickle process, never be afraid to ask questions. Often, the builder (that's you!) is on his or her own when it comes to complying with regulations, and zoning officials may not be able to spot problems before they arise. A couple I know—both experienced builders—built a small barn. When they

FIGURE 1–2

Before a project can be considered, zoning boards often require a site plan drawn to scale and containing the kind of information shown here.

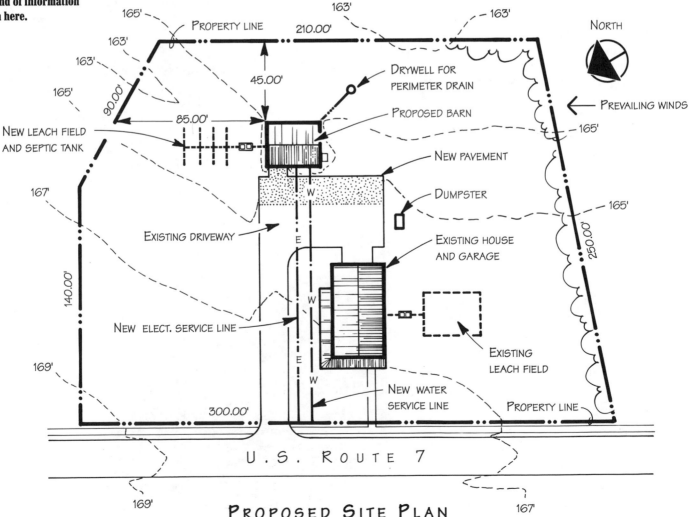

PROPOSED SITE PLAN

added a porch, it came within 75 feet of the road, a violation of their town's zoning code. Even though the barn builders owned the land the road crossed, the zoning official required that they take the porch down. But this official didn't realize he was dealing with resourceful Yankees who solved the problem with a chainsaw. They cut the porch from the house. Even though the porch still stands where it was built, its being cut legally "detached" it from the main structure, making it "portable" and in compliance with zoning regs.

As for building codes: nearly every structure of any substantial size falls under the jurisdiction of a building code. Codes present minimum requirements for building details, thereby assuring that a building is constructed to minimum standards of quality. Check with your municipality to see which of the standard codes it has adopted. Once you learn which one you must follow, you may want to obtain a code book from the sponsoring organization. Since such books can be costly (sometimes $50 or more), you may opt to find one at the library or borrow it through interlibrary loan.

When you draw up plans for your barn or modify plans in this book, you may have to show town zoning officials that your plans meet at least minimum code requirements. When you are building your barn, in all likelihood your local building inspector will visit your site. The building inspector is familiar with the code and will look over your methods and materials to make sure you are building to its minimum standards of quality.

Check with your town or district, because often you must arrange for the building inspector to visit your site—most don't show up automatically. Visits can take some planning, as the building inspector may be required to come by at different stages of the project, such as before the slab foundation is poured and later, after framing is finished. Some municipalities have no such inspection requirements, but don't risk a violation. Find out what's required of you.

In planning for our barn, we'll do our utmost to design up to code. But ultimately, the responsibility of building to code and answering to your building inspector falls upon you, the builder.

Some towns require that your plans be approved by an architect or structural engineer, and that the party show approval by "stamping" the plans with his or her professional seal. It may be difficult to find someone who will stamp and approve plans he or she didn't draw. This is particularly true for architects, who may look at plans brought in for stamp approval as food taken from their mouths. Structural engineers are sometimes more willing to approve plans. But check with your town to see if stamping is required and find out who must examine the plans for approval.

If you do make changes in the plans presented in this book, have those plans approved by a structural engineer. Reason: the plans presented here have been reviewed for structural detail and run through computerized spanning programs to make sure the structure is not overstressed (overloaded). If, for instance, you want to add second-floor dormers, you will have to remove

TABLE 1–1

Building Code Organizations

The three main building codes are

Building Officials and Code Administration International
4051 Flossmoor Road
Country Club Hills, IL 60478
☎ (708) 799-2300

Southern Building Code Congress International
900 Montclair Road
Birmingham, AL 35213
☎ (205) 591-1853

International Conference of Building Officials
5360 Workman Mill Road
Whittier, CA 90601-2298
☎ (310) 699-0541

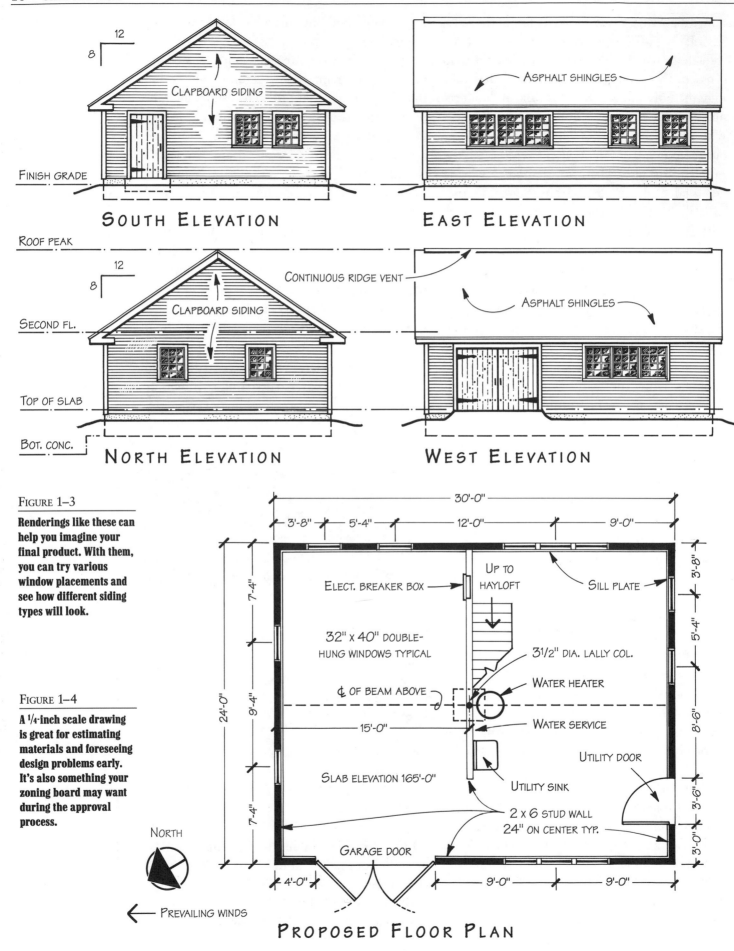

SOUTH ELEVATION

12
8

Clapboard siding

FINISH GRADE

EAST ELEVATION

ASPHALT SHINGLES

NORTH ELEVATION

ROOF PEAK

12
8

Clapboard siding

SECOND FL.

TOP OF SLAB

BOT. CONC.

WEST ELEVATION

CONTINUOUS RIDGE VENT

ASPHALT SHINGLES

FIGURE 1–3

Renderings like these can help you imagine your final product. With them, you can try various window placements and see how different siding types will look.

FIGURE 1–4

A ¼-inch scale drawing is great for estimating materials and foreseeing design problems early. It's also something your zoning board may want during the approval process.

NORTH

PREVAILING WINDS

30'-0"

3'-8"   5'-4"   12'-0"   9'-0"

7'-4"

24'-0"

9'-4"

7'-4"

3'-8"

5'-4"

8'-6"

3'-6"

3'-0"

ELECT. BREAKER BOX

UP TO HAYLOFT

SILL PLATE

32" x 40" DOUBLE-HUNG WINDOWS TYPICAL

3½" DIA. LALLY COL.

WATER HEATER

¢ OF BEAM ABOVE

WATER SERVICE

15'-0"

UTILITY DOOR

Slab elevation 165'-0"

UTILITY SINK

2 x 6 STUD WALL
24" ON CENTER TYP.

GARAGE DOOR

4'-0"   9'-0"   9'-0"

PROPOSED FLOOR PLAN

Typically installed over an unheated space, a metal roof on purlins doesn't require venting.

roof rafters from your plan to make those dormers fit, and that may compromise the load-bearing capacity of the remaining rafters and put extra stress on your ridge beam. An engineer will tell you what you must do to compensate for your modification. If you widen or lengthen your barn, you change the joist and rafter spans, and that means upsizing these and other members. Don't take plan modifications lightly. Buildings do fall down, especially when they're loaded with snow or tested by wind. We've done all we can to assure that the structure presented in this book is a sound one, but if you change it, have an expert review your changes to make sure you don't need to compensate for them.

Any outbuilding will likely increase your property taxes—if you live in a community that has them. A little research can save you some real money, particularly if you realize your yearly savings extend over the life of the barn. There are good books on the topic such as Steve Carlson's *Your Low-Tax Dream House: A New Approach to Slashing the Cost of Home Ownership*, (Hinesburg, Vt., Upper Access Press, 1989) where you may find pointers on simple ways to avoid or reduce taxes.

FINISHED SPACE

When choosing what type of structure to build, decide early on whether you are going to finish off the second floor (or even your first floor) for a living space. A finished-off second-floor living space requires a much different structure than a second-floor space left unfinished. Why? An unfinished second-floor space allows you to use a less-expensive roof system, and, of course, you won't have to invest in all the other materials a finished space requires (sheetrock for the walls, plumbing, wiring, heating, and flooring materials). Our barn's second-floor space can be left unfinished, allowing use of a simple, water-shedding agricultural metal roof, which is a relatively easy roof to frame for and install. Such a roof can be nailed on purlins (structural members attached horizontally to the rafters) and doesn't require plywood decking (figure 1–5). You can use metal roofs over plywood decking if you feel you want to deck the roof to give your building more stability and heat-retention value. But a simple metal-roof system in an unheated structure requires no venting above the rafters (more

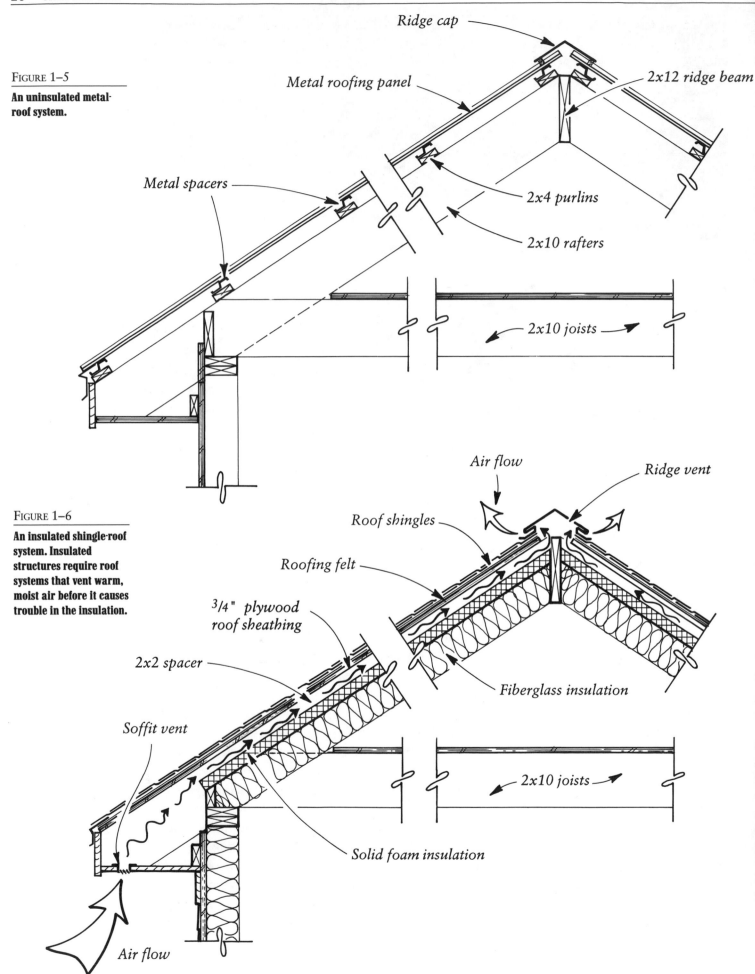

FIGURE 1–5

An uninsulated metal-roof system.

Ridge cap

Metal roofing panel

2x12 ridge beam

Metal spacers

2x4 purlins

2x10 rafters

2x10 joists

FIGURE 1–6

An insulated shingle-roof system. Insulated structures require roof systems that vent warm, moist air before it causes trouble in the insulation.

Air flow

Ridge vent

Roof shingles

Roofing felt

3/4" plywood roof sheathing

2x2 spacer

Fiberglass insulation

Soffit vent

2x10 joists

Solid foam insulation

Air flow

on venting later), nor does it require insulation.

If you do plan on finishing off the second floor for year-round living, the roof structure must be built such that it can vent out the moisture created in your living space. All insulated, heated structures have moisture buildup, and not preparing to vent and remove moisture can cause huge problems. Moisture originates from people in the structure and from such things as clothes dryers and showers. But the moisture you really have to worry about is that which condenses from outdoor air infiltrating a heated building—a natural occurrence. If you plan on finishing off your barn as living space, you must frame it differently to allow for insulation and venting. Among other things, you must vent the ridge and eaves, so air is drawn across the top of your roof insulation and moisture is pulled away before it builds up and soaks the insulation or runs down the sheetrock and pools behind your walls (figure 1–6).

A further warning: This building strategy adds cost. You'll have to deck the roof with plywood and then apply shingles or some other roof type that allows venting. In addition, you'll have to buy soffit and ridge vents, solid foam insulation, and roll insulation for the rafters. And there are added costs involved in preparing the rafters to receive these vents and insulation.

A finished second floor also requires more investment in upgrading your utilities. You'll have to modify your house's septic system, possibly expanding it to allow for sewage from an additional bathroom. In fact, you may have to install an independent septic system just for your barn. You'll have to wire your barn to accommodate up-to-code outlets (yes, there are electrical codes, too) and also answer code and zoning requirements for living space.

Aside from the added cost of a stove or furnace and a heat delivery system, you may incur the additional cost of sheetrock or panelling for the structural walls and ceilings, framing and sheetrock for any interior partition walls (bathroom, bedroom, office), flooring, and all the extras a living space requires: thermal-pane windows, a heated stairway and lockable exterior door, interior doors and wood for trim—the list goes on...and on!). In chapter 8 we'll look more carefully at finishing out your barn's interior, but now as you prepare your plans, be sure you know all that is required for the finish work you intend, including those relevant zoning or code requirements.

Planning for the future.

If you think you might want to put a heated living space in the second floor *in the future,* it is both possible and desirable to frame the roof appropriately now, even if the finished space is years down the road. A roof for a heated space is somewhat more costly than one for an unheated space, so look at your budget carefully, as you will have to pay for plywood, shingles, and vents now, and insulation, sheetrock, and other finishing materials later.

Venting a simple storage barn is not an issue; the roof system presented in this book allows for a free flow of air, and moisture buildup isn't the problem that it is in a closed living space. Building such a barn—for storage, animals, or unheated work space—uses simple, relatively inexpensive construction methods. And the finished structure can be heated to an extent—with a woodstove, or a gas-fired furnace, for instance. Understand, however, that once you start to insulate your barn to retain heat, you must also consider how you'll vent to eliminate moisture.

MATERIALS AND WASTE

When constructing our barn, we'll try to use *standard dimension lumber* wherever possible. Standard dimension lumber is cut at the mill and sent to your lumber yard in lengths of 8, 10, 12, 14, 16, 18, and 20 feet. Many builders like to obtain lumber they will use as structural members (joists and rafters) that is a foot longer than what they need. They reason that by trimming 6 inches off each end, they remove badly split or checked ends and square up the ends with clean cuts. (Factory ends—square cuts made at the mill—aren't always dependable for square.) As much as possible, we'll use wood at its full length to reduce waste.

Waste

Even if you do trim off the ends of lumber, you don't have to throw those cutoffs away. When you're building, establish a bin for scrap lumber. You'll find lots of construction uses for these scraps along the way—for cutting shims or blocking, for example. At the end of the job, if you still have a big bin of wood, you can burn it for heat in a wood stove, or if you don't have one, give it to someone who does. Be sure to separate out any wood that's been pressure treated with pesticide. All *chromated copper arsenate [CCA]* wood, the green-colored lumber, falls into this category. Burning this wood creates especially dangerous fumes. In addition, avoid throwing any wood in your landfill. With

From shims to blocks to kindling, scrap wood has many uses.

a little thought, you can find a good home for it.

Invariably, building creates lots of waste. Some of it, such as cardboard packaging, can be recycled or cleaned and reused. If you choose latex paint for your siding, those buckets can be washed out for use as containers on a later project. Sheetrock "mud" buckets have many uses, and they're easy to hose out. Use your imagination.

Still, there will be some waste you just don't know what to do with, and these non-recyclable wastes build up onsite. It may pay for you to rent a dumpster during construction. Dumpsters can be costly, so shop around. Be sure to tell the vendor that you intend to fill the dumpster with construction debris, not household trash. That can change the price, and it would be a drag to have the guys in the truck come to pick up your dumpster and demand more payment, claiming they didn't know what you were filling it with. If you do get a dumpster, be sure to pack it carefully to optimize space usage.

Salvage

I'm always shocked by what people throw away on construction sites. Perfectly good materials—even appliances in working condition—are often simply trashed. Some of the materials you'll need for your barn can be found on the junk heaps of local sites. Don't be shy about walking up and asking the foreman if you can salvage their junk. Lots of people do it, and it can save you real money.

Though it's hard to salvage wall studs—2x4s or 2x6s—you can occasionally find some good ones that are destined for the junk heap. That may mean sorting through a heap of assorted debris to find your wood, and it may not be worth it. You're more likely to find windows, doors, and sections of large beams that might make good headers. Even if all the glass in a window is broken, a little glazing and some repair and paint can save you hundreds of dollars. Old doors often just need to be stripped of their paint with some solvent or a propane torch. Hollow-core doors (the ones used in interior doorways) are often punctured, but you can strip

them of their hardware, and, even if only one side of the door is intact, you can use it as a tabletop or deep shelf (though be warned: Hollow cores don't support much weight).

You'll also likely find countertops, cabinets, plywood—though rarely whole sheets—and truckloads of assorted scrap lumber. On one kitchen remodeling job near my house, I recently salvaged two perfectly good and sizable laminate countertops (one of which is serving in my kitchen right now) as well as a dishwasher, a sink with a working disposal, an inwall oven, stove hood, and cabinet doors. With a little work, many things discarded from construction sites can give another full lifetime of service.

A recent phenomenon are businesses that salvage construction debris (not just fancy architectural material) and sell it to you at a reduced rate. Look in your Yellow Pages under "Surplus" or "Salvage." Besides useful basics you may find some nice materials to personalize your barn, such as antique windows or doors.

SCHEDULING

When planning your barn, remember that delivered materials should be put in a place where they won't have to be moved again. If you receive a lumber delivery before your slab is poured, make sure it isn't in the way of the concrete truck's path when it delivers your concrete. If you have rebar dropped off, try and get it placed close to where you'll be tying it for your slab. (Backing a delivery truck 15 feet closer to a site can save a great deal of back pain!) If you take delivery of something that has to be kept out of the rain, gang it with other items that have to be kept dry and create a semi-permanent shelter to protect everything.

In addition to planning where you'll put your materials, I strongly recommend you draw a time line so you can anticipate when you'll need certain materials and services. A good time line can help you avoid scheduling mishaps like taking delivery of framing lumber the day you're supposed to finish your slab, or watching a truckload of sheetrock get rained on as you try to rig up some temporary plastic tenting.

A time line can also be extrememly helpful for scheduling subcontractors. For instance, if you are going to hire an electrician to wire your barn, you'll want to make sure all the building components important to the electrician's job are in place and ready before he arrives; otherwise you may have to pay him show-up time, or pay him to return for a second day. The same is true for any plumber you might hire to install your furnace or bathroom fixtures. If the finished walls aren't in place, he's got nowhere to put the sink. If the floors aren't ready, he can't set the toilet. A time line can show you the best times to schedule subs—and save you dollars in the process.

I've seen a good planning system where different colored highlighters were used to indicate the duration of each part of a project. On a large wall calendar where you could see three months at a glance, a yellow marker indicated how many days the foundation would take, with written notes as to when the excavation needed to be done, the forms should be in place, the rebar

A time line can show when job phases overlap. You can also use it to alert you to a sub-contractor's arrival or material deliveries.

MON	TUE	WED
2 Do Batter	**3** boards) →	**4** EXCAVATOR Pick Up Septic Permit
9 & REBAR) → ☆ Call for Lumber	**10** CONCRETE POUR	**11** HOOK UP GFCI Drying Days
16 START FRAMING) ☆ Call for Windows	**17** →	**18** FIRST FLOO
		25

tied, the gravel poured, the concrete ordered, and so on. The framing schedule was indicated with a red highlighter and its time line began just as the foundation line was ending—at about the time the J-bolts that anchor the frame to the slab got placed in the damp concrete. Similar notes on tasks, duties, and deliveries were also made. A different set of highlighters indicated the different subcontractors, when they would arrive, and what had to be ready for them. A time line isn't absolutely necessary but it's a great way to keep track.

INSURANCE

Call your insurance agent about insuring your barn and materials during (and after) the building process. If you borrow money to build your barn, the bank may require insurance for the entire project. But getting insurance is a good idea anyway, because you can never predict the unexpected. A blowtorch used in plumbing can tip over while you're not looking. Before you know it, all your work and planning is up in smoke.

5 GRAVEL DELIVERY

*Call in Concrete Order

6 GRADE SITE)

Dig Short Electrical Trench)

7

12 BUILD LUMBER STORAGE

13 LUMBER DELIVERY

14

19

20

21

26

27

28

FIGURE 1–7

As this rendering shows, your 24x30-foot barn can easily become a gardening center complete with greenhouse, potting bench, and garden vehicle storage.

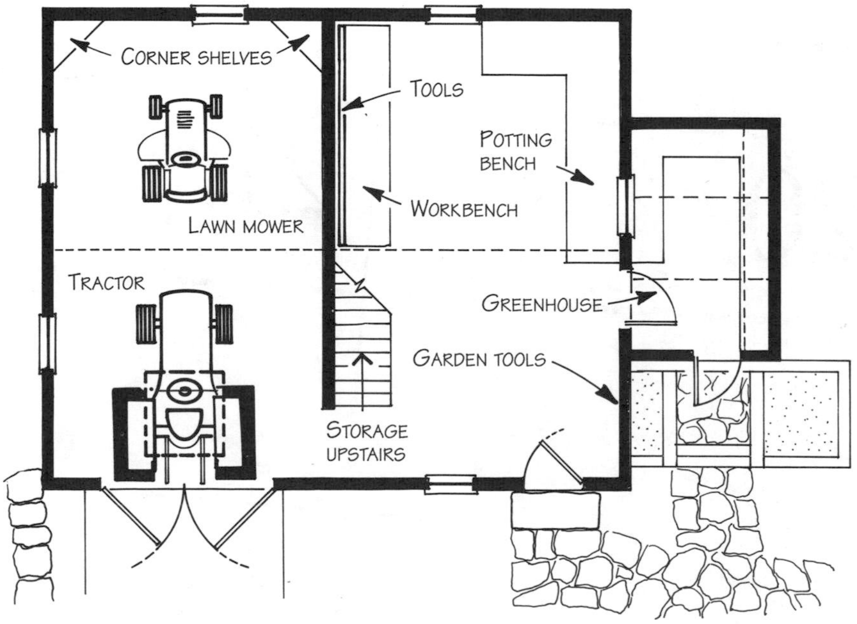

CORNER SHELVES

TOOLS

POTTING BENCH

WORKBENCH

LAWN MOWER

TRACTOR

GREENHOUSE

GARDEN TOOLS

STORAGE UPSTAIRS

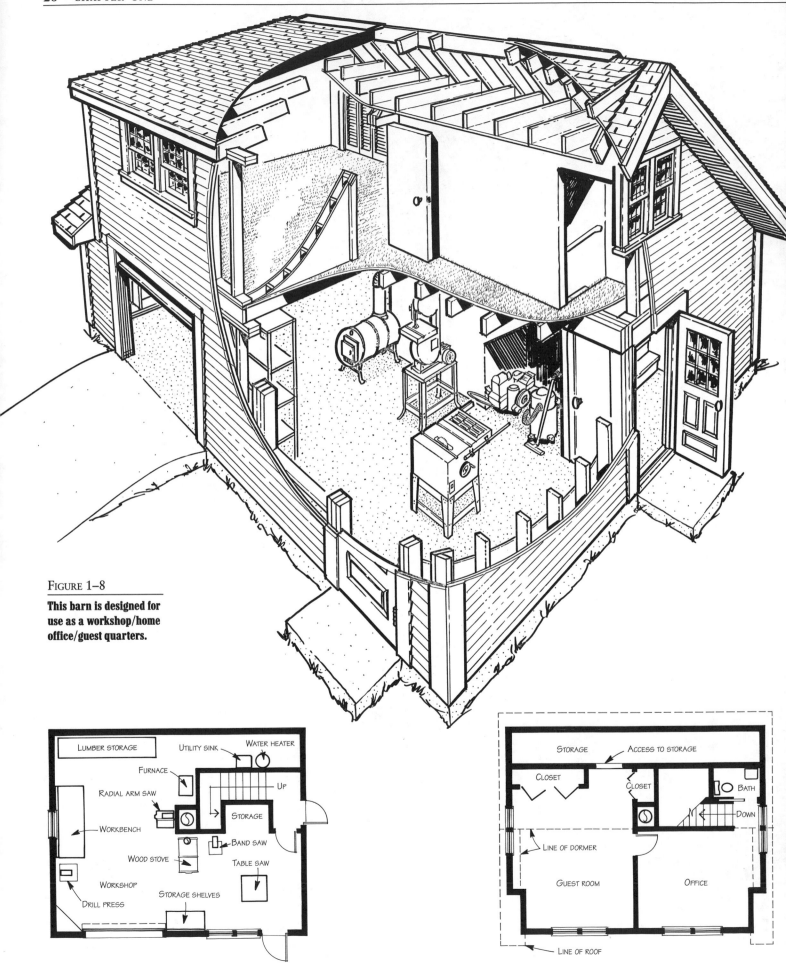

FIGURE 1–8

This barn is designed for use as a workshop/home office/guest quarters.

LUMBER STORAGE

UTILITY SINK   WATER HEATER

FURNACE

RADIAL ARM SAW

UP

WORKBENCH

STORAGE

BAND SAW

WOOD STOVE

TABLE SAW

WORKSHOP

DRILL PRESS

STORAGE SHELVES

STORAGE   ACCESS TO STORAGE

CLOSET   CLOSET   BATH

DOWN

LINE OF DORMER

GUEST ROOM   OFFICE

LINE OF ROOF

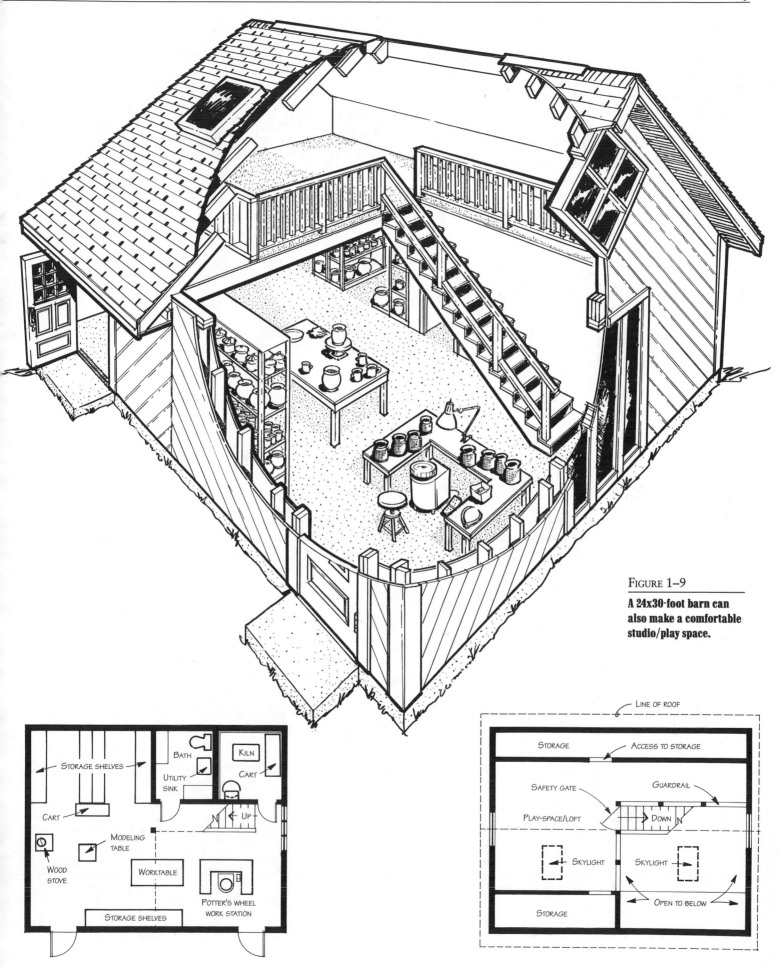

FIGURE 1–9

A 24x30-foot barn can also make a comfortable studio/play space.

STORAGE SHELVES

BATH

KILN

UTILITY SINK

CART

CART

Up

MODELING TABLE

WORKTABLE

WOOD STOVE

POTTER'S WHEEL WORK STATION

STORAGE SHELVES

LINE OF ROOF

STORAGE

ACCESS TO STORAGE

SAFETY GATE

GUARDRAIL

PLAY-SPACE/LOFT

DOWN

SKYLIGHT

SKYLIGHT

OPEN TO BELOW

STORAGE

2 Siting

Where do you put the barn?
Unfortunately, we can't always erect buildings where we'd like. For you it may be possible, but you should consider a number of factors before you determine where on your property your barn will sit.

If your lot has a level site with stable soil, you're in luck. Unfortunately, most sites aren't perfect for the type of foundation we're going to use. In some cases, we can modify the site by grading it with a bulldozer or backhoe and modify the soil by adding gravel. But sometimes there are conditions that will prohibit building, unless you are willing to pump lots of money into site preparation. Luckily, for most of you reading this book, your site should be able to support a barn, although first we must consider—and possibly correct—some basic site conditions.

In the last chapter, we created a lot plan, positioning the barn where we felt it suited us best. Once you have chosen this place for your barn, it's time to evaluate the soil on the site for its ability to support the barn's weight.

For our barn we will be using a *slab-on-grade foundation*. The word *slab* in slab-on-grade refers to the concrete monolith we'll pour as the barn's foundation. *Grade* refers to the soil the slab is poured on. (In building, grade can also refer to the process of smoothing soil to an intended level, as in "Grade this soil so it slopes downhill.")

When choosing a site for your barn, consider the site's soil type, frost depth, grade, access to utilities, and location relative to the sun and prevailing wind.

A slab-on-grade foundation is perfect for the type of structure we are building because the slab serves not only as our foundation but also as our first floor. Further, it is versatile when you get to finishing off your interior (more on slab versatility in chapter 3). Before we pour it, though, it's important to know how your foundation relates to the soil it will sit on. In our case, a slab-on-grade foundation imposes the lowest soil loading in pounds per square foot (psf) of all foundations. Why? Because it spreads the load of the building over a wide surface area of soil, as opposed, for instance, to a standard basement wall foundation, where the weight of the entire building rests on concentrated points over a small surface area of soil.

But no matter what kind of foundation we use, we have to make sure the soil can bear the building load. If the soil cannot bear the load and it compresses under the weight of the building, it will likely do so unevenly, and the building will rack, twist, and shear, causing potentially huge, expensive problems. Even if the building sinks evenly—that is, if it sinks as a single, level massive unit—problems can still result if the sinking is radical (over an inch or two) and ongoing. For our barn we can expect some minimal sinking (called *settling*), but we want to control it as much as possible.

If you are building on *bedrock* (solid rock),

you are in great shape, because there is no question whether your "soil" can support the barn. But as we start to move across the scale, from the most desirable soil, "bedrock," to the least desirable "organic soil," or "peat," we have to commit more and more energy to preparing the soil for our construction project.

There are different ways to categorize and determine soil type. For our barn we'll use the BOCA code's soil table, but you may find other sources that employ different tables with slightly different categories. BOCA has five categories of soil: (1) crystalline bedrock; (2) sedimentary rock; (3) sandy gravel or gravel; (4) sand, silty sand, clayey sand, silty gravel, and clayey gravel; (5) clay, sandy clay, silty clay, and clayey silt. As you can see in table 2–1, each soil type has a bearing pressure. Through rules of thumb, we can roughly calculate the weight of our barn, and predict a safe range of soils to build on. If the soil you plan to build on falls into a category of unstable soil (BOCA categories 4 and 5), you can modify it by excavating the questionable soil and substituting more stable, gravelly soils and thereby move it up the chart into a better category. For our purposes, gravelly soil is soil stable enough to support our barn, so the closer to that category we come through modifying soil, the safer we are for building. Since our barn is a relatively lightweight build-

TABLE 2–1

Building Officials and Code Administration International's ratings for various soil types. Soils closer to "bedrock" are more stable and, therefore, more desirable than those closer to "clay."

BOCA's Presumptive Load-Bearing Values of Foundation Materials

CLASS OF MATERIAL	LOAD-BEARING PRESSURE
1. Crystalline bedrock	12,000 *(lbs. per sq. ft.)*
2. Sedimentary rock	6,000 *(lbs. per sq. ft.)*
3. Sandy gravel or gravel	5,000 *(lbs. per sq. ft.)*
4. Sand, silty sand, clayey sand, silty gravel, and clayey gravel	3,000 *(lbs. per sq. ft.)*
5. Clay, sandy clay, silty clay, and clayey silt	2,000 *(lbs. per sq. ft.)*

Frost Chart

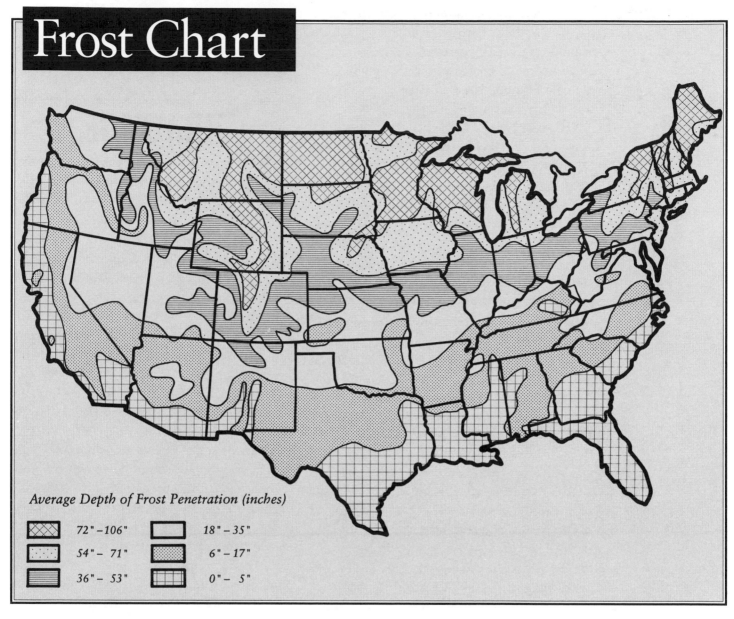

Average Depth of Frost Penetration (inches)

72" –106"   18" – 35"

54" – 71"   6" – 17"

36" – 53"   0" – 5"

ing, we can use standard calculations to determine when the soils are safe enough to support it. However, many experienced builders recommend modifying the soil with gravel additives no matter what type of soil is there to begin with, and we recommend that approach, too.

Before we get into soil-modification specifics, we have to consider something else: frost. For those of you who live in areas where there's frost (chart 2–1), you must prepare your building for the upward movement of soil that frost creates. This movement is called *frost heaving,* and it occurs when water-saturated soil freezes. Frost-heaved soil may increase in volume by as much as 25 percent, and that can cause your foundation to buckle and crack severely.

The finer the soil beneath your foundation, the greater the *capillary action* (distortion of liquid in contact with the soil) and the greater the potential moisture content. The greater the potential moisture content, the more probability there is for freezing and frost heaving. Therefore, because of its fineness, silt is the soil most susceptible to freezing, while bedrock—since it can absorb and hold very little water—is the least.

Well-drained gravelly and sandy soils aren't as likely to heave, since there's not enough water in the soil to expand and cause trouble. And, obviously, soils that are kept warm don't have a chance to freeze and heave. If you plan on heating your barn 24 hours a day during the

CHART 2–1

Frost depth changes geographically. This chart indicates how deep you must dig to get below frost line.

months frost can form, you probably won't have much problem with frost heaves. But if you have ground that holds water—as many soils do—and you are not going to heat your building *all* the cold months, you will have to modify the soil before you put down a foundation.

The real problem soils are clay and silt, as they not only retain water but can draw it from other sources. Still, given the right conditions, any soil can heave. Naturally well-drained sands and gravels are less likely to do so, but clayey and silty soils on your site will have to be excavated and replaced with a layer of ³/4 *gravel* (gravel containing ³/4-inch stones and smaller) which itself must be compacted with a *jumping jack* or vibrating plate type of compacting machine. That will provide a layer of drained soil beneath your foundation.

How deep should you make this layer of gravel? For unheated buildings, the rule of thumb calls for excavating and replacing the native soil to 50 percent of the frost depth (75 percent for highly frost-prone soils (chart 2–1). Even if the native soil is well drained, and you are in a frost-free area, as a general rule you should excavate out at least 12 inches of the native soil and replace it with a 12-inch layer of compacted ³/4 gravel. That will give you well-drained soil that can easily support a slab.

If you are unsure of what type of soil you are dealing with, call a soils engineer and have a soil analysis done. Obtain recommendations from the engineer for modifying your soil.

STEEP SLOPES

If you are able, plan to build your barn on a level or nearly level site. Sites that are minimally sloped can be excavated and graded to level. But steeply-sloped sites present problems that are expensive to solve when preparing a foundation. For these steep sites, a slab-on-grade foundation may be out of the question, unless you combine it with a retaining wall system. You may very well end up using another type of foundation instead of slab-on-grade. In fact, you may want to hire a professional excavating company to handle the preparation of your foundation. But once your foundation is in place, you can follow the other principles in this book for building the barn structure.

DRAINAGE

All sites must drain well, and it's important that you give water an opportunity—often artificially created with pipes and landscaping—to drain away from your structure.

A structure of nearly any kind displaces water artificially with its foundation and concentrates water with its roof. Water that used to fall naturally to the ground before your building was there now falls on a roof, flows off the eaves, and falls to the ground in concentrated amounts. Your foundation drainage system and landscaping must be prepared to drain this water away. That means providing for both the surface water that collects and the water that seeps into the ground.

Consequently, with a slab-on-grade foundation, the gravel you put down beneath your foundation should extend not only to the limit of the slab, but beyond, to catch rain or meltwater from the roof eaves (figure 2–1). Directing surface water away from your foundation can be done by grading the soil away from your foundation, and ideally, creating a swale that will take the water to a stream, pond, or drywell (figure 2–2).

But even with the gravel bed extended to catch runoff water from the eaves and a grade to take the water away from the building, you have to take care of the water that seeps into the gravel or otherwise collects near your foundation. In many cases it is wise to install a *perimeter drain*. A perimeter drain is simply a perforated 4-inch polyvinyl chloride (pvc) drainpipe system that encircles the foundation below grade at the lower level of your gravel replacement fill. A properly-installed perimeter drain collects seepage through its perforations and carries it away by sloping in the direction either of a stream, pond, or drywell. (More on perimeter-drain design in chapter 3.)

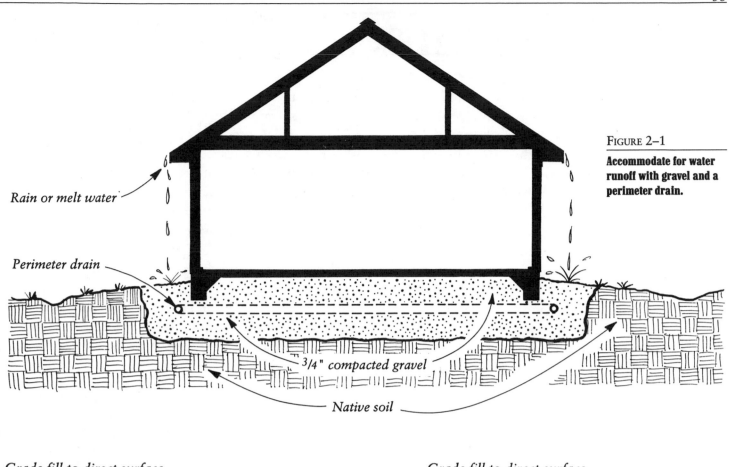

FIGURE 2–1

Accommodate for water runoff with gravel and a perimeter drain.

Rain or melt water

Perimeter drain

3/4" compacted gravel

Native soil

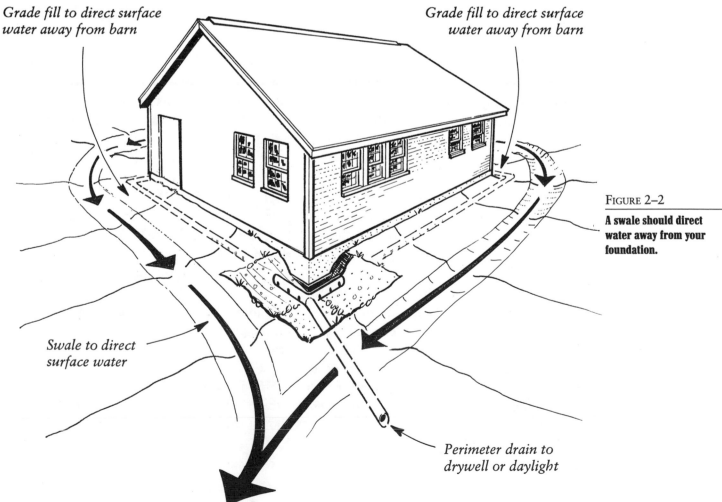

Grade fill to direct surface water away from barn

Grade fill to direct surface water away from barn

FIGURE 2–2

A swale should direct water away from your foundation.

Swale to direct surface water

Perimeter drain to drywell or daylight

VEGETATION

When planning for excavation and the delivery of materials like gravel or concrete, be aware that large machines, like backhoes, dump trucks, and concrete trucks are unwieldy and massive. They can make a real mess of a site, especially if they deliver or work where the ground is muddy. Backhoe buckets and shovels can mash and scar trees. Weighty concrete trucks leave tire marks. I still have the imprint in my lawn from where a concrete truck backed in to deliver concrete for a sidewalk at the side of my home a year ago. And that was with the truck backing in just once. Imagine how the soils around your barn will compress when a backhoe is driven repeatedly over the land. If you do have heavy equipment dropping off materials, try to contain this damage by designating paths for the trucks to take. After the project, you may find you have to recondition soil that the heavy machinery has inadvertently compacted.

If you plan on preserving trees that exist close to your site, be aware that the soil compression around the roots from repeated passes of heavy machinery can easily kill a tree. Warn your machine's operator away from certain areas, or protect the delicate soil with some platform that distributes the weight of the machinery over a wider surface area. You may want to take a few sheets of stacked ¾-inch plywood and lay them down over particularly sensitive areas, though even then you'll find that this measure offers little protection from something as heavy as a backhoe, plus it's potentially expensive.

When you are excavating for your foundation or simply clearing a patch for your equipment to use, you may want to remove grass in the form of sod patches to be used later when you landscape your barn site. Smaller trees, too, can be removed and saved, but you must do a little research on how to remove and store them properly.

If you remove fill from an excavated area, be careful how you redistribute it. Soil is a delicate thing, and throwing loads of fill on top of soil that already supports plant and tree life is disruptive; it can easily wipe out existing trees. For advice, call your local university and see if there is an agricultural extension service representative who can come out and appraise your site. Or contact the National Forest Service.

With respect to vegetation and water supply, be sure not to wash solvents, paints, or washout from concrete tools into soil that supports plant life or borders streams, ponds, or other natural water sources. Though latex paint and cement seem to "disappear" when you wash out brushes or trowels, all that runoff goes into your soil and sometimes on into water supplies. Wash out concrete in a sandy area, not on the lawn. Clean brushes in a drain. And request that your concrete trucker not wash out his trough anywhere runoff will disrupt the soil.

EROSION AND EXCAVATED EARTH

Erosion from rain during construction can cause topsoil loss and general erosion at an alarming rate. Any time you remove the natural covering over soil, you run the risk of losing that soil to rain runoff. Additionally, once you start altering the topography of the area around your barn, the dynamics of the land change, however slightly, and rain can run off or gather in unpredictable ways. When excavating, avoid as much as possible disturbing the natural soil covering and think ahead by trying to protect the dirt you do disturb from being washed away—or back into your freshly excavated ditch—by rain and runoff. Hay is a good, cheap way to protect soil. A few bales of hay spread on the ground around a site can help prevent erosion and protect the soil from being assaulted by rain.

If you have topsoil where you are going to excavate for your foundation, you can and should save it for reuse. Scrape it off with a backhoe and put it in a mound when you start to excavate for your slab. (Make sure the mound

TIP

WASH OUT CONCRETE IN A SANDY AREA, NOT ON THE LAWN. CLEAN BRUSHES IN A DRAIN. AND REQUEST THAT YOUR CONCRETE TRUCKER NOT WASH OUT HIS TROUGH ANYWHERE RUNOFF WILL DISRUPT THE SOIL.

of dirt is out of the way!) Then, lay either a layer of sod or hay on top of the mound, or plant grass seed, or cover it with a tarp. An unprotected mound will erode or flatten—especially if you have children playing on it—and the runoff will be hard to regather to put around your finished barn.

TOPOGRAPHY, ORIENTATION, AND WEATHER

When siting your barn, be sure to look at the lay of the land, keeping in mind the barn's end use. If you plan to raise animals, be aware that runoff from manure piles and feeding areas will travel downhill and potentially contaminate streams, lakes, or even your own well or spring water.

If you plan on piping water to your barn, determine the water source and be mindful of its location. You don't want to be too far—or too many vertical feet uphill—from your water source, as this distance can mean added expense for piping, and pumping water uphill can create problems, including insufficient water pressure at the user end.

As for orientation, it's best to site your barn on a north-south axis, or with your building turned slightly clockwise so it faces south-south-east. The barn should sit with its longer walls running north to south. As we mentioned in the preceding chapter, the north side of the building will be buffeted by the chilliest winds and receive the least light. The south and east side of the building will receive the most sun and the warmest breezes. Since wind and sun are the two natural factors that most affect us, why not benefit your barn by positioning it and designing its openings for the most solar gain and the warmest wind, while simultaneously shutting out the cold?

Of course, not every barn can be positioned on a north-south axis. Other factors—road access, site conditions, the amount of land you have to spare for outbuildings, the relative position of existing structures, to name a few—must also be considered. It makes little sense to build your barn on a north-south axis if it means building on unstable soil or blocking the sun that already pours in your home's southern windows. Surely, your barn will not ice over and fall down rotting wet if you can't situate it north to south. North to south is the optimum alignment, and if you can so site your barn, great; if you can't, so be it.

If your property is hilly, you will experience the most solar gain by putting the building on the south-facing slope. That is because the sun's rays have the greatest warming effect when they land at an angle approaching perpendicular to the ground. The closer you move toward the equator, or the more you can tilt your building toward the equator, the more physical warmth you will feel. Since the sun's altitude increases roughly 1 degree per 70 miles displacement to the earth, ground sloping 5 degrees to the south receives the same radiation as level ground 350 miles to the south. So, even a minimally sloped site can give you substantially more solar gain than a flat site. Building your barn on a south-facing slope—if you have the option—has other advantages as well. If you decide to install solar hot water heaters or photovoltaic collectors on your barn, you will be in good shape, as your roof will be well positioned.

If you are building in the south and you don't want the added heat from solar gain, you would obviously align your building with the walls containing the fewest openings to the south and east.

Besides the sun there is also the factor of prevailing wind. You may live on a lake shore, on a hillside, or in some other location where there is a prevailing wind. Don't ignore this when positioning your barn, as a wind blasting in your barn or garage door can negate many times over any solar gain you receive by aligning your barn for the sun, irrespective of the wind. Often, prevailing wind directions can change from season to season. If the change in direction exceeds 90 degrees (let's say it comes from the west in the fall, and from the north-east in the winter), no matter how you position your building, you will not be able to protect against it entirely. You may have to enlist nature's contribution here—planting shrubs and trees can provide very good protection against the wind.

If you are curious about the weather and have not really paid attention to it (how many of us can point to the direction of prevailing winds for the four seasons?) you may be able to obtain this information from your local airport, local newspaper (research microfilmed back issues to discover a pattern from the daily forecasts), or the National Weather Service.

WHERE DO YOU REALLY WANT YOUR BARN TO SIT?

In the end, since this barn we're designing may end up serving any number of functions, weather considerations can be secondary to personal siting desires if you are willing to let convenience of position override the advantages of positioning relative to the sun and wind. With some modification—adding insulation, or adding or removing windows—you can compensate for the advantage you would have gained from the more "sensible" alignment.

UTILITIES

When siting your barn, remember that you will have to bring power, and, probably, water to it. If you are designing a simple storage barn, power is an enormous convenience you'll never regret hooking up. For you readers planning on animals or serious gardening, water is an absolute must.

If you hook up your barn for electric power with a new metered service, your utility company will be involved. *Call your utility company while you are in the early stages of planning for your barn* and learn what they require

of you before they'll come out for a hookup. They will probably supply you with drawings showing the required specifications for a service, but be sure to find out where inside your building you will be placing your breaker panel. Utilities usually insist that the distance from the meter to the breaker panel be as short as possible. If you erect walls, install your breaker panel without concern for utility specs, and start wiring, you may find your utility rep insisting you move your panel before power will go in. When planning your barn, you must have a firm idea of where your breaker box should go.

Getting Temporary Power to the Site

If you are building your barn near a house that already has electrical power, temporary power might be a simple matter of running an extension cord out a back window. But when using power tools, be aware that the longer the extension cord, the heavier its gauge of wire must be. The line loss (from friction in the wires) causes a voltage drop in higher-gauge (thinner) cords that can damage your power tools and make them run poorly. A 12-gauge wire is recommended for cords up to 100 feet long that supply 1-horsepower (hp) motors. For 1.5-hp motors, the maximum recommended length of 12-gauge is 50 feet. If you think you can string cords end to end over hundreds of feet to reach your barn site, think again. It may be worth your while to buy a long, low-gauge line and wire yourself a four-socket *ground fault circuit interrupter (GFCI)* box, specifically for this project. (You'll never be sorry you have this heavy-duty extension cord around the house.)

I highly recommend that you get GFCI sockets. A GFCI can detect when power is not being returned in the natural cycle (as when power is being grounded out through your body in an electrocution) and the socket turns off the power. It can be reset like a circuit breaker. This power shutdown all happens in milliseconds (the faster the GFCI response, the more costly the device). But it can save your life if, say, your saw's wiring is faulty and gets grounded to its own metal casing and then to your hands, or if you, your cord, and your power tool all somehow get soaked with water. GFCIs are a good idea under any circumstance.

If you are building your barn far from regular power sources, you have two choices. You can make your own power—by running a gasoline-powered generator or having a temporary power pole installed by your utility company. A temporary pole is a metered electrical service that includes a *conduit mast* (the wooden pole itself—usually a length of 4x4), a piece of plywood to mount the meter on, GFCI breakers, power outlets, and a ground. You may have to build and install your temporary pole yourself and then call the utility company to come out and wire it. Be sure to call them in advance to learn the specific requirements. Those can vary from region to region, so call and find out what's required. As for cost, a 100-amp pole with 220 and 110 outlets will run you around $50 a month, with a minimum multi-month contract and a set-up fee.

If you can borrow power from a neighboring house, you may be in luck. It's customary for the borrower to offer to pay *all* power bills during the time you're borrowing power. This avoids confusion and, on your part, shows good will. (Before making such an offer, though, take a quick look around to be sure the household is not an energy hog, with air conditioners in every window and meat freezers wall to wall in the basement!)

Water and Sewage

Water is another story. A simple year-round water supply for animals and gardening may not be so simple when you consider that you must bury the pipes below the freeze line and dig down and poke a hole through the foundation of your house to run the pipes from it to the barn. At the barn itself, you'll have to bring the water line in through the foundation, having prepared for that necessity before the slab pour. Once the water line is into the barn, you can go about your business of hooking up sinks, faucets, and drains. (More on water lines and

A ground fault circuit interruptor outlet helps prevent shock and electrocution. It is an invaluable safety feature at any job site or in any home.

hookups in chapter 7.)

For those of you finishing off your second floor and installing a bathroom, there are additional considerations. Besides supplying year-round water to your second floor, early on in the planning you must evaluate your septic system and, with the consultation of a good plumber, determine if it can handle the additional sewage from an apartment. You may have to expand your septic system or modify it, or even install a new septic system (nothing is as unpredictable, in terms of cost and work, as a new septic system, because the soil and its ability to *perk*—short for percolate—or absorb water properly, can cost real bucks to get right). You must know your septic needs *before* you start nailing together the form boards for your foundation, as your septic may require some substantial digging. Minimally, it will involve laying sewage drainage lines from your barn to the septic system, with all the digging that that entails.

In any event, you should estimate how much water you think your barn will require at peak demand and, in consultation with your plumber, prepare to supply that water to your barn with an up-to-code delivery system that won't freeze in the winter or be crushed when vehicles drive over the pipe's underground path (more on plumbing in chapter 8).

Estimating Peak Water Demand

The type of barn you intend will affect how much water you need to prepare to deliver. If you estimate your *peak demand*—usually defined as the amount of water flowing when all your water-using devices flow at the same time—and prepare to deliver peak demand at all times, you are probably overdoing it. Peak demand is rarely reached, unless you go water crazy and run all your sinks and showers and washers at the same time. Still, your barn will demand water, sometimes lots of it, so let's look at the rule of thumb: A small cottage or small home should have water supplied at the rate of between 200 and 250 gallons per hour. By comparison, a large home, with more than one lavatory or bath, should have a supply of about 300 to 375 gallons per hour.

Now, let's look at this more scientifically, analyzing water demand for two types of barn: a simple, unheated one, and a finished-off barn with living space.

For the simple barn, estimate how much water you'll need for your animals or, if you plan on running a garden hose off the barn's water supply, how much water you want to use on your garden. You should research animals' water requirements in a good guide on how to raise them, but as an example: a horse drinks 10 gallons a day; a dry cow, 12; a milker, 35; sheep, 2. Your garden can drink—really drink—water as well. Eight gallons of water will sprinkle a 100-square-foot lawn, and 16 to 20 gallons will saturate it. But as you can see, a barn for raising animals, or for housing your gardening projects, does not require anywhere near the 200 to 250 gallon per hour "rule of thumb" estimate for a small cottage. Even if you supplied your barn with 100-gallons per hour you will probably never have a problem.

If you finish your barn for a living space, your peak demand comes closer to that 200 to 250 gallons-per-hour figure. Installing a toilet, shower, bathroom sink, and kitchen (perhaps with a dishwasher) can draw quite a bit of water. A shower usually draws 200 gallons per hour or 30 gallons per bathing. A standard toilet draws up to 6 gallons per flush, and a kitchen sink can draw as much as 75 gallons of water per day! Since the shower delivers the 30 gallons you use per bathing at the 200 gallon-per-hour rate, your shower alone will demand at least the low-end rule-of-thumb estimate for cottages. But if you wish to be able to do dishes while someone else flushes the toilet and then jumps in the shower, 200 gallons per hour may be too low a rate. If you live modestly and decide to do only one water-consuming activity at a time, the 200-gallon-per-hour rate is probably on the low end of a safe rate of supply.

If you combine your finished living space with a garden/animal barn below—an interesting combination!—and decide to bathe and water the animals, do dishes, shower and flush the toilet all at once, then you'll be grateful for a 250-gallon-per-hour supply, and even wish you had more.

After you do your analysis, take the figures to your plumber and inquire about the best method for delivering your required gallonage.

TABLE 2–2

Water Demand Rules of Thumb

HOUSE SIZE	PUMP CAPACITY
Small house	200-250 *gals. per hr.*
Large house *(more than 1 bathroom)*	300-375 *gals. per hr.*
Working farm	300-400 *gals. per hr.*

WATER DEMAND INFORMATION			
Shower	200 *gals. per hour*	Horse	10 *gals. per day*
Bath	30 *gals. per filling*	Cow *(milker)*	35 *gals. per day*
Lavatory	1.5 *gals. per filling*	Cow *(dry)*	12 *gals. per day*
Toilet	3.5-6 *gals. per filling*	Hog	2.5 *gals. per day*
Kitchen sink	75 *gals. per day*	Sheep	2 *gals. per day*
Person	35-50 *gals. per day*	100 Chickens	2 *gals. per day*

To fine-tune your analysis, consult a water-supply chart, available through water companies; such charts break down water usage by fixture and appliance.

WHEN TO BUILD

It's best to build in the late spring (after the ground dries) for a number of reasons. First, it allows you the longest stretch of good weather to get your barn roofed, sided, and weather-proofed for the coming winter, and it gives you the previous fall and winter to plan. You can line up your permits, resolve zoning issues, draw your building plans (if you need to draw them), and generally think out how you will schedule different parts of the job.

Start planning early, not just two weeks before you build. If you psych yourself up to erect a barn instantly, you'll be chomping at the bit to smell the exhaust and hear the roar of the excavator's backhoe long before you've put the proper time into planning and siting the structure and carefully picking your materials. Rushing a project invites mistakes, perhaps costly ones. And just like the unthrifty vacationers who always buy their gear or reserve lodgings at the height of the season, you may end up paying more. At the very least, scheduling a busy subcontractor on short notice can be difficult, sometimes impossible.

Constructing a scale model of your barn and placing it on a site plan can give you a good idea of how the real thing will affect other buildings nearby. Here, a flashlight imitates the path of the sun across the property.

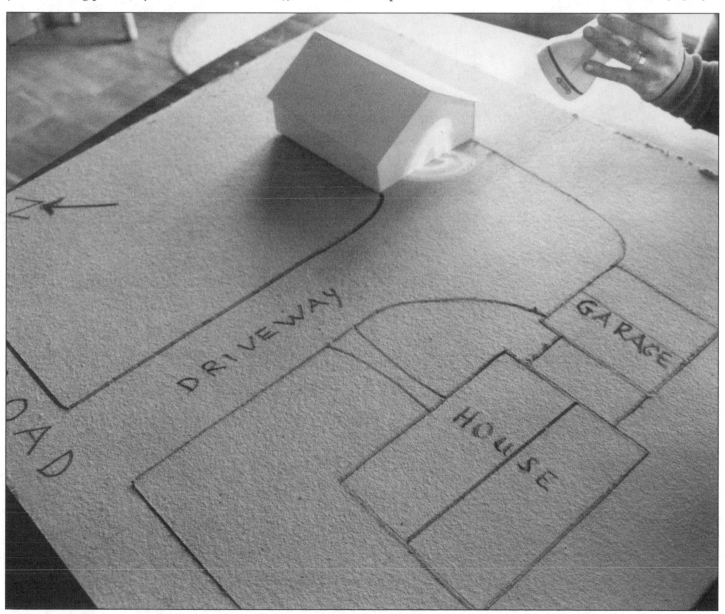

3 Foundation

A square and level foundation for your barn is essential. A racked or out-of-level foundation will fight you the entire project, forcing you to make adjustments at every stage. Laying out and forming a foundation is relatively simple, but it's no place for shortcuts, and you want to do lots of double-checking as you undertake the process.

In the preceding chapter, we looked at excavation considerations and how to prepare the soil by modifying it with gravel. In this chapter, we'll learn how to prepare for and lay out your foundation, how to excavate, measure for grade, prepare for the pour, and pour and finish the concrete.

THE SLAB DESIGN

The foundation we'll pour is a *monolithic* slab, meaning that the slab and *footing* (the band of thicker concrete that runs around the slab's edge) will both be part of the same massive piece of concrete. Another common slab type, the *floating slab,* involves pouring the footing first, then pouring a slab within the box that footing creates. For our barn, and for simplicity's sake, a monolithic slab will suit our purposes just fine.

Our slab will be 4 inches thick, 24 feet wide, and 30 feet long, but if you were to view the finished product with X-ray vision (figure 3–1), you'd see a foot-wide, 2-foot-deep concrete band—the footing—running all the way around the slab. With X-ray vision you'd also see a pad 3 x 3 feet and 1 foot deep in the center of the

Pouring a slab for your barn requires detailed preparation and calculation.

slab. Our barn's center load-bearing post will sit atop this thicker concrete which we'll call the *load-bearing pad*. Your X-ray vision would also show that the slab and footing do not meet at a 90-degree angle. The underside of the slab must taper down to the footing, as this design offers better distribution of the building's weight.

To strengthen the perimeter footings and pad, we'll use reinforcing rods known by builders far and wide as *rebar*. Rebar comes in various thicknesses; we'll use #4 rebar, which is a half inch in diameter. We'll reinforce the main part of the slab itself with *#10 mesh*, also called *WWF*, or *welded wire fabric*, which is patterned in six-inch squares. We'll also put #4 rebar where the foundation tapers from the slab down to the footing, but we'll bend it to follow the slab. Later, we'll look at how to place this rebar and mesh, but for now let's understand why

we're using it. As a building material, concrete is very strong in compression, but not as strong in tension, meaning that it can withstand being pushed, but pulled hard enough, it might break. Rebar and mesh supplement the concrete's tensile strength and help to contain the concrete if cracks start to form.

Besides reinforcing our slab's strength, we should also protect it from moisture. Moisture infiltrating the slab from the ground can cause damage and possible heaving, so it's smart to lay a *vapor barrier* to keep the moisture in the ground. We'll use a sheet of 4-mil polyethylene plastic. Some builders place this vapor barrier directly on top of the gravel before a pour. If you are careful not to puncture it when you're walking around during the pour, you won't have a problem. Other builders advocate placing the vapor barrier between the gravel and the ground, well beneath the actual slab. To me,

FIGURE 3–1

The slab for any structure should be thickened where it carries the most weight. For our barn, the slab is thicker around the edges for the walls and in the center for a supporting post.

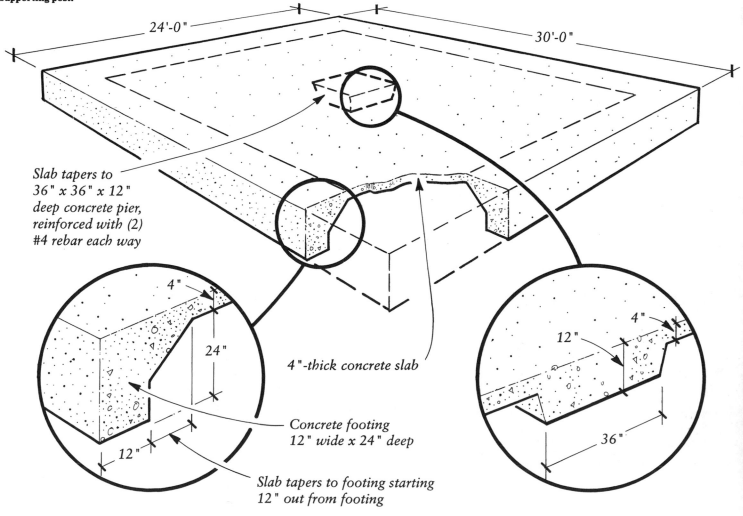

Slab tapers to 36" x 36" x 12" deep concrete pier, reinforced with (2) #4 rebar each way

24'-0"

30'-0"

4"-thick concrete slab

4"

24"

12"

Concrete footing 12" wide x 24" deep

Slab tapers to footing starting 12" out from footing

4"

12"

36"

that's the better idea for maintaining a consistent vapor barrier that won't be punctured accidentally and will keep water well away from the slab.

If you want a warm slab (if you'll live directly on the first-floor concrete, for instance) you can insulate the slab by putting 2-inch rigid foam insulation commonly called *blueboard* on top of your gravel before you pour. Blueboard can be purchased with tongue and groove fittings, so you can lock panels into each other to form a continuous insulation barrier. The concrete then covers up and seals this insulation. If you plan to put down rigid foam insulation, be sure to calculate its height when figuring the height of your gravel. Two-inch-thick foam means you use two inches less gravel, *not* two inches less concrete—otherwise your slab will not be the required thickness. Two more warnings: Some builders contest this practice of placing foam in a foundation because ants sometimes make their home in it. After a few years, the ants can actually eat out the foam and open up a void between your gravel and slab. Also, rigid foam is expensive, and installing it will drive up the cost of your slab. An uninsulated slab is not the end of the world (you can always put an insulated floor on top of the slab), and those of you who won't live on the first floor don't need to insulate anyway. True, there is some thermal loss through the slab, and the insulation helps to slow it, but you should weigh rigid foam's pros and cons before committing to it.

UTILITIES

Before pouring a slab, be sure you plan ahead for any utilities or piping that need to be brought through it. This includes the *soil pipe* that runs from the bathrooms to your septic (if you are installing bathrooms), and the *water supply line* (if you are running one below frost depth from your water supply—well, spring, or municipal line). For your soil pipe, you'll find yourself trenching out to your septic system so that your plumber can hook it up later. For the purposes of pouring the slab, you don't have to hook up the soil pipe to the septic before you pour. You must, however, position the soil pipe at the slab end very precisely, because its placement will dictate where a first-floor toilet is positioned. If you are running soil pipe up to the second floor, you want it to travel as direct a route as possible. Consult your plumber and make sure you are working with the proper measurements when positioning your soil pipe and read ahead in chapter 7 of this book to get a better grasp of plumbing design.

The same is true for your water supply line. In northern areas, water supply lines must be buried beneath the frost line; otherwise they'll freeze in winter. Installing a water supply line involves real planning because you have to dig a trench for it early on and then have your plumber (or you) perform the actual installation between the time you excavate for the slab and the time you start pouring gravel. Your plumber can help you decide where to have the pipe emerge from the slab to accommodate your plumbing needs later.

It's all right for soil pipes, which are usually made of cast iron, to come in direct contact with concrete, but beware of other pipes you intend to bring through the slab. Concrete can corrode some metals, aluminum among them. You may have to make special provisions for your pipes, such as covering them with insulation, or running them through a non-corroding *chase* (a housing or tunnel) to prevent concrete from coming in contact with them.

Overall, it's better to avoid placing service pipes directly, or indirectly via a chase, into the concrete unless you absolutely must. Electrical conduits and baseboard-heating water-delivery pipes, for instance, can all be run above your slab. But if you want to create housing for pipes in the concrete, a simple chase can be made of polyvinylchloride plastic pipe called *schedule 40*. Of course, you can't have sub-slab 90-degree-angled chases that you intend to run plumbing through later—the plumbing pipes just won't pass through sharp angles. But you can build the chase around preassembled plumbing pipes that are in place when you pour

Bring pipes or wiring up through chases in the slab and cap or crimp the tops to protect them until it's time for hookups.

and that you hook up later. It's probably o.k. to run uninsulated pipe above what would otherwise be the frostline below a heated slab, but if, for some reason, your chase will run through an area above the frostline in an unheated portion of earth or gravel not under the slab, then insulate the chase and insulate and heat (with wire heat strips) the pipes within the chase to prevent them from freezing.

Wiring can be pulled through a chase, either by shooting a string through an assembled chase with compressed air (you tape one end of the string to a Ping-Pong ball and blow away at it) and then pulling wires through with that string, or by placing a string in the chase as you assemble it. The *National Electrical Code (NEC)* may prohibit certain wire services from using a PVC chase (they may require an insulated aluminum conduit instead), so check with your electrician and make sure that your chase plan is up to code.

Once the pipes or chase is in place be sure to cap both ends to keep out dirt, varmints, and debris, only uncapping them when they are ready to be permanently hooked up.

DRAINAGE

In the last chapter we showed how perimeter drains are a good means of directing ground water away from your foundation. Plan for your perimeter drains before you excavate, and keep in mind this salient information: Ideally, you want to use a perforated 4-inch PVC pipe. If you can buy it cheaply, an easy-to-work-with version of this pipe comes in flexible coils, starting at 100-foot lengths. But if you want to economize, use the cheaper, rigid, schedule 40 PVC pipe. With schedule 40, you lose the convenience of laying flexible pipe around your foundation's corners, and you'll have to buy fittings and assemble the sections with glue, but you'll save money, and the fittings really aren't all that hard to work with.

Whichever piping you choose, you'll want to install it 4 inches away from the base of your footing and sloped to a dry well, drain, or daylight at a minimum slope of 1 inch for every 20 feet. When you excavate, be sure to accommodate for this pipe, and lay it in after the pour—

specifically, after your form boards have been removed but just before you backfill. As you backfill, you surround the pipe as well as the slab with gravel. You will need about 115 feet of pipe to surround the foundation of your 24 x 30 foot barn, and whatever additional footage to outlet the water to your drywell, drain, or daylight.

LAYOUT AND EXCAVATION

Before you can excavate, you have to lay out your foundation so your heavy-equipment operator knows where to dig, and you know where to build the concrete forms. The best method is the batter-board system, using string and some 2x4s. For this two-step process, you'll need a ball of mason's string (don't skimp; get the real stuff), a 50-foot tape measure, a 10-foot tape measure, a hammer, a handful of 8d common nails, and four good-quality wooden stakes 30 inches long (rip a good 2x4 in half, cut four 30-inch stakes, and sharpen one end of each).

To start your layout, go out to your barn site and drive a stake in the ground where you want one corner of your barn to be. With the stake *firmly* driven, drive an 8d common nail halfway into the center of the top of the stake. This is stake #1, and the nail establishes the outside edge of one corner of your foundation. From here on you will be aligning your barn, so if you want to have the walls face a certain direction, now is the time to break out your compass and use it to establish the direction and placement of the next stake.

With a 50-foot tape measure hooked on the nail of stake #1, measure out the length of one 24-foot wall and drive a stake in at that point. This is stake #2. After you've driven the stake, remeasure from the nail on stake #1 to stake #2 and drive a nail into the top of stake #2 precisely at the 24-foot mark. This establishes the outside edge of your foundation at this second point.

The line drawn between stake #1 and stake #2 represents the alignment of one of your walls. If you don't like the way the barn is facing, now is the time to change it!

Stretch the mason's string taut between stakes #1 and #2 and tie it to the base of these nails. (Don't cut the mason's string up in pieces; use one big piece for all four walls for this procedure.) If simply pulling the mason's string bends your stakes, or if the nail bends, you may have to start over with a more firmly driven stake or a heavier nail. With this string in place between stakes #1 and #2, you have established the foundation dimensions of one wall.

This next step is particularly crucial because the next wall you will establish with mason's string must be 90 degrees to the existing wall between stakes #1 and #2. *Do not use a small framing square to establish this 90-degree angle*—it isn't exact enough. Instead, use the following simple, but more precise way to determine 90 degrees, called the *3/4/5 method*.

A triangle with dimensions of 3 feet by 4 feet by 5 feet will always give you a right angle (90 degrees) where the 3- and 4-foot sides meet. (This triangle will give you a right angle whenever the sides are exact multiples of 3, 4, and 5, such as a triangle that has 9x12x15-foot sides.) You can either build a wooden 3/4/5-foot triangle in your shop and use it as a square to guide your strings, or you can create a 3/4/5 triangle with a tape measure to get the same results. Here's how you do the latter: From stake #2, stretch your mason's string in the direction you want your next wall to go (your 30-foot "length" wall). Have your helper hold this string roughly in place for now, 30 or so feet down the line.

From stake #2, measure 3 feet up the string that connects stake #1 to stake #2 and drive a temporary stake. Remeasure this 3-foot distance and put a nail exactly at the 3-foot mark. Attach your 10-foot tape measure to this nail and lay it down in the grass.

Next, from stake #2, measure 4 feet down the string that will attach stake #2 to stake #3 (#3 is the one you're just about to locate and drive into the ground). Mark this string exactly at the 4-foot mark (use duct tape, or a colored

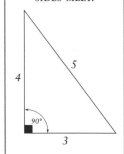

A TRIANGLE WITH DIMENSIONS OF 3 FEET BY 4 FEET BY 5 FEET WILL ALWAYS GIVE YOU A RIGHT ANGLE (90 DEGREES) WHERE THE 3- AND 4-FOOT SIDES MEET.

marker, but be exact). Now, have your helper pull this 30-foot length of string taut and as level as possible.

Next, take the 10-foot tape that's attached to the temporary stake at the 3-foot mark (the tape measure that's lying on the ground), and measure out 5 feet diagonally toward your "length" wall string until your 5-foot tape reading meets the 4-foot marker on the outgoing string. If you measure precisely, you establish a 90-degree angle when the 5-foot mark on your tape intersects the 4-foot mark on your outgoing string.

Next, with your 50-foot tape, measure 30 feet along your "length" wall string, and—with the string's 4-foot mark and the 10-foot tape's 5-foot mark exactly matching—drive stake #3 at the correct wall-length measurement.

Remeasure your wall length and check your 90 degree angle. Now, drive a nail to establish exactly the third corner of your barn.

Repeat this same process for the string you'll put up between stake #3 and stake #4, measuring out 24 feet for a "width" wall.

Finally, if everything else is where it should be, the string that runs between stake #4 and #1 will necessarily be the right distance, and at 90 degrees to the walls you've established.

Double-check *everything*. Make sure you have four 90-degree angles and that the distance from nail to nail to nail to nail represents the respective lengths of the outside of your foundation dimensions. Finally, measure diagonally from stake #1 to stake #3, and from stake #2 to stake #4. These diagonal distances should match each other exactly, *with no margin of error*. If they are not the same, the square is racked and you need to remeasure and adjust the stakes and string (figure 4–3).

Once your string rectangle is perfect, you can build your batter boards. With the exact dimensions of the foundation established, we'll erect a superstructure to suspend a second string box exactly above the one we've just established. The string box we've established will soon be removed, enabling you to dig on your site without disturbing the string outline (figure 3–2).

FIGURE 3–2

Getting the four corners of your barn perfectly square is essential to building a sound structure.

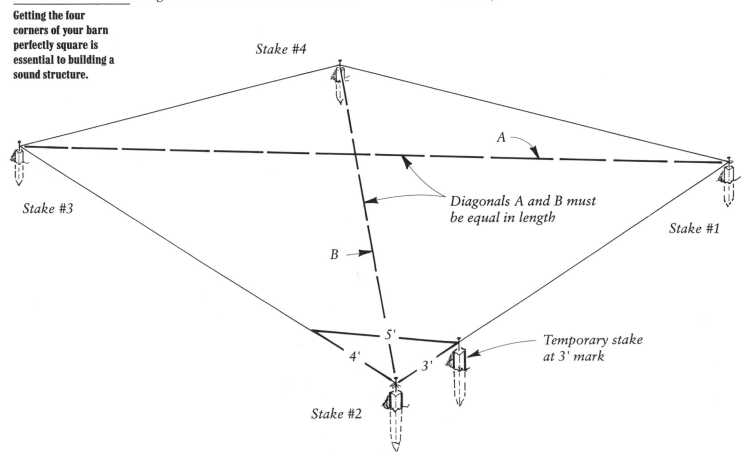

To construct the batter boards, you'll need sixteen 4-foot 2x4s, and eight 3-foot 2x4s. Let's look at how to build one batter board, and then you can build them for all the corners.

Step back 5 feet from stake #1 along the line that runs between stake #1 and stake #4. To your left and right, drive in a 4-foot 2x4 so that its 4-inch side is 90 degrees to the string that runs between stakes #1 and #4. Now nail a horizontal 3-foot 2x4 between the two 2x4s you just pounded into the ground. This horizontal board should be 3 feet off the ground and level before it is nailed into place. Use a spirit level for that purpose.

Now do the same thing 5 feet back in line with the string that runs between stake #1 and stake #2. Drive in your next pair of 4-foot 2x4s (or just drive one and use one of the 2x4s from your first batter board) and nail a level, horizontal, 3-footer between them, making sure this horizontal board is *at the same height* as the other horizontal board you just nailed up.

You should now have two h-shaped batter boards, each at 90 degrees to the string facing the level horizontal board. Construct these batter board sets for each of the four corners. The object here is to suspend a second string box above the one you made with the stakes. But this second string box will be out of the way, removable, and supported by structures that are 5 feet back from the corners of the foundation.

Once you have the batter boards built, stretch four pieces of mason's string between them so that the string sits exactly above the already existing string box you created with the stakes. To position the string exactly, drop a plumb bob from where the batter-board strings overlap and be sure to place the corners of your new string box exactly above the corners of the stake box.

Secure these strings to the batter boards with a nail in the back side of the horizontal 2x4. Once you have the strings positioned exactly, mark the position of the batter-board string on the horizontal batter board with a saw kerf mark, so you always know where the string belongs if it gets knocked out of place or if you want to remove it to allow equipment to enter

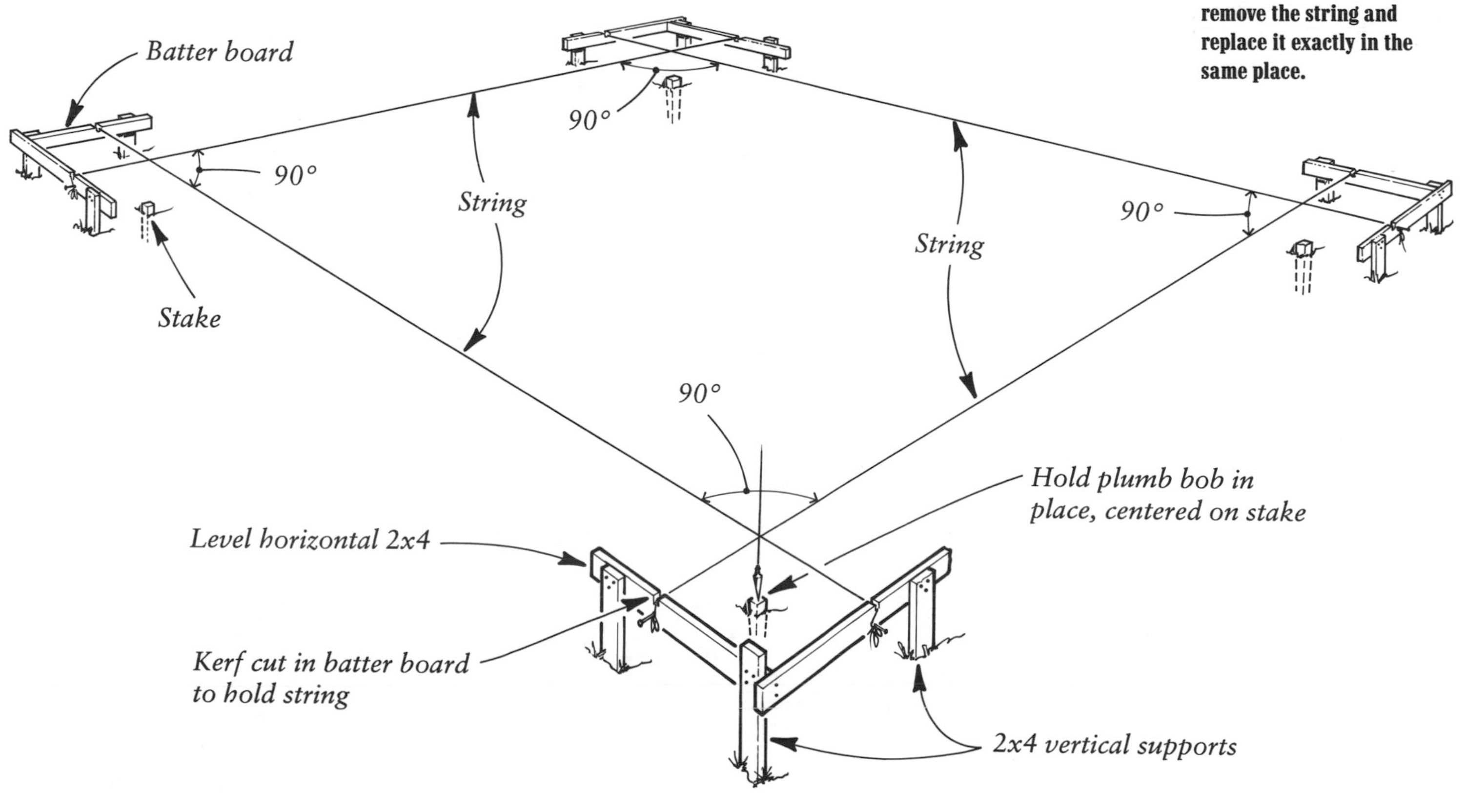

FIGURE 3–3

If you need to excavate inside the string box, the batter boards let you remove the string and replace it exactly in the same place.

Batter board

90°

90°

String

Stake

String

90°

90°

Hold plumb bob in place, centered on stake

Level horizontal 2x4

Kerf cut in batter board to hold string

2x4 vertical supports

your slab area.

In the end, you should have eight batter-board structures (two in each corner), and they should sit 5 feet back, behind the corners their mason's string creates. You should have a batter-board string box that is exactly the same size and dimension as the string box you created with your stakes. Once you've made the batter-board string box, you can safely remove the stake string box below.

Now if you need to remove the batter-board string box to let a backhoe or truck on your site, you can do so without hesitation because the box can always be perfectly restrung by laying the string along the kerf marks on the horizontal boards and retightening the string.

Transits and Dumpy Levels

You will have to rent a *transit to shoot the grades* on your foundation site. With it, you will be able to double-check your batter-board lines for square. Let's look at how to do that and simultaneously learn a little about transits.

A transit is basically a telescope mounted on a horizontal scale that indicates the scope's degree setting. Transits are rated in *minutes*. A *5-minute transit* has a level-line accuracy of $\pm^1/_8$ inches over 100 feet, for instance. For measuring angles, when you spin a 5-minute transit 90 degrees, it will accurately determine that angle within $1\,^2/_3$ inches over a 100-foot distance. Not bad. A *15-minute transit* is less exact, and a *1-minute transit* more so. A 5-minute transit will suit our needs just fine.

When you spin the transit scope from left to right (it moves in a level plane), you can track on the scale how many degrees you have turned it. If your transit is facing exactly north, and you spin it clockwise, you will know it faces directly east because the scale will show you that you've moved it 90 degrees. The transit smoothly spins 360 degrees in one plane, like a gun turret.

A transit can tilt up and down too, like a telescope. A second scale on the transit indicates the degree of tilt up or down. A similar instrument, called a *dumpy level* or *builder's level* can tell you how many degrees you turn left to right, but it can't tilt up or down.

Both these types of instruments are powerful telescopes made for reading tape measures and *story poles* (sticks marked at precise intervals and used at foundation sites for measuring elevations) from great distances. (They're also great for birdwatching or seeing what your neighbor's cooking on the grill!)

For all practical purposes, you can rent a dumpy level for shooting your grades. But if you rent a transit, you can use it to check your batter-board lines for square. To do that, place your transit so its tripod straddles one corner of your string box. Drop a plumb bob down from the center of the transit so its center is positioned exactly above one of the batter-board string box's corners. Then level your transit both north-to-south and east-to-west by adjusting the transit's leveling screws (see "How to Level a Transit"). Since the transit's eyepiece has a cross hair (like a hunting rifle sight), you can exactly line up your string with the center cross hairs. When you tilt the transit scope up and down, you should be able to sight the entire length of your string, and it should not vary from left to right within your scope.

Sight one "wall" with your transit so that the string is in the center of your cross hairs. Using the horizontal degree scale on the transit, swing your instrument exactly 90 degrees to sight the "wall" perpendicular to it. This string should stay in the center of the cross hairs for its entire length as you tilt the instrument up and down. If your strings are out of whack and vary from true lines 90 degrees to each other, your transit can show you by how much. Set the transit up in all four corners to check for square.

Excavation

Schedule your backhoe operator as far in advance as possible so you're not stuck with your layout finished and nobody to dig the hole for you. (Since layout isn't time consuming, you can pretty closely guess when you'll be ready for your heavy equipment.) After you've fin-

How to Level a Transit

IT'S CRUCIAL THAT YOUR TRANSIT BE perfectly level before you shoot grades. If it is the slightest bit off, and you project that error out over 50 or 100 feet, it can add up to a substantial measurement. One side of your foundation could be two inches higher than the other side, and you wouldn't know it until you went to frame the building and found you couldn't get square doorways to fit tightly.

The ultimate object in using a transit is to be able to shoot a perfectly level line in any direction. Thus, your transit must be able to turn 360 degrees (a full circle) and maintain level throughout that circle.

When you have decided where to place your transit (out of the way of the backhoe), set the three tripod legs firmly into the ground. The legs are pointed, so setting them shouldn't be a problem. As you set the legs, look at the base of your transit. Just below the four leveling screws, there is a plate the transit rests on, called the *leveling plate.* Set the tripod so this plate is as close to level as you can make it. (Some transits have a *bubble-in-a-circle* leveling indicator for this stage.) This is the first step in leveling your transit: getting it roughly level with the tripod legs.

Next, using your level locks, lock your transit scope into the *level* position indicated by the Vernier scale (the scale located below the transit's scope that indicates degree of tilt). At this stage, even with the transit locked at "level" it may not look as though the scope is actually

shooting a level line. We're about to correct that.

Spinning your transit scope, aim it "north" or at a zero-degree setting on the horizontal indicator scale.

Now look at the bubble-vial leveling indicator on your transit, mounted just under or on your scope. Using the leveling screws (the four screws that support the transit above the leveling pad), adjust the transit so the bubble is exactly in the center of the vial. With that done, the first half of the transit leveling is complete.

Next, rotate the transit scope 90 degrees, so the scale reads either 90 degrees if you've spun it clockwise ("east") or 270 degrees if you've spun it counterclockwise ("west"). You will see that the bubble in the vial has changed position. Correct that in both directions. Use your leveling screws to center the bubble.

Spin the scope in 90-degree increments and adjust the leveling screws each time until the vial's

bubble indicates level no matter where you spin the transit. But only adjust the leveling screws with the scope positioned at 90-degree intervals to the last reading of the bubble.

Be careful not to snug up the leveling screws too tight. Too-snug screws will eventually warp the pads they sit on.

Leveling a Builder's Level

Since a builder's level is permanently "locked" in a level position (it's made that way), you can skip the "lock-at-level" step listed above. Otherwise, a builder's level is leveled in exactly the same way as a transit. Plant your tripod's legs so the leveling plate is as level as you can make it, then perform the same steps outlined above. Using the vial bubble as a reference, level the transit with your leveling screws. Then, turn the transit 90 degrees and level it with your screws again.

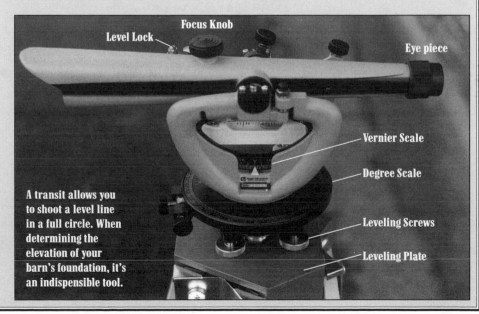

Level Lock • Focus Knob • Eye piece • Vernier Scale • Degree Scale • Leveling Screws • Leveling Plate

A transit allows you to shoot a level line in a full circle. When determining the elevation of your barn's foundation, it's an indispensible tool.

ished your layout and prepared your site for the arrival of a large, heavy machine, review the previous chapter to determine how deep the excavation will need to be to get below the frost line and avoid frost heaving.

Since the backhoe can't get inside the string box you have created, you have to take the string down for a brief time. Don't remove the batter boards, though! To indicate to the backhoe operator where you want the excavation done, use lime to outline the area to be excavated. Remember, you are excavating not only for your foundation, but beyond it in all directions so you can have a gravel area for drainpipes to absorb water runoff.

At minimum, backhoe operators usually charge $40 to $50 an hour. They're worth every penny. To excavate with hand shovels is extremely hard work, and it's amazing what a backhoe can do in a short time. You'll never regret hiring a backhoe to do the work you would otherwise have to do with shovels.

Before you dig, be sure to find out if there is anything important your backhoe driver could possibly hit with his shovel or scoop. Underground powerlines, telephone lines, sewage lines, or gas lines can cause you enormous amounts of danger, delay, and grief. A few quick calls to your utility companies, or one quick call to a "dig safe" number, a week in advance can help both of you avoid oodles of problems.

How do you know how deep you are?

Before excavating, calculate how far down into the ground you want to place your form boards (your *form depth*) so that the top of the slab—determined by the top of your form boards—sits at the right elevation. A 4-inch slab should sit 8 inches above your original grade, so you'll increase the original grade by 4 inches using gravel. Add to this form depth the amount of gravel you intend to add to protect against frost heaves. That will be the excavation depth.

Consult with your backhoe driver to let him know how deep you want your excavation. The backhoe driver may want specific depths to dig for, but chances are you or the driver's assistant will be "shooting grades" as the driver digs.

BEFORE YOU DIG, BE SURE TO FIND OUT IF THERE IS ANYTHING IMPORTANT YOUR BACKHOE DRIVER COULD POSSIBLY HIT WITH HIS SHOVEL OR SCOOP.

This you can do with the transit or the builder's level.

Place your transit far enough away from your foundation so it won't be in the way of the backhoe. Once it's stable, level it.

The transit you rent should come with a *story pole*. As mentioned earlier, a story pole is basically a long, round, stiff tape measure or stick with large numbers for the transit to read. You "shoot" the story pole by looking at it through the transit.

Before your backhoe gets to the site and to minimize your nervousness over the impending expense, shoot some grades so you get an idea of how much soil the backhoe has to remove. To do this, have a helper hold the story pole at the *high* point of the lot where your foundation will sit. There's not much excitement in this process for the helper, but he or she must concentrate on holding the story pole exactly vertical.

This high-point story pole sighting is where you should calculate your frost depth. Now look at the story pole through the transit scope. The scope's cross hairs will indicate a height on the pole. (This height is relative, so it doesn't really matter what it says, so long as the scope is level, but it does establish the relative height of your transit instrument.) Let's say the reading is 5 feet 6 inches. That means that your transit is 5 feet 6 inches above the highest point on your foundation lot.

Suppose your frost calculations tell you that you want to remove 3 feet of earth (you have calculated this ahead of time in your soil analysis). You therefore want the story pole to "sink down" 3 feet. You will know the backhoe has excavated enough dirt when your story pole reads 8 feet 6 inches. As long as the pole reads 8 feet 6 inches wherever you place it, your site will be, for practical purposes, level and at the right depth.

Incidentally, you may be able to rent or borrow a rotating laser level for this part of the job. They're convenient but not absolutely necessary. A laser level is a rotating beacon that sends out a stream of light—like a lighthouse. If you establish your instrument height, and then set up a rotating laser level so the laser shines in a level plane at the instrument height, you don't have to keep looking at your story pole through your transit. The laser will shine on the story pole at the instrument height level, and, as you excavate and the story pole "sinks down," the laser will indicate by how much. It's convenient because you can hold the story pole anywhere on the site and the laser will cast its light upon it. While you are excavating, you leave the laser on, and it rotates away casting out a beam at the level you've established. You only need one person—the story-pole holder—in order to determine how you are progressing with your excavation.

As the backhoe operator scoops out dirt, take occasional readings with your transit and story pole and see how close you are coming to your desired grade. Once you reach the desired grade in one area, let your operator know exactly what that point is and have him grade the rest of the foundation to that depth. You may end up grooming some areas by hand, but try to get as close as you can to the right depth with your backhoe. If you go a little too deep, no problem, because you will be filling the hole with gravel. But then, why put in more gravel than you have to?

PLACING THE GRAVEL

After you have excavated out dirt, you want to replace it with gravel. First, lay down a 4-mil plastic vapor barrier on top of the soil. Overlap it *at least* 6 inches where two sheets meet. Dump and spread your gravel to the desired depth (you will be shooting the gravel height with your transit and story pole). As you approach the desired gravel height, slow down, because if you put in too much gravel, the thickness of your slab will be compromised. Gravel that is an inch too high will mean a slab that is an inch too thin since the height of your slab is "fixed" at 8 inches above previously existing grade. Be sure to level your gravel consistently

and accurately and stop when you have enough.

As your gravel is spread, make a few passes with your compacter for every eight inches of gravel depth. (If you wait until all the gravel is spread, you'll be compacting just the top 8 inches of gravel.) Then dig out a 3 x 3 x 1-foot trench in the center of the slab for the center post's load-bearing pad. Slope the gravel side walls of this trench at about 50 degrees. If you are building in a low-frost area and are not using much gravel, make sure that you have at least 4 inches of gravel between the bottom of this trench and the soil beneath.

Using the batter-board string box as a guide, dig out an extra-deep trench around the edge of your foundation for the footing of your monolithic slab. The gravel in this trench will form the underside of a footing 12 inches wide and 24 inches high. The outside perimeter of this footing will be board-formed, but there is no way to use board forms beneath the slab to form the inner wall or the underside of your footing because they would be encased in concrete, leaving no way to remove them. That's why we're using the gravel itself to form the underside of any part of the slab. When trenching the gravel for footings—at the center and around the perimeter—shoot grades to get exact gravel depths at these parts of the slab.

Your slab will be 4 inches thick, so you should shoot your gravel to be 4 inches below the top edge of where the perimeter board form (your ultimate slab height) will be. But as you near the outer edge of the foundation, you don't want the slab to meet the vertical footing in a perfect 90 degree "L". Instead, for optimum load-bearing strength, you want the slab to slope, or taper, down to meet the footing. Since the gravel *is* the form for the underside of the slab, it must slope down to form where the tapered slab meets the inside wall of the footing. This taper should start 24 inches from the slab's edge and descend 4 inches over a 12-inch distance. Where the inside wall of the footing will be, you should create a nearly vertical wall of gravel (it will be about 8 inches high), and that inside wall should be 12 inches in from the perimeter form boards (figure 3–4).

TIP

As you approach the desired gravel height, slow down, because if you put in too much gravel, the thickness of your slab will be compromised.

FORMING THE SLAB

With your compacted gravel leveled in the slab's interior, sloped at the edge, and packed to form the underside and inner wall of the footings and center pad, you are ready to form the slab's perimeter footing with boards. The form boards need to be 24 inches high. Two 2x10s and one 2x6 will do nicely.

When the concrete is poured against these boards, it tends to stick to them, making them hard to remove. Before you form up the slab, spray the inside of the form boards with *form oil,* available at any good building store. It makes the boards easier to remove. (Be warned: When you remove these form boards, they won't be good for much besides similar rough work because they'll be encrusted and oily.)

To form your slab's perimeter, the strings on your batter boards must be in place. First, drive perfectly vertical 2x4 stakes into the ground around the outer edge of your slab at 4-foot intervals. You will nail your horizontal form boards to the inside of these stakes; the stakes hold the form boards in place (figure 3–5). Account for the width of your form boards when you calculate where to drive the 2x4 stakes. The measurement from the inside of one stake to the inside of another stake directly across the slab from it should be the width of the slab, *plus* the width of the form boards (add 3 inches—that is, 2 x 1½ inches—for the form boards' width). To calculate this another way, drop a plumb bob from your batter-board string above one of the stakes. With your form boards in place and nailed against these 2x4 stakes, the plumb bob should point to the exact inner edge of the form board.

Since concrete is heavy, you'll want to drive in a lot of these stakes along the form boards, especially where the form boards meet end to end. You don't want your form boards blowing out on you when you are pouring concrete, nor do you want them to bow. It's a good idea to drive in diagonal supports *(kickers)* behind each of the 2x4 stakes.

You will be using the top of the form boards to sight how much concrete to pour in. So, the top must be at exactly the desired height for the top of your slab. As you place the top form board, shoot it with your story pole and transit to make sure it's at the proper elevation and level all the way around the slab. For this work, you may want to use a *water level.*

A water level is a transparent hose with water in it; since water seeks its own level and you can't fool gravity, the water level at one end of the hose will match the water level at

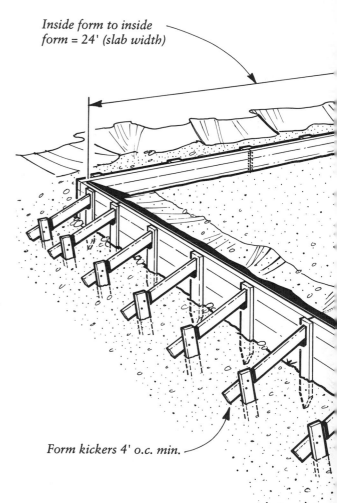

Inside form to inside form = 24' (slab width)

Form kickers 4' o.c. min.

the other end, no matter the length of the hose. Hold the transparent hose up against the top of the form board and have your helper hold the hose against another at any point on the form's surface. The water levels should match. You can use clear plastic tubing to make your own water level or buy a more sophisticated one (with grade marks on end vials) at a good building-supply store.

Once the form boards are in place, you should be able to sight exactly down the inside edge of each from your batter-board strings.

Once everything is tight, nailed, and shored up, you can remove your batter-board string completely.

Now you should have a formed space for your slab, with compacted gravel—protected from beneath with a 4-mil poly plastic vapor barrier—forming the slab-to-be's underside. The gravel should taper down to form your load-bearing center pad and your 12-inch-wide perimeter footing. Your footing's perimeter should be formed with level boards that define the top elevation of the slab.

FIGURE 3–4

The slab's edges are formed with boards. The underside is formed with gravel.

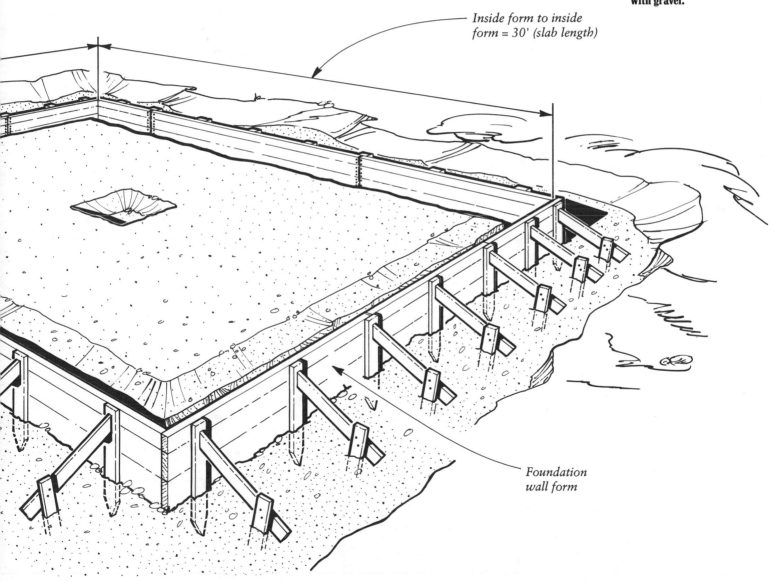

Inside form to inside form = 30' (slab length)

Foundation wall form

PLACING THE REBAR AND MESH

Make sure that none of the form oil you sprayed on the form boards comes anywhere near the rebar or mesh (or for that matter anything else the concrete must stick to). Form oil will keep the concrete from adhering properly to the metal. Also, make sure your rebar and mesh are clean. They can have some rust on them, but no large rust flakes or paint.

Take two pieces of #4 rebar and lay them lengthwise next to each other in the trench where your footing will be poured. The rebar should be about 3 inches in from the edge on each side, with 6 inches between them. But don't lay the rebar right on the gravel. Instead, prop it up on half bricks or metal rebar stands so that it sits a few inches up into the footing (figure 3–6). Where the rebar meets, overlap the ends and fasten them together with tie wire in three places. The rule is, overlap 24 times the diameter of the rebar. Number-4 rebar has a half-inch diameter (determined by multiplying the designation number, 4, by 1/8 inch). A half-inch x 24 equals 12 inches, which is how much each length of rebar should overlap.

You will have to bend the rebar at right angles for the corners. Either use a rebar bender (you can rent one), or invent one (slip the rebar in the Y of a tree, and pad the bark against injury).

The #10 wire mesh should be laid in sections as large as possible. Since you want the mesh to sit in the center of the slab, prop it on half bricks, just as you did with the rebar. It's best to put down the mesh and then go back and prop it up afterwards with the bricks.

Mesh comes in rolls, usually 4 feet wide and it's most easily cut with a bolt cutter. Roll out sections, overlap them by three or four squares, and tie these overlaps every 10 squares of so with tie wire. Lay the mesh as close to the edge of the slab as possible. Wear work gloves when handling this stuff; it can cut your hands badly.

You also want to lay angled #4 rebar where the slab starts to thicken and turns down toward the footings at the taper sections (figure 3–7). This rebar is rather tricky to support, so tie it to the mesh with flexible wire.

Once the concrete pour begins, be careful not to let the weight of the concrete pin the mesh to the gravel anywhere on the slab, and be sure the rebar doesn't move around when your concrete sloshes into the footing or your helpers are clomping around on top of it.

FIGURE 3–5

Cross-section: board-and-kicker arrangement used in forming the slab.

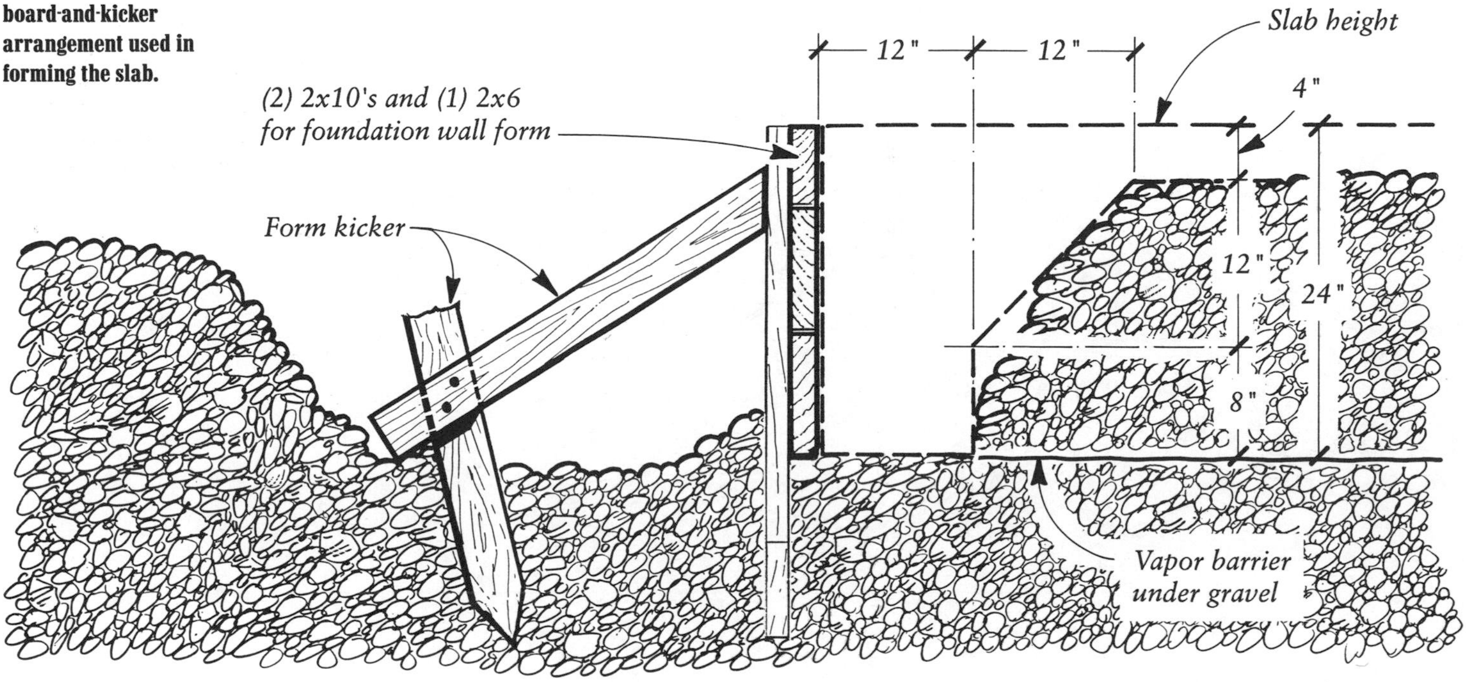

(2) 2x10's and (1) 2x6 for foundation wall form

Form kicker

12" 12"

Slab height

4"

12"

24"

8"

Vapor barrier under gravel

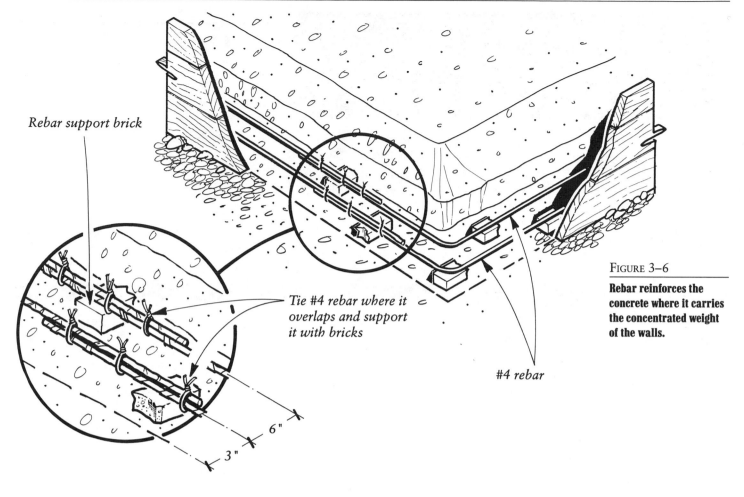

Rebar support brick

Tie #4 rebar where it
overlaps and support
it with bricks

#4 rebar

6"

3"

FIGURE 3–6

**Rebar reinforces the
concrete where it carries
the concentrated weight
of the walls.**

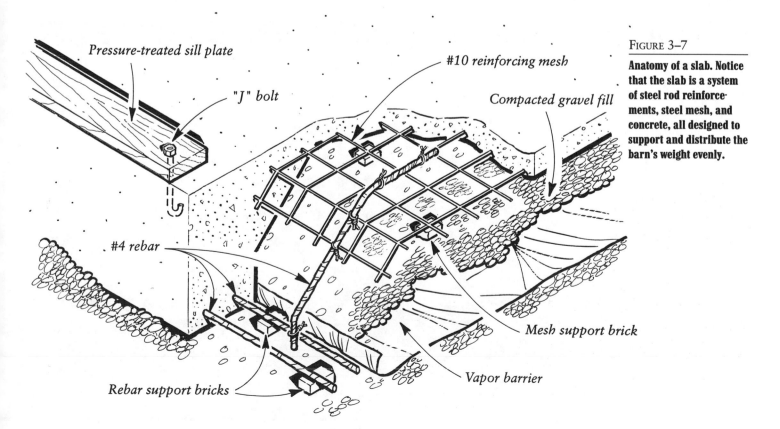

Pressure-treated sill plate

"J" bolt

#10 reinforcing mesh

Compacted gravel fill

#4 rebar

Mesh support brick

Vapor barrier

Rebar support bricks

FIGURE 3–7

**Anatomy of a slab. Notice
that the slab is a system
of steel rod reinforce-
ments, steel mesh, and
concrete, all designed to
support and distribute the
barn's weight evenly.**

How Much Concrete Should You Order?

WHEN ORDERING CONCRETE, YOU must indicate how much you want. Calculate the volume of concrete using this formula: length × width × depth of slab and express your answers in cubic yards. For your barn's slab, you must make four calculations: one for the area of your slab, one for the area of your footer and pad, one for the area where your slab tapers down to the footer, and one that totals those previous three answers.

Some figures you'll need to know:

27 cubic feet = 1 cubic yard (3 × 3 × 3 feet)
1,728 cubic inches = 1 cubic foot

CALCULATION 1

First, let's do the calculation for our 24 × 30-foot slab. Start by converting the length and width to inches, since our depth is in inches, and we'd rather not work with decimals.

length	24 feet	= 288 inches
width	30 feet	= 360 inches
depth		= 4 inches

288 × 360 × 4 = 414,720 = our slab's volume in cubic inches.

Since 1 cubic foot = 1,728 cubic inches, divide by 1,728.

$$414,720 \div 1,728 = 240 \text{ cubic feet.}$$

Now divide by 27 to find cubic yards.

$$240 \div 27 = \boxed{8.8 \text{ cubic yards. ANSWER.}}$$

Thus, our slab (without the footing or pad below the 4-inch depth or the tapered part of the footing) will require 8.8 cubic yards of concrete.

CALCULATION 2

Now let's calculate the footing volume. Since our calculation for the 4-inch slab included the area over the footing, our footing dimensions are 12 inches × 20 inches (not 12 × 24 inches because our slab-depth calculation incorporated those 4 extra inches). If we consider it as a single straight object, the footing is 104 feet long.

First, convert the dimensions to inches.

$$104 \text{ feet} = 1248 \text{ inches}$$

Now, multiply the three dimensions to obtain cubic inches.

$$1248 × 12 × 20 = 299,520 \text{ cubic inches}$$

Now, divide by 1,728 to obtain cubic feet.

$$299,520 \div 1,728 = 173.3 \text{ cubic feet}$$

And divide this figure by 27 to obtain cubic yards.

$$173.3 \div 27 = \boxed{6.4 \text{ cubic yards. ANSWER.}}$$

This 6.4 figure is the volume in cubic yards of the entire footing *minus* the 4-inch slab height already factored into our first calculation. At this point you could add the totals you already have (6.4 yards + 8.8 yards = 15.2 yards), and guess an amount for the tapered section of the footing. But let's calculate that volume mathematically.

CALCULATION 3

An object 12 inches × 12 inches × 360 inches (our 30-foot wall is 360 inches long) equals the area of two right triangles with an altitude and base of 12 inches and a length of 360 inches. Thus, if we calculate the volume of an object 12 inches × 12 inches × 360 inches, we will have the volume in cubic inches for the taper along both sides of the length of our slab. If we make a similar calculation for an object that is 12 inches × 12 inches × 22 feet long (264 inches), we will have the area for the tapered sections along the two shorter walls as well.

For the length walls:

$$12 \times 12 \times 360 = 51{,}840$$
$$51{,}840 \div 1{,}728 = 30$$
$$30 \div 27 = 1.1 \; \textit{cubic yards}$$

For the width walls:

$$12 \times 12 \times 264 = 38{,}016$$
$$38{,}016 \div 1{,}728 = 22$$
$$22 \div 27 = .8 \; \textit{cubic yards}$$

Our pad is 3 × 3 × 4 feet or 36 × 36 × 12 inches, but from its height we must subtract the 4 inches already accounted for in our first calculation. Thus,

$$36 \times 36 \times 8 = 10{,}368 \; \textit{cubic inches.}$$

If we divide that number by 1,728 (the number of cubic inches in a cubic foot) we obtain an answer of 6 cubic feet.

$$10{,}368 \div 1{,}728 = 6 \; \textit{cubic feet}$$

Divide that number by 27 (the number of cubic feet in a cubic yard), and our answer is .2 cubic yards—the amount of concrete we'll need for our pad.

$$6 \div 27 = .2 \; \textit{cubic yards}$$

1.1	+	.8	+	.2	=	**2.1** *cubic yards required for our pad and all the tapered sections of our footing.* ANSWER.
length wall taper area		width wall taper area		pad area		

CALCULATION 4

Now we add together all our previous answers:

$$6.4 + 8.8 + 2.1 = \boxed{\textbf{17.3} \; \textit{cubic yards of concrete.} \; \text{ANSWER.}}$$

If you order **18 YARDS**, you'll be all set.

Before you place your order, you may want to think about ordering some extra concrete for other jobs around the house you've left sitting, like that cracked slab in your sidewalk or the new pad for your barbecue patio. Now's the time to take stock and add whatever extra volumes you need.

PREPARING FOR THE ACTUAL POUR

When the concrete truck finally pours concrete into your slab form, prepare to move the wet concrete around; the truck can only get so close. Stone rakes work well, as do simple clean spades. Have a wheelbarrow ready to cart some concrete to the corners the truck's trough can't reach. (Make sure you wet all your tools before a pour to minimize the concrete's sticking to them.) For massaging the concrete and moving small amounts of it around by hand, a *mag float* is handy. It's really a trowel, but it's made of thick magnesium, and it's often used in the early stages of the finishing process to push rocks below the concrete's surface. A handy tool to have by your side.

You also need to have a *screed* or *strike board* ready for the pour. You use the screed board to swipe off excess concrete and level the slab, much the way you can remove excess sand from the top of a beach pail and level the rest by swiping your hand across the top. The screed board not only swipes extra concrete away and levels the slab, it also serves to indicate when you've reached grade with your pour. As you pass the screed board over the wet concrete, it will show you both high and low spots, so for best results choose a good straight board for your screed board, not a piece of junk lumber.

As the concrete is poured it will mound up. Level it with your stone rakes, then make a pass over the area with your screed board, using a sawing motion. Ideally, a screed board should stretch from one side of the form to the other,

FIGURE 3–8

Pour wide slabs in sections and use removable screed guides to indicate the proper slab height.

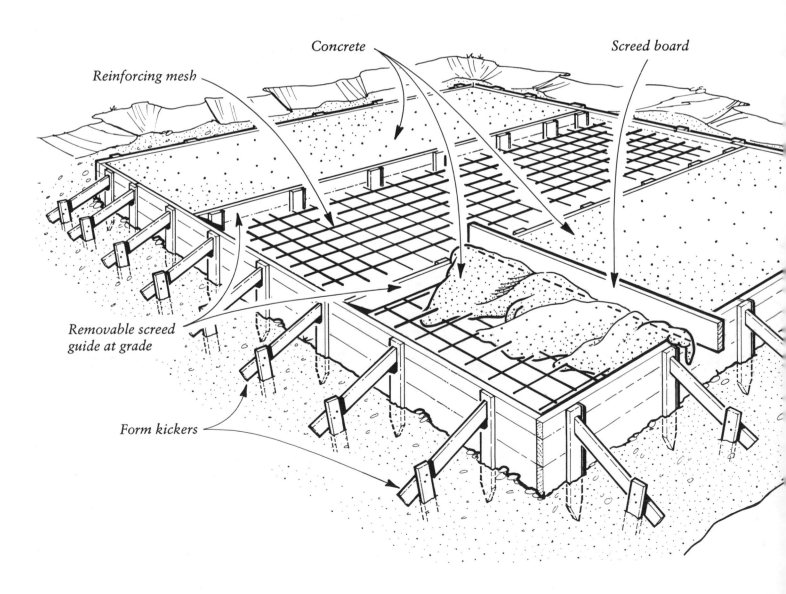

Concrete

Screed board

Reinforcing mesh

Removable screed guide at grade

Form kickers

widthwise, but since a 24-foot board is awkward and will bow, you should plan on using a 12-foot board and setting up a sectioned, temporary guiding rail in the center of your slab so the screed board will have something to rest on. This guide board can be supported by temporary stakes, but however you support it, the top of the temporary rail needs to be shot for grade so that it is at the exact height of the slab's top grade. Build the guide in sections so that you can remove them as you go. As the concrete is poured, you will work down both sides of the screed guide and remove each section as you finish with it (figure 3–8).

A temporary screed guide can make for tricky work, so you may want to pour your slab over a two-day period. If you do, plan on pouring the outer two sections of the slab one day and the center section a few days later.

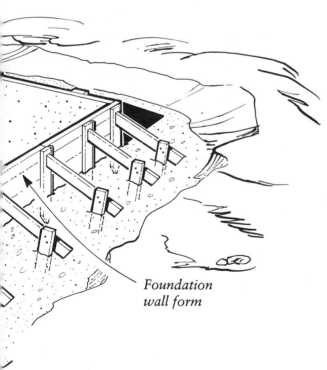

*Foundation
wall form*

FACTS YOU SHOULD KNOW ABOUT CONCRETE

Concrete is a mixture of sand, gravel, portland cement, and water. There is an entire science surrounding its strength and what you can add to enhance it. For our barn, we will need *type I* (also called *class A*) concrete. Type I concrete comes in different strengths measured in pounds per square inch, or psi. For your slab, order concrete with a psi rating of 3,500. Other types of concrete include types II and III, but those are for specialty applications, requiring rapid hardening or sulfate-resistance.

When dry concrete is mixed with water, it begins to harden, in a process called *hydration*. It takes 28 days for concrete to fully harden, though in most cases you can walk on concrete and remove form boards after three days.

Hydration is greatly influenced by temperature, so ideally you want to keep your sub-slab and slab at 70 degrees Fahrenheit throughout the process, though 50 to 90 degrees Fahrenheit is a safe range for hydration to occur. (Hardening concrete below 40 degrees Fahrenheit violates the temperature range set by the BOCA code.) Just as important, you want to keep your slab wet throughout the process—more on that in a moment—and sub-50-degree water only hinders an effective drying process.

When the concrete company mixes your batch of concrete, they will put in more water than the concrete actually needs for complete hydration. Concrete needs only 28 pounds of water for every 100 pounds of concrete (a .28 ratio) to completely hydrate. But a mix of .28 would be unworkably stiff and it wouldn't flow from the truck. So more water is added, usually up to a .45 ratio to get the concrete to flow and to make it workable enough that you can smooth it out with your *bull float* (a surface-smoothing tool) or trowel. The more water you add, however, the weaker the concrete gets. Researchers have found that concrete with a

.40 ratio and a psi rating of 5,600 is weakened to a 2,100 psi rating when the water ratio is increased to .60. Your concrete company will do all these calculations for you so you get concrete at the 3,500 psi strength. But be wary of adding water just to make your concrete workable or because you think it's getting too dry.

Once your concrete is poured into the form, you want it to retain its water for as long as possible, to give it every opportunity to hydrate properly and completely. If you pour your slab on a hot day and your slab sits in the hot sun, or if your concrete is poured on sunbaked gravel, you will have a weakened slab—the required water will evaporate too quickly and compromise the hardening process. Thus, you may want to shade your site completely with a tarp or wait to pour on a cloudy day. Anything you can do to keep the slab out of direct sunlight is desirable.

After you have poured and finished your concrete, it's best to shield it from rapid evaporation by containing the moisture. Putting poly plastic over your finished, wet slab is a good idea. Where the poly touches the concrete, the latter will discolor but its strength won't be affected. If you can, build a poly tent very close to the concrete or stretch and staple the poly to the form, being careful to seal up all the holes. Another approach is to spray your slab with curing compound. This is a solution that helps the slab retain water by cutting down evaporation. Curing compound is available at any good building-supply store.

POURING AND FINISHING

Early on, call your concrete truck company and ask them what the lead time is for getting a truck to your site. In busy areas, especially at the beginning of the summer, you may need to call a week or two ahead of time to guarantee a date. You don't have to tell them exactly how much concrete you need when you schedule a truck that far in advance. But they'll pencil in the delivery and you can call in your exact quantity later.

When the truck arrives, you should have everything ready to go, because if the pour takes more than a standard delivery time, the company may start to charge you a per-hour overtime charge. Once the pour starts, however, take your time no matter what. Even if you do have to pay an overtime charge, it's worth it to get the job done right, at your pace. After all, this is one of the few times when your work—and possibly your mistakes—will be set in stone.

If you can, have the truck back right up to the form and run its trough out into the center of the slab form. The truck trough pivots, enabling it to pour the concrete over a wide area. Also, concrete trucks usually carry trough extenders (you might want to request one) so the pour can reach even farther. When the trough is positioned, though, the concrete should not be allowed to splatter from a great height. Splattering can cause the concrete to separate, compromising its strength.

The thing you really have to watch out for is pouring in too much concrete. You can always add more, by the shovel or the wheelbarrow. But if your truck pours out its load and you start to screed across a consistently high slab of wet concrete, you and your helpers may find yourselves ankle deep in it, shoveling the excess out of the form, which is hard, messy work. Even worse, you'll be stepping all over your carefully-placed mesh. The best approach is to work an area with the concrete trough and patiently make your way from one side of the form to the other, screed-boarding the concrete as you go.

Rent a *concrete vibrator* to use during your pour. A vibrator is used to jiggle the concrete and make sure it settles into every little part of the form. The vibrator has an engine—about the size of a chainsaw's—and a cable with a weight on the end. You dip the weight into the concrete and turn on the machine. As the vibrator shakes, the concrete visibly settles out.

Another tip: To get a good finish on the exposed footing walls, whack the form a few times in 3-foot intervals all the way around the slab with your hammer. This will bring some concrete *cream* up against the form and propel the large rocks into the concrete and out of sight.

As you will learn—maybe the hard way—gaining access to the middle of the slab isn't easy once the pour has been completed. As the slab is poured, you will alternatively be working to the left and right of your screed guide and removing it in sections as you go. That way you won't have an indentation that's inaccessible to filling and smoothing when you pull out the screed board guide. The object is to work your way down, screeding both sides of the slab, not screeding on one side of the guide and then the other.

FINISHING YOUR SLAB

As soon as you have poured and screeded off the concrete, you'll want to smooth it further with a *bull float*. A bull float is essentially a large, thick trowel mounted on the end of a sectioned aluminum pole. The bull float skims over the concrete, bringing up *cream* (the portland/sand mix free of large rocks), while simulta-

neously pushing rocks down. Using a bull float is tricky, though, and you really ought either to apprentice with someone on another slab to learn how to use it or have an experienced person come on your job to help you. The object is to push the bull float across the slab and pull it toward you using a slight jerking or jitterbugging motion. In its path, the bull float should leave a swath of smooth concrete.

For slabs that are just for agricultural use, bull-floating may be enough of a finish, and after a few passes with it, you can take a wet, clean garage broom and drag it across the damp concrete to give a brush finish.

Once your slab is bull-floated, it's time to put in anchor bolts (we'll use *J-bolts*). A few days after you pour your slab, when you start framing, you need a way to attach your wall's *bottom plate* (or *sill*) to the concrete. The J-bolts will hold this bottom plate in place and tight to your slab.

Before you even pour your slab, you have to calculate where to put the J-bolts, and then be ready to place them before the concrete has hardened. J-bolts should be placed at 5-foot intervals. To make sure they go in the right place, roughly lay out your walls. You don't want J-bolts to be located in the middle of a

Smoothing freshly poured concrete with a bull float forces down rocks and brings up "cream." For many barns, that's all the finishing required.

When installing J-bolts in the wet concrete, place them at a point roughly half the width of your sill plate. Try to leave about 2 inches of the bolt exposed for a nut and washer.

pedestrian or garage-door opening. And you don't want them poking up where studs will be (see chapter 4, "Framing," for the proper distance between studs and how to calculate where your doors will go).

You also want to make sure the J-bolts will poke through the center of the plate. Our bottom plate board is a 2x8, so your J-bolts should be 4 inches in from the slab's perimeter edge.

Tap your J-bolts in with a hammer, first protecting the bolts' threads from mashing with double nut heads, and do your best to have them sit perfectly vertical. Also, make sure not to drive them in so far that you won't have enough thread with which to suck up your sill plate. The bottom plate will be 1 1/2 inches high. And you have to account for a washer and the height of the nut on top of that. (If for some reason you botch the J-bolt installation, take heart: you can always drill out some holes later with a hammer drill and add expansion bolts.)

Finer Finishing

Some of you may want a finer finish than a bull float offers, and that will involve some trowel work. Soon after you pour the concrete, you will find that you can put a small piece of plywood on it and kneel on the plywood without sinking into the wet concrete. At this point, you can begin to trowel the concrete to put a finish on it.

Gauging when a slab is ready to be troweled takes a knowing, experienced eye. I suggest that you either apprentice with someone on a few other slabs or hire someone who knows finish work. The actual art of troweling is also not as easy as it looks. You don't simply swipe the trowel back and forth a few times and call it a day. You have to know how much to trowel the concrete, how much "cream" to work up, and when to stop. Over-troweling can cause small cracks to appear later. Troweling isn't a technique you can pick up on your first slab and expect to do right. To get some experience, call a local mason and see if he or she will let you help finish a slab. (Who ever turned down a free laborer?) Try for a smaller company, run by a single person. You may find larger construction companies are all business and have insurance complications. Another option, of course, is to hire a mason for a day and have him or her help you finish the slab. If you pour on a weekend, you might interest someone in an extra day's wages for giving advice.

Adding Control Joints

While the concrete is still fresh, you will want to *edge* it and put in *control joints*. Edging is rather simple. With an edge-shaped hand tool called an edger you walk around the slab, working the edger between the wood form and the slab. The edger gives a nice, rounded edge and makes a 3-inch-wide path of smoother, indented concrete all around the slab's perimeter. Look at any sidewalk; the rounded edges were made by this tool. It isn't a bad idea to edge while the concrete is quite wet. I once worked on a big job for a veteran foreman who would edge just as soon as the concrete was poured. This amused others on the crew who told him, "Edge later; get the concrete in the form first!" He told me edging that early got the big rocks down while the concrete was still wet, and it saved lots of arm work later. He was right.

You also want to put *control joints* in your slab. These are relief cuts in the concrete that confine and control cracking that's caused by the slab expanding and contracting. You can cut control joints with a trowel designed just for that purpose or you can use your edger. Run

it one way to cut the joint, and then rotate it 180 degrees and run it back the other way. (The relief joint looks like a double edge.) Again, take a look at any sidewalk: The control joint is the relief cut defining the sidewalk sections.

A control joint should be spaced every 15 to 20 feet, and it should have a depth of one quarter the thickness of the slab. In our case, we should put in inch-deep control joints. As for their spacing, quarter your slab, running a control joint lengthwise at the 15-foot mark on the 30-foot walls, and at the 12-foot mark on the 24-foot walls.

Once your slab has been bull-floated and trowel-finished, edged, and control-jointed, you may want to put on a brush finish before the concrete gets too dry. (Some people claim a brush finish makes the slab dusty after it's been in use a year, though that's never been my experience with them). Duct-tape a handle extension on a driveway broom and get the broom wet but not dripping. With one smooth pass, drag the broom across the slab, working at a right angle to one of the walls. Wash concrete off the broom after each pass and redampen the broom. You'll find yourself dragging the broom over the edges and control joints, but running your edger over these areas again is

easy, and this technique yields an attractive finish with tight lines between the joints and edges and the broom finish.

As we mentioned before, you may want to put up a poly tent or simply cover the slab with poly to keep the water in. But at this point you can leave the concrete itself alone.

Immediately after you finish the concrete and for the first few days after the pour, periodically mist your slab with water. Use a lawn sprinkler. This provides water for the surface to cure properly and it cools the slab, slowing water evaporation. If you spray it down with a hose, be careful at first that its spray is not so intense that it takes the finish off the concrete or washes any of it away. After a day or so, you can spray your slab down without worry.

BACKFILLING

After three days, you can remove your form boards. With the form boards removed, you can install your PVC perimeter drain as we explained earlier in this chapter. After you have covered your PVC pipe with a layer of gravel, it's time to backfill.

You know that you want your slab to sit 8

inches or so above the original ground level. With some of the soil that you excavated, fill in around your slab and grade this soil so it will take water away from your slab. You may even want to use gravel as backfill. This is especially true if you are not going to use leaders and gutters to concentrate and direct rainwater and snow melt. Water pouring directly off your roof will quickly erode your soil. If the water hits gravel instead, it seeps in and is carried away by the perimeter drain.

You may find that the backfill will settle over time and you will have to add a bit more after several months. Also, now is not the time to plant anything, because you'll be walking all over this backfill as you frame your building. Save landscaping for a little later.

BRING ON THE LUMBER!

Now we're really cooking. With the level, square slab in place we're well on our way. After you've backfilled, cleaned up, and graded your site, you are ready to take some deliveries of lumber and finally start banging nails!

Use this worksheet to estimate the costs of materials and services discussed in this chapter.

WORKSHEET

FOUNDATION COSTS

CONCRETE AND REINFORCEMENT

Concrete:
_____ PER-YARD COST X _____ TOTAL YARDS = _____

Rebar:
_____ PER-FOOT COST X _____ TOTAL FEET = _____

Mesh:
_____ PER-ROLL COST X _____ TOTAL ROLLS = _____

Poly:
_____ PER-ROLL COST X _____ TOTAL ROLLS = _____

Blueboard:
_____ PER-SQUARE COST X _____ TOTAL SQUARES = _____

Gravel:
_____ PER-YARD COST X _____ TOTAL YARDS = _____

Extra delivery charges:
_____

CONCRETE FORM AND LUMBER

2x10s for slab form:
_____ PER-FOOT COST X _____ TOTAL FEET = _____

2x6s for slab form:
_____ PER-FOOT COST X _____ TOTAL FEET = _____

Utility 2x4s:
_____ PER-FOOT COST X _____ TOTAL FEET = _____

Batter boards:
_____ PER-FOOT COST X _____ TOTAL FEET = _____

Screed board and guide:
_____ PER-FOOT COST X _____ TOTAL FEET = _____

2x4 stakes: _____ **Nails:** _____

UTILITIES

Cast waste pipe:

_____ PER-FOOT COST   X _____ TOTAL FEET   = _____

PVC for chase:

_____ PER-FOOT COST   X _____ TOTAL FEET   = _____

PVC for drain:

_____ PER-FOOT COST   X _____ TOTAL FEET   = _____

PVC fittings and glue:

_____

**Plumber's fee for
septic hookup:**

_____ PER-HOUR COST   X _____ TOTAL HOURS   = _____

**Water supply line
pipe and fittings:**

_____ PER-FOOT COST   X _____ TOTAL FEET   = _____

**Plumber's fee for water
supply line hookup:**

_____ PER-HOUR COST   X _____ TOTAL HOURS   = _____

EQUIPMENT RENTAL OR PURCHASE

Backhoe:

Bull float:

Edger:

Lime:

Mason's string:

Tie wire:

Transit and story pole:

Trowels:

Vibrator:

Form oil:

Curing compound:

J-bolts, nuts, washers:

Poly tent:

Duct tape:

Support bricks:

For easy access, store framing materials near your barn site and work station but away from delivery traffic and excavation machinery.

4 Framing

Framing is fun. Sawing boards, pounding nails, and erecting walls is truly satisfying work. At the end of each day, you can look at what you've done and think, "Hey, not bad! I really *am* building my own barn."

At this point in the process, your barn becomes more than just plans on a table, as string outlines transform into real walls. You might even start to understand why full-time contractors put up with long hours and fickle clients: building is pleasurable. Since you're a builder now, why not look the part? Dig out that beat-up tool pouch and strap it on. Heck, you may even want to tie a red bandana around your neck, put out a water cooler, or carry your coffee from the house to the barn in an insulated jug, just like they do on the big jobs.

GETTING READY

While your slab is hardening, you'll have a few days to focus on preparing to frame. You must call ahead to the lumberyard to arrange delivery of lumber—something you should do even before you start pouring concrete. Sometimes lumberyards need a few days—especially in the busy season—to gather and deliver your wood. In the meantime, you should prepare an area for storing the lumber piles. You'll be receiving quite a variety of wood for your barn; separate it out upon delivery. You'll at least take delivery of 2x6s for the walls, 2x10s for rafters and joists; 4x8-foot plywood sheets for your sheathing; 2x12s

for headers and ridge beam, and whatever siding you choose.

You don't want the wood sitting directly on the ground—it'll absorb moisture—so get some scrap 2x4s (better yet, some old pallets) ahead of time and lay them out so they're ready to support the stacks of wood upon delivery. After delivery, you may want to erect a temporary polyethylene plastic tent over the lumber to keep it dry. Allow air to circulate around and through the stack to help remove moisture, especially if

the wood is green, and never cover the ends of the wood with plastic.

Tools

A radial arm saw can be very handy during construction. If you don't have one, a good circular saw will do just fine. In either case, establish a *sawing station* where you can erect level sawhorses or your radial arm saw and its extension table. The station's ground should be level and

A safe, stable work station and a knowledge of electric cutting tools such as circular saws and chop saws help make framing fun.

If you feel comfortable using one, a pneumatic nailing gun can be far less strenuous to use than a hammer.

firm, with lots of room to walk around. Also, keep this location in mind when you choose your lumber storage site. Carrying 12-foot 2x6s an extra 20 feet 40 times a day will wear out even the fittest crew member.

In chapter 2, we discussed how to run electricity to the site for powering tools. If you are running power, be mindful that you must use the proper-gauge wire for long runs of extension cords lest you damage the motors in your electrical tools. Review the section, "Getting

BASIC TOOLS NEEDED FOR BUILDING A BARN

Hammer

Square

Circular saw

Level

Speed square

Tape measure, snap line

Cat's paw, flat bar

Carpenter's pencil, razor knife

Temporary Power to the Site" on pages 38-39 in chapter 2 for specifics.

Pneumatic nail guns are also potentially convenient and rentable. Swinging a 25-ounce hammer 600-plus times a day during a construction job produces awesome cumulative stress on the hand, wrist, arm, and shoulder. Pneumatic nail guns can reduce a lot of that stress for you. But you pay the devil with the weight of the guns. If you use pneumatics, you won't be swinging your hammer as often but you will be lugging a heavy gun.

These guns get their nail-driving punch from compressed air. You use different guns for different nail types (framing, finish, staples). When nailing, you place the gun where you want the nail to go, and pull the trigger. It's that simple. But pneumatic guns are costly: their nails are sold at a premium, and you need an air compressor and hoses to run them. More important, the guns can be dangerous, packing real power. Wear safety glasses if you use one (in fact, you should wear safety glasses at *all* times during construction) and watch your every move. Years ago a building trade magazine showed the X-ray of a nail shot into the skull of a worker by a pneumatic gun. The worker was climbing a ladder and bumped his head against a nail gun held by another worker above him. Fortunately, the victim recovered. But be careful with nailers! If renting a nailer makes sense to you, practice with it before using it on the job.

There aren't many other specialty tools you'll need for framing besides your circular saw, hammer, handsaw, chalk line (snap line), drill, socket set, and other standard carpenter's tools. But you will need a *framing square* and a *speed square*. A *bevel square* comes in handy too. We'll put these squares to use in just a little bit.

Choosing Your Lumber

There are a number of types of lumber: *kiln-dried, native green, air-dried,* (with subcategories *S-dry, S-green, and MC-15),* and *pressure-treated.* Each type of lumber has a different moisture content, milling quality, and inherent strength. Not all of it is suitable for framing.

Kiln-dried lumber is dried at the sawmill and cut to consistent, predictable dimensions. Barring shrinkage, a 2x4 measures 1 ½ inches by 3 ½ inches; 2x6s measure 1 ½ inches by 5 ½ inches; 2x8s, 1 ½ inches by 7 ¼ inches, and so on. (Note, for 2x8s and up, you may lose as much as ¾ inch off the full dimension—larger dimension stock can vary!)

Native green lumber—usually available from local sawmills—isn't cut as precisely. A 2x8 can measure 2 ¼ inches by 8 ½ inches, for instance. Nor is native green lumber structurally as stable as kiln-dried lumber. It's heavier and harder to work with; it cracks and splits as it dries. Native green's advantage: it's cheaper. But since it's not "graded for structure" or "appearance," it should be avoided for framing unless you are building a very rough structure. Keep in mind, though, native green lumber is good lumber for board-and-batten siding, or traditional barn board siding (more on these in chapter 6.)

S-dry, S-green, and MC-15 are categories of air-dried lumber found most often near the coasts or in the western United States. Because of its relatively high moisture content, some builders use it for framing and let it dry over the course of a summer before enclosing it.

Another kind of lumber is known as *pressure-treated.* Pressure-treated lumber, often called PT, is southern yellow pine pressure soaked in an insecticide and fungicide solution (usually a form of arsenic, though borates are becoming popular). The most common type is called *CCA,* for *chromated copper arsenate,* which is the name for the insecticide solution used in the wood.

For the barn design presented in this book, use either 0.40 or 0.60 CCA PT wood for the *sill plate* (0.25 and above is rated for above-ground use; the 0.25—one of nine categories in all—refers to the CCA concentration). In general, plan on using pressure-treated lumber anywhere the wood will come in contact with moist earth or concrete.

Some people insist that pressure-treated CCA wood is dangerous. Though an airtight legal connection between sickness and CCA use has not been proven consistently, people have become ill after working with CCA lumber. To be safe, wear a dust mask when you cut CCA, don't breathe or compost the sawdust, and wash your hands and face after working with it. Don't burn the scraps. Also, be aware when picking up the wood at the lumberyard that some of the insecticide solution may have precipitated out as the wood dried on the stacks. The precipitant commonly looks like white powder. Avoid touching it, and wash your hands thoroughly after loading the wood.

Non-pressure-treated lumber is the wood most people are talking about when they refer to common lumber, and it's the wood we'll be using for the majority of our barn. So let's look at specifics. Non-pressure-treated kiln-dried lumber comes in two types: *structural grade* and *common yard grade* (sometimes called *construction grade* or *framing grade*). Structural grade comes in five categories, number 1 being the best (knot-free, no defects) and number 5 the worst (full of knots and blemishes). Common yard grade comes in four categories, with number 1 the best, number 4 the worst. Which should you use? For our barn, use *kiln-dried, No. 2 & BTR (better) common yard grade* for structural framing (joists, rafters, and ridge beam) and *kiln-dried, Standard and Better* (marked: *STND & BTR* at the lumberyard), for the wall framing. This wood typically comes in spruce, pine, or fir and is sometimes actually referred to as *spruce-pine-fir.*

In the past, most lumberyards charged for delivered wood by the *board foot (bdf)*. One board foot is a board 12 x 12 x 1 inches. A 12-foot 2x4 is 8 board feet (2 x 4 x 12 ÷ 12 = 8). Your lumberyard may still charge by the board foot. But more and more yards are charging according to the dimensions of the individual sticks ordered. Yet another twist: You may get charged by the board foot, and then find a premium added for longer lengths of larger dimension lumber. For peace of mind—and budgeting purposes—ask your yard for its pricing system.

With our wood type chosen, let's look at how we'll lay out our walls and roof and at the end of the chapter calculate our lumber needs for framing.

The Sill Plate

When you erect the frame for a wall after nailing the frame together on the ground, you have to nail it to a piece of wood that's firmly and permanently attached to the slab. This piece of wood is called the *sill plate,* and it's attached to the slab with the J-bolts we earlier tapped into the concrete. Before we can begin framing, we have to bolt the sill plate down.

For starters, use two 12-foot 2x8 CCA pressure-treated boards. Lay them end to end along one of the 24-foot walls, to the inside of the J-bolts. With the ends of the 2x8s flush to the outside of the foundation walls and abutting each other in the center, use a framing square to mark where along the 2x8s your J-bolts will poke through, and how far in on the 2x8 the holes should be drilled (figure 4–1). Then drill holes for your J-bolts where you have marked. Hint: Make the holes small enough to receive your washers but big enough so that each plate has a bit of wiggle room should you need to make adjustments.

At this point, you should know exactly where your barn's doors will go. Later, after we've erected our walls, you'll have to cut out the sill plate in each door's passageway. To make that job easier, take your circular saw now and cut an inch-deep *kerf* (saw blade width) mark on the underside of the sill plate to either side of where your door will go. (As you read on, you will see that this kerf mark should come where the inside of the doors' jack studs will be.) Later, after our walls are erected, we can go back with a straight-bladed electric saw called a *sawzall* or a handsaw and easily cut through the plates without risking our blade to the slab or binding the saw at an awkward angle.

Next, place the 2x8s over the J-bolts and suck up the nuts and washers with a socket wrench so the 2x8s are secured. No matter how snug you make these nuts, you will have to retighten them just before you raise your walls and just before you sheetrock. Why? The wood dries and the nuts lose tension. Here's another tip: In the inevitable rush of the pour, you may have installed your J-bolts too low. There might not be

Right

Wrong

HOLDING A HAMMER AT ITS BASE GIVES YOU MORE SWINGING POWER.

enough thread to grab with a nut. In that case, drill out the wood above this bolt with a 1 ½-inch spade bit before drilling the bolt hole. This gives you room for your socket wrench and gains you enough room to start the nut. Or, start the nut without the washer, compress the sill wood with it, then unscrew the nut and see if you can get a washer and nut on.

If you are going to insulate and finish your first floor, you may want to get a strip of plastic foam called a *sill seal* and install it around the slab edge before bolting down your sill plates. Push it gently over the J-bolts and onto the slab. When you tighten the nuts, the foam strip creates a seal between the slab and sill plate that helps stop air infiltration.

For your 30-foot wall sills, avoid waste—use three 10-foot 2x8s. Since the sill plates on your 24-foot wall extend to the edge of the slab, the length of a plate required along the 30-foot wall is shortened by twice the width of one 2x8,

or 14 ½ inches (figure 4–1). Measure and bolt these sill plates down the same way you did for the 24-foot walls. Do not miter 45-degree angles where the two sill plates meet.

Laying Out Walls

With the sill plates bolted snug, it's time to lay out the walls. But first let's look at a wall's design.

The walls in our barn will be framed with 2x6 studs. You can use 2x4s for your wall studs, but they will be only marginally cheaper, and your building won't be as sturdy. If you plan to insulate your building, you should definitely use 2x6s. These deeper studs allow for thicker insulation.

If you follow the design presented in this book, your first floor ceiling will be 8 feet high. That's standard. If you want a higher ceiling, adjust the stud height accordingly. (If you want

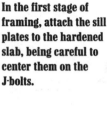

FIGURE 4–1

In the first stage of framing, attach the sill plates to the hardened slab, being careful to center them on the J-bolts.

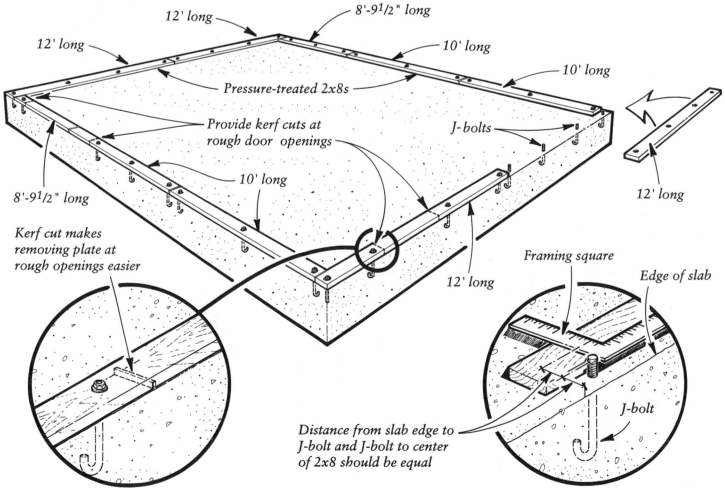

12' long

12' long

8'-9½" long

10' long

10' long

Pressure-treated 2x8s

Provide kerf cuts at rough door openings

J-bolts

10' long

8'-9½" long

12' long

Kerf cut makes removing plate at rough openings easier

12' long

Framing square

Edge of slab

J-bolt

Distance from slab edge to J-bolt and J-bolt to center of 2x8 should be equal a wall higher than 10 feet, check your code books. Some codes require *fire blocking*—horizontal blocks designed to prevent fire from rising uninhibited—every 10 feet in the *stud bays*—the spaces between studs.) Since 8-foot ceilings are so common, there are studs that are precut for walls that height, called *precuts,* and their length accounts for the bottom plate of the wall and the double top plate to give you the right wall height. If you use a 91 ¹/₂-inch precut, and you have a double top plate width of 3 inches (2 x 1 ¹/₂ inches = 3), and a single bottom plate (not counting the sill) of 1 ¹/₂ inches, then you get a wall 96 inches high, from its bottom plate to the top of its double top plate; 96 inches is 8 feet. It is also what a section of 4x8 foot drywall will cover perfectly with no waste (figure 4–2). Such easy fitting applies to the interior walls only. The exterior walls need more than two 4x8 sheets (more later).

Rough Openings

When laying out your walls, you must account for windows and doors and give them rough openings to fit into. When you buy a new window or a prehung door, the manufacturer will indicate the required size of the rough opening. (We'll cover more on the fine points of window and door installation later in this chapter.) A rough opening should be 1 ¹/₄-inches larger than the window sash or door, on all four sides. That allows for a standard ³/₄-inch jamb, and it also leaves room for any shims that you'll use to level and square up your door or window. For manufactured windows or prehung doors that come with pre-built jambs, you need only allow for the half-inch shims on all four sides. If you do buy manufactured windows or prehung doors, be sure to get units that have the proper jamb width for your size wall. A door's or window's jamb width for a 2x4 wall is *not* the same as for a 2x6 wall. Often these days, manufacturers supply a standard window unit, and customers are left to order the jamb extensions they need for their walls.

If you are using salvaged windows or doors, check ahead to the window/door installation section of this chapter to see what kind of jamb you should build and how much space you should allow for it. No matter what kind of door or windows you are using, calculate the rough openings required and account for these when you lay out your studs.

Ideally, you want the tops of your windows and the tops of your pedestrian doors to be the same height (figure 4–2). With our 8-foot ceiling design, we can use *headers* that are all the same height and thickness, whether they are used above a window or a door. A *header* is a horizontal structural member that supports the building load otherwise carried by studs we've removed to make room for a window or door. Since windows and doors are not structurally strong supports, a header spans their width and carries the weight above them. Using 2x12 headers for windows and doors will make the tops of all our windows and doors the same height above the slab. (They also save the work of having to cut short (*cripple*) studs for any remaining section of the wall above the headers.)

A 2x12 header puts the tops of your windows and doors at 81 ³/₄ inches. We obtain that figure by subtracting 11 ¹/₄ inches (the header height and 3 inches (the double plate height) from 96 inches (the wall height).

We'll assemble all headers the same way. Since the header must be as thick as the wall (5 ¹/₂ inches), we'll sandwich two pieces of ¹/₂-inch plywood between three 2x12s to obtain a header of exactly the right thickness (figure 4–3). Because the 2x12s may be bowed, cut the plywood pieces at 10 ³/₄ inches so they don't sit flush with the 2x12s' tops and bottoms. Nail the header together using 16d nails 8 inches o.c. Notice in the wall layout that to either side of a header you nail two types of studs: The *king stud* goes from the bottom plate to the top plate; a *jack* or *trimmer stud* goes from the bottom plate to the underside of the header, to carry the header load. When you mark your plates for stud position, remember that the stud you are marking on the top plate is the stud that will go on the outside of your header. It's the shorter jack stud, marked only on the bottom plate, that actually determines the width of your rough opening.

TIP

A TAPE MEASURE HELD ON THE END OF A BOARD CAN GIVE INACCURATE READINGS. FOR MORE PRECISION, START YOUR MEASUREMENTS AT THE ONE-INCH MARK, MAKING SURE TO COMPENSATE FOR THE DIFFERENCE.

Anatomy of a Wall

FIGURE 4–2

Notice how headers support the gaps created by windows and doors, and framing members occur every 24 inches on center.

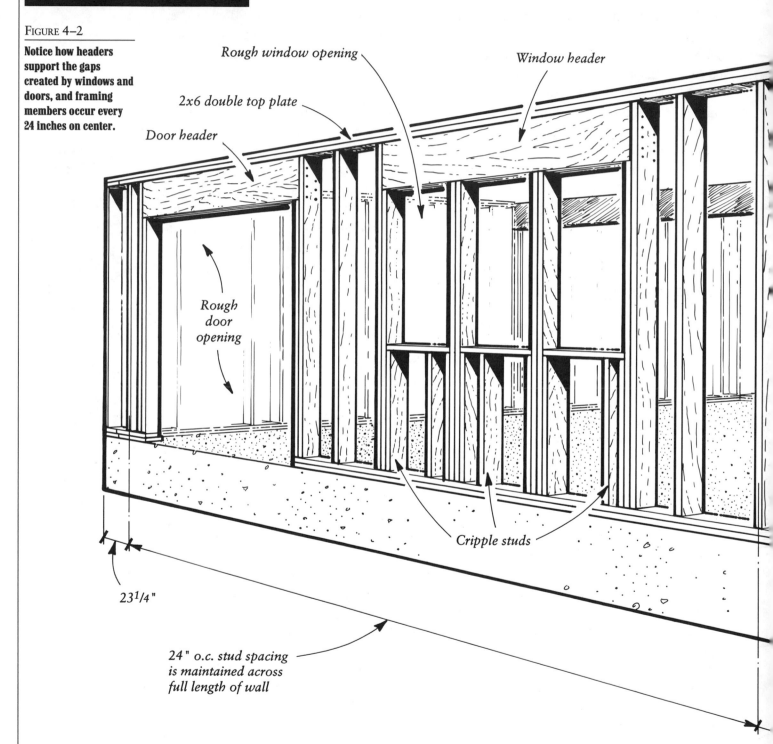

Rough window opening

Window header

2x6 double top plate

Door header

Rough door opening

Cripple studs

23¹/4"

24" o.c. stud spacing is maintained across full length of wall

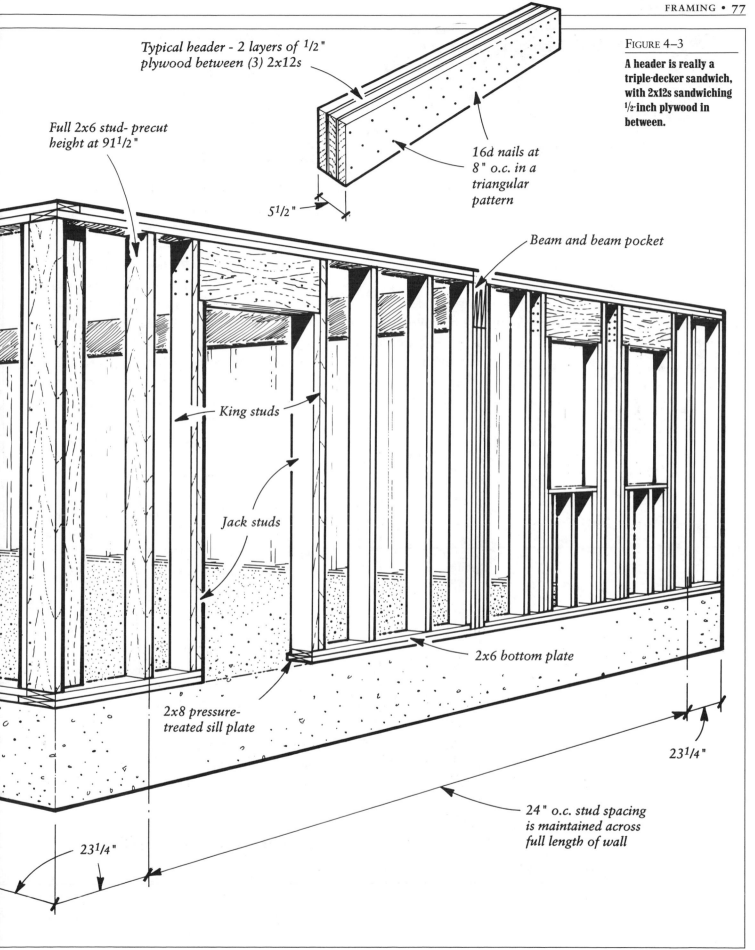

Typical header - 2 layers of ¹/2"
plywood between (3) 2x12s

FIGURE 4–3

A header is really a
triple-decker sandwich,
with 2x12s sandwiching
¹/2-inch plywood in
between.

16d nails at
8" o.c. in a
triangular
pattern

5¹/2"

Full 2x6 stud- precut
height at 91¹/2"

Beam and beam pocket

King studs

Jack studs

2x6 bottom plate

2x8 pressure-
treated sill plate

23¹/4"

23¹/4"

24" o.c. stud spacing
is maintained across
full length of wall

SHORT-WALL LAYOUT

Now, let's lay out a 24-foot end wall. Refer to figure 4–4 as you go. In laying out these walls, everything we do to one we'll do to the other. They are mirror images of each other, only differing where you choose to create rough openings for doors and windows. The same is true for the 30-foot walls; they, too, are mirror images of each other.

Each end wall will actually be built in two sections, with each section 11 feet 9 ³⁄₄ inches long. These sections will be built with 12 foot top and bottom plates trimmed back 2 ¹⁄₄ inches. Where the two wall sections meet in the middle—to the left and right of the slab's center, we will make a support or *pocket* where a beam will sit.

FIGURE 4–4

The center beam sits on a post made of three 2x6s at the midpoint of the end wall. As shown here, joists eventually rest on the beam.

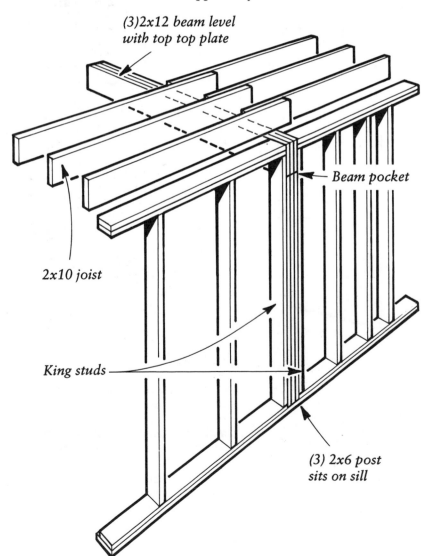

(3)2x12 beam level with top top plate

2x10 joist

King studs

Beam pocket

(3) 2x6 post sits on sill

The beam will run lengthwise from one end wall to the other, only resting midway on a load-bearing post (figure 4–4). Remember, our foundation is thicker along the center line where this post will sit.

Beam Support

Why are we installing this beam? When we finish our outside walls we will run ceiling joists widthwise across the barn and parallel with the end walls. Without the beam, the ceiling joists would have to span 24 feet—the full width of the barn. Since 24 feet is an awesome distance for a piece of wood to span (it would have to be a *very* wide joist), we can ease the strain by having the joists span 12 feet, from the top plate to the mid beam. Since each ceiling joist will rest on the beam in the middle of our barn, the top of the beam will have to be flush with the top of the wall's top plate.

Build the beam pocket support out of three 2x6s, each 7 feet ¹⁄₂ inch long. Nail them flush to each other using 8d nails. These 2x6s will create a seat 11 ¹⁄₄ inches below the top of the double top plate. When the 2x12 beam sits in the pocket, the top of the beam will be flush with the top of the top plate.

When it comes time to erect your end wall sections, sandwich this beam pocket support between them so the center line of the beam pocket is exactly at 12 feet from either end of the wall, at the midpoint of the barn.

Warning: A center beam made of three 2x12s should be beefed up if you intend to place heavy loads on your second floor. For example, a second floor loaded to the rafters with hay bales requires a center beam composed of *five* 2x12s. Check with a structural engineer if you have doubts, and, obviously, modify the beam pocket to accomodate the wider beam.

The Bottom and Top Plates

Back to the end walls themselves. Pick out two 12-foot 2x6s, making sure they are the straightest boards in the pile. These will be your top and bottom plates. Lay them down on your slab beside each other. Square them up so you'll be able to draw lines at the same points with your framing square across both boards simultaneously.

Using a tape measure, let's first measure out where each stud will go and mark either side of those points with a *carat* (an upside-down V, with the point aiming directly where your measurement falls). Afterwards, we'll use the framing square to draw straight, square-line outlines in which the studs will go (figure 4–5).

With our two 12-foot 2x6 top plates lying on the slab, first mark and trim off 2 1/4 inches from each. (Remember, we need plates that are 11 feet 9 3/4 inches to make room for the beam pocket.) Since not all 12-foot boards are exactly 12 feet, square off and cut an inch from one end, then measure 11 feet 9 3/4 inches and make a second clean square cut to give you fresh square cuts at both ends (see "Cutting Clean, Square Lines with Your Circular Saw").

Our studs will be 24 inches *on center,* or 24 o.c. That means that the center-to-center—*not* the edge-of-one-to-the-center-of-the-next—measurement will be 24 inches. (If you are using 2x4s, run them 16 inches on center.) Having established a rule, here's an exception: The first studs (the corner stud) will go at the end of the plate, but the second one will not be 24 o.c., in

Cutting Clean, Square Lines with Your Circular Saw

IT'S NOT EASY TO CUT CLEAN, SQUARE lines with a circular saw—the blade can stray from the cut line. Want the perfect saw guide for each cut? Here's a technique that might help. All you need is a *speed square* and your circular saw.

A speed square is a small, solid, heavy-duty square, usually made of aluminum, with just one small slot cut in the center of it, and angles and inches etched on both sides (see page 72).

To perform this technique, you also need to know about your circular saw's *sole plate,* that flat metal plate at the base of the saw that rests on the wood when you make a cut.

If you hold your speed square against a board, to the left of where your saw will pass, you can see it establishes a guideline along which your saw's sole plate can run.

Before you make a cut, and before you even turn on your saw, rest your saw against the board as if you were going to make a cut, and push the resting blade right up against the cut line. You'll see that the sole plate is now substantially on the wood.

Snugly rest your speed square to the left of the sole plate and hold it firm. Back your saw up an inch, start the blade, and begin your cut. As you push your saw through the cut, keep the outer edge of your sole plate square with your speed square and your cut will be square.

You'll soon realize that the distance between your speed square and your cut line is the same, cut for cut. Place your saw on a table, and tilt it up. The distance between your speed square guideline and your cut line happens to be the distance between your saw's blade and the left of your sole plate. If you want, you can measure and mark this each time you mark a cut line.

By holding a speed square up to the board you are about to cut and backing it away from the cut line exactly the distance between your saw's blade and the left edge of the saw's sole plate, you establish a guide for your circular saw. The quickest way to do this: Hold your saw up to the cut line, then place your speed square up against the board and flush with the left side of your saw's sole plate. Hold the speed square firmly in place and run your saw through the cut with the square as the guide.

order to account for how the half-inch plywood sheathing will fall on the studs once the framing is done. If you put your second stud at 23 1/4 inches from the end of the plate and a third stud 24 o.c., from there, a 4-foot panel will fall exactly in the middle of the third stud once the panel material is lined up properly with the half-inch plywood sheathing on the opposing wall. (Measure for this 23 1/4-inch stud from the outside corners of the four walls, *not* where wall sections meet in the middle of the slab.)

For this next step you have to know where you want your doors and windows, and how big each rough opening should be (read ahead to the section in this chapter on doors and win-

dows). For rough openings, mark the king studs on the top and bottom plate. Where jack and cripple studs occur, mark only the bottom plate. Mark each stud location with an X for a full stud not part of a rough opening, a K for king, a J for jack, C for cripple, and an O with a line through it for the center of window and door headers.

Once you have laid out a rough opening, measure from the corner and make sure you have some kind of stud occurring at each 24 o.c. location (except for doorways, of course). Below windows, place your cripple stud at 24 o.c., even if it is not in the center of the windowsill. You will be running plywood and sheetrock from the

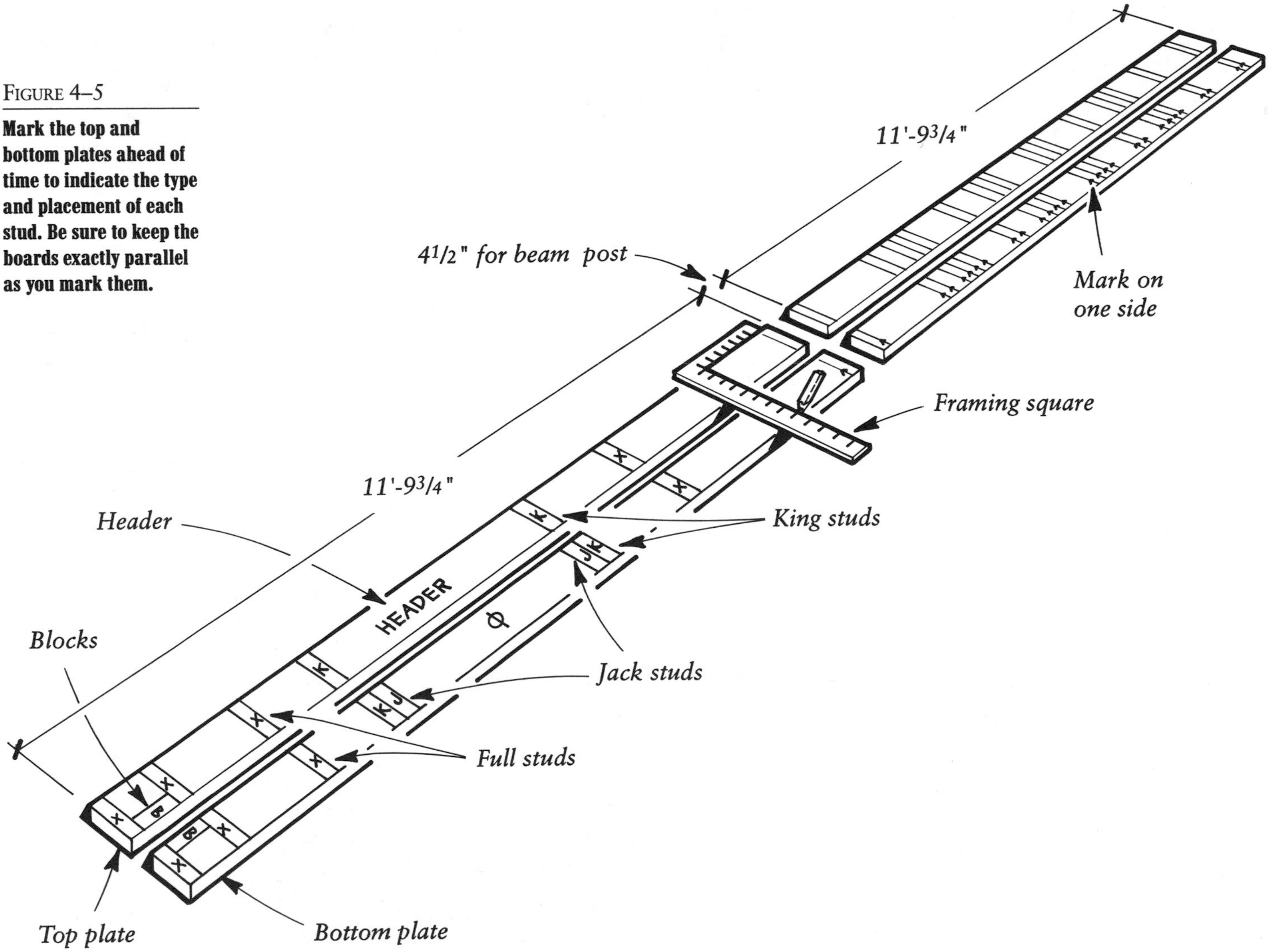

FIGURE 4–5

Mark the top and bottom plates ahead of time to indicate the type and placement of each stud. Be sure to keep the boards exactly parallel as you mark them.

11'-93/4"

Mark on one side

4 1/2" for beam post

Framing square

Header

11'-93/4"

HEADER

King studs

Blocks

Jack studs

Full studs

Top plate

Bottom plate

corner, and you need to have some stud to nail to at each 24 o.c. location.

You will be cutting out the section of bottom plate where the doorways occur after you erect the wall. Make a 1-inch kerf mark on the underside of the plate just as we did in our pressure-treated (PT) sill plate so we can later saw through to remove that section of plate without difficulty.

Corner Detail

When laying out the studs for your 24-foot end walls, the stud at the end of the plate (where the corner of the building will be) is actually a double stud. One 2x6 sits flush with the end of the plate. At a right angle to that stud and flush with the interior wall face, place a 2x6 widthwise (figure 4–6). The 2x6 you turn widthwise is just a sheetrock nailing surface and can be a full 2x6 or four 2x6 blocks. A full stud is easiest.

This configuration establishes two things: (1) when adjoining walls meet, there is something substantial to nail to; (2) 4x8 sheet goods such as sheetrock will snug in without cutting at the corner, on a good nailing surface.

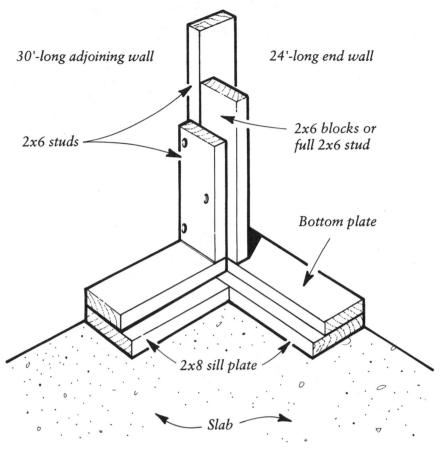

FIGURE 4–6

Extra studs are needed at corners to ensure a good structural connection where walls meet and to provide a nailing base for interior panel materials, like sheetrock.

LONG-WALL LAYOUT

When laying out your 30-foot wall, you'll find you might not want to build it as a single long unit unless you have enough crew to lift the entire wall easily. Instead, you may choose to build the wall in sections. If you do, have the top and bottom plates break on a stud (or on a header) so the plates aren't hanging in the air between studs. This is not a concern on your 24-foot end walls, because the beam-pocket supports will occupy the walls' dead center, and the wall sections to either side of them will be composed of two complete independent sections.

Remember, your long walls won't measure a full 30 feet. Because they will abut the already-standing 24-foot end walls, the long walls will be shorter by two wall widths (the end walls are each 5 1/2 inches thick, so, the long walls will be 30 minus 2 x 5 1/2, or 29 feet 1 inch long).

DRILLING OUT FOR J-BOLTS

Once you have your stud locations marked on your plates, pick up the bottom plate and put it on the sill where it will sit when the wall is erected. Note where the J-bolt stubs will pop up into the wall's bottom plate. Measure and drill out a relief anywhere the J-bolts will stab into the bottom plate.

NAILING YOUR WALL TOGETHER

Time now to bang some nails! We'll assemble each wall on the slab, sheathe it, cut out our rough openings, and then erect it when it's done.

Important to any barn raising is finding jobs for *everyone* who wants to help. Here, two aspiring craftsmen ready framing nails for use by dulling the sharp points so they won't split the wood.

TIP

PLACE A BLOCK
BENEATH YOUR
HAMMER WHEN
PULLING NAILS. IT
GIVES MORE LEVERAGE
AND PROTECTS
THE BOARD.

Take out some precuts and lay out one for every set of stud lines on the top plate that has a corresponding set of lines on the bottom plate (you won't be putting in your jack studs just yet). Stand your top and bottom plates up on edge and separate them. Place precuts at opposite ends of your plates and nail them. Use 16d nails, two for each stud. If the nails split the wood badly, dull them first by tapping the pointy end with your hammer. (Note: This is a gr*eat* job for that younger member of the crew who is looking for something important to do.)

With those first two precuts in place, you should have a box comprised of on-edge 2x6s. Just get the wall approximately square for right now because nailing on our sheathing later will force the wall to be truly square. Nail in the rest of the precuts, and build your corner as shown in the corner detail illustration.

Nail your headers in now as well. After your headers are in, you can install your jack studs. Once the jack studs are in, you can nail in your 2x6 window sills. With the window sills in place,

you can install your cripple studs. Nail a cripple next to each jack stud, at either end of the window sill, and one in the center of the sill or wherever is required to establish a nailing surface at 24 inches o.c.

Do not install the topmost top plate at this time. That will go on after all the walls are up and plumb.

SHEATHING

Once you have your wall studs nailed together, it's time to put on the sheathing. The sheathing will act to square the wall. Once you lay your sheathing down on your studs, you will easily discover where the wall is out of square.

Your siding preference determines the kind of sheathing you will use; for most of you that will be plywood sheathing. (Look ahead to the siding section of this chapter to see sheathing requirements for different kinds of siding.) If you are going to use native rough-sawn barn boards for board-and-batten siding, you won't have to sheathe with plywood but you will need blocking and diagonal bracing to keep your walls square (more later). If you're using clapboards, shakes, or even just a plain plywood exterior finish, sheathe now with plywood.

Use half-inch plywood for the exterior sheathing, but realize there are many types of plywood finishes to choose from. At the lumber yard you'll run into all manner of multi-letter combinations, such as AB and BC. For our barn, let's use CDX plywood, unless you want your plywood sheathing to be the actual siding. In that case, you may want to upgrade to a better finish. Consult your lumberyard. CDX is quite common, of good quality, and available in the thicknesses we need. (Note: the only way we won't be using CDX is as an underlayment for tile or linoleum floors. Otherwise, use CDX plywood of the appropriate thickness for all sheathing and decking. More later in this chapter.)

Sheathing is a simple task, and the only real requirements are a couple of strong backs and an ability to cut panel material in a straight, square line (see "Cutting Square Lines on Panel Materials"). Our barn is 24 feet wide and 8 feet high. You'd think you could just use exactly six vertical 4x8 foot plywood sheets on each end wall, but unfortunately we need to cover a few more structural members than just the stud walls. To see how you put sheathing on, refer to figure 4–7. Notice that you want the sheathing to extend down over the bottom plate, and then over the sill plate, and actually sit 2 inches down below that, overlapping the slab. This sheathing overlap will help seal the weather out. When you lay your sheathing down on the stud wall, run it horizontally. At the bottom plate, account for the sill (1 1/2 inches) and the distance you want to overlap the slab (2 inches) and then have the sheathing stick out below the bottom plate 3 1/2 inches. When you nail it on, you will see along the edges of the sheathing if the stud members are square because the sheathing is naturally square. Move your stud members until they line up squarely with the edges of the sheathing.

You will also notice from figure 4–7 that

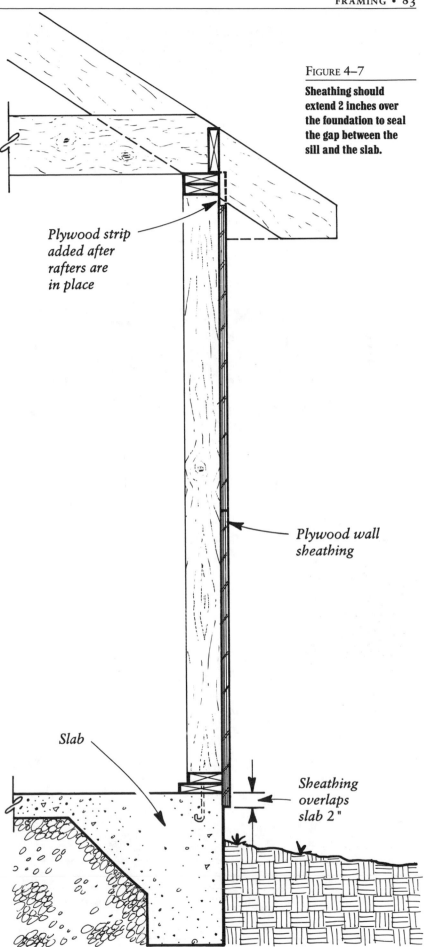

FIGURE 4–7

Sheathing should extend 2 inches over the foundation to seal the gap between the sill and the slab.

Plywood strip added after rafters are in place

Plywood wall sheathing

Slab

Sheathing overlaps slab 2"

sheathing extends upwards to cover the two top plates. Abut a second piece of sheathing to the piece you just nailed on and nail it on, too. You'll notice that there is a gap above this second piece because the wall is more than 8 feet high. Rip a piece of plywood to cover this gap. (Don't put one piece of plywood at the bottom of the wall and one at the top, leaving a gap in the middle. Let the gap fall at the top of the wall.)

Use 8d nails for all your sheathing. Drive nails every 6 inches along the four perimeter edges of the plywood and every 12 inches for studs within the panel. To prevent buckling and allow for expansion due to moisture, leave a ⅛-inch gap between the plywood panels.

Rough openings? Sheathe right over them. And sheathe right over the outside edge of your beam pocket support. Then nail around the rough opening studs and headers using our perimeter nailing schedule of one nail every 6 inches.

When you are ready to cut your rough openings, use a drill with a long, thin bit and drill out holes at the four corners of the rough openings. Snap a chalk line between the drilled holes. With your circular saw cut out the plywood along these chalk lines but leave the plywood on the outside of the beam pocket in place.

Cutting Square Lines on Panel Materials

GETTING A CLEAN, SQUARE CUT ON panel materials is difficult. Most people measure for their cut, snap a chalk line, and run the saw freehand. Well, here's a tip for getting clean, square panel cuts every time.

Go ahead and make your measurements and snap a chalk line to indicate your cut line. But don't cut the panel freehand with your circular saw. Instead, clamp in place a reusable *shootboard* or *fence* as a saw guide.

A shootboard consists of two strips of 4-foot plywood, one 4 inches wide, the other 8 inches wide. When you cut the strips (it's best to use a table saw for accuracy), be sure the lines are true and square—this shootboard will be your saw guide for multiple cuts. Nail the thinner board on top of the wider one so your saw's sole plate fits snug against the 4-inch board and the saw's blade sits snug against the outer lip of the wider 8-inch

FIGURE 4–8

A shootboard made from two pieces of plywood, one 4 inches wide, and the other 8 inches wide, serves as a fence or guide for your saw when cutting panel materials. The shootboard is temporarily clamped in place and then reused.

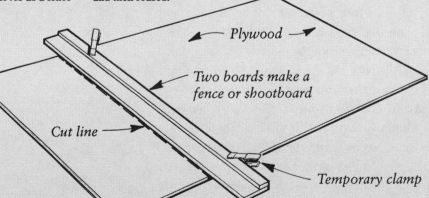

board (figure 4–8).

Once you've built your shootboard, go to the panel you want to cut. With your chalk line snapped, clamp the shootboard onto the plywood with spring clamps so the outer edge of the wider board lines up with your

chalk line. When you run your saw along your fence, the blade will protrude enough to cut the plywood but will be guided by the shootboard. Besides ensuring a straight cut, a shootboard also helps prevent the plywood from splintering.

CHECKING THE WALLS FOR PLUMB AND SQUARE

Once the wall has been assembled, muster your crew and stand the wall up on top of the sill where it will permanently sit (figure 4–9). Using 16d nails, you may want to install 10-foot 2x6 braces at the top of the outside of the wall section you're about to raise. These braces will slide along the slab as you raise the wall and are ready to brace the wall once it is upright. You can also use them to secure the wall when you plumb it. Once the wall is up, check it for *plumb*—that is, make sure it is standing perfectly vertical. That requires a 4- or 6-foot level, but you shouldn't just put the level directly against the wall for your reading because it won't be accurate enough. Take a perfectly straight piece of 2x4, or rip a piece of plywood in a perfect rectangle

and hold your level against it. This piece of wood effectively extends your level. You may want to put "feet" on the bottom of the level extender, so you have a place to grab your level.

Before you put your level against the stud wall, nail a diagonal brace with one nail into the outside stud. You should be able to move this diagonal brace up and down like a pump handle. You will eventually secure this brace by nailing it to the PT sill plate. While you hold the level against the wall, have a crew member press the diagonal brace against the sill plate and drive a nail into the brace so it is one hammer blow away from being nailed into the plate. As you pull or push the wall, watch the level. When the level indicates vertical, shout "Nail it!" The crew member on the diagonal brace drives the nail into the sill, thus bracing the wall in a plumb position. Now run an additional brace from the sheathing to a stake in the ground outside your slab. Nail a temporary 2x4 cleat on the outside of your sheathing to give something for this outside brace to grab.

FIGURE 4–9

Once walls are erected, brace them by running diagonal 2x6s either to the sill or to stakes hammered into the ground.

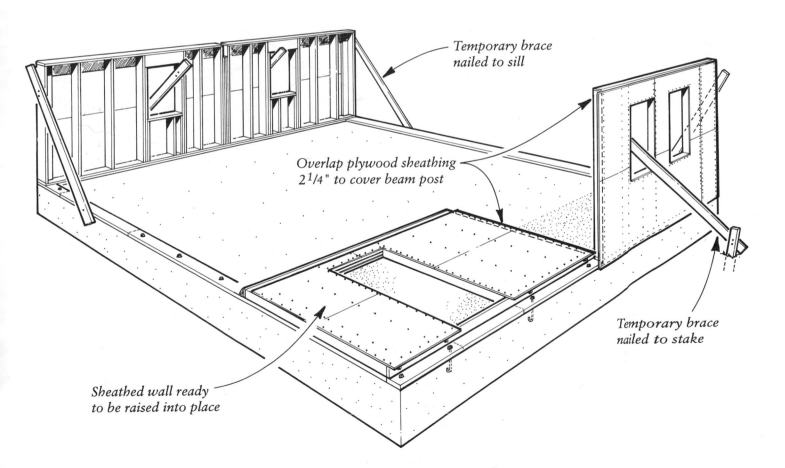

Temporary brace
nailed to sill

Overlap plywood sheathing
2¼" to cover beam post

Temporary brace
nailed to stake

Sheathed wall ready
to be raised into place

ADJOINING WALLS

The walls that will run the length of the barn are slightly different from the 24-foot end walls. For one thing, there's no need to accommodate for the support beam in the middle of the wall. For another, these longer walls have a different design at their ends, where they tie into the end walls (see figure 4–6). The end walls have a double-stud configuration, but our long walls have a single stud at their ends. Also, as shown in figure 4–11, the topmost top plate of the long walls extends so it can overlap the top plate of the end wall. We won't install this topmost top plate until all the walls are up.

Using the same principles discussed above, lay out your studs and plates for the 30-foot walls. This is the wall where you might have a garage or barn door opening, so be sure to calculate the rough opening from the manufacturer-supplied specs or plans. (Again, check ahead in this chapter for door installation information.) Use the same measurements you used on the end walls for other rough openings and windows. Use the same 2x12 headers to maintain consistent door and window height.

As mentioned, a full 30-foot wall will be extremely heavy, so you'll want to build the wall in sections and nail those sections together. Where the wall sections meet, there'll be a double stud (one end stud from each wall).

FIGURE 4–10

A string blocked to stand 2 inches off the corners creates a guide for checking if your walls are out of line. Run a 2-inch block under the string from one corner to the other. If the walls are in line, the block should just fit.

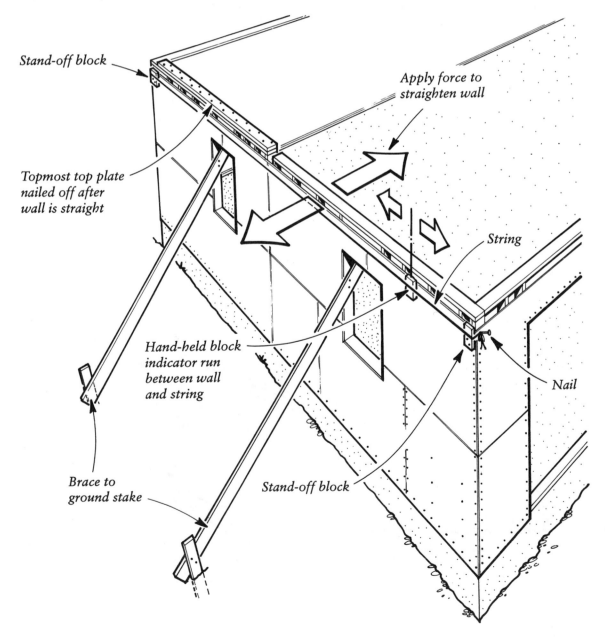

Stand-off block

Apply force to straighten wall

Topmost top plate nailed off after wall is straight

String

Hand-held block indicator run between wall and string

Nail

Brace to ground stake

Stand-off block

CHECKING THE WALLS

Once you have all your walls erected, it's time to check them one side at a time to make sure the sections in each are all in a line. Here's a simple way to do that. Cut three 2-inch square pieces of wood, making sure they are exactly identical in dimension. Tack one piece of wood to the outside of your top plate at either end of any wall. Run a mason's string between them. The string should stand out from the top plate of the wall. Now, take your third piece of wood and run it under the string. Since the string stands off the top plate by 2 inches, you should be able to just fit a 2-inch block between the string and top plate, all the way down the wall, from wall section to wall section (figure 4–10). If the wall varies, correct accordingly. How do you tie the walls together in a line? The topmost top plate will do that, and now is the time to put it on.

You may find that you have to push and pull walls to get them to line up. But once they are in line, have the top plate ready to nail through and set the walls in place.

For the topmost top plate, use boards as long as possible. Ideally you want two topmost plate boards touching end to end over a stud or a header, but this is not as crucial as with the lower top plate. Where the end walls and long walls meet at the corners, extend the topmost top plate of the long wall 5 ½ inches so it overlaps the end walls, tying the walls together. If the topmost top plate board that you use at the corner is a shorter board, make sure it extends back over your long wall *at least* two full stud bays (48 inches).

BUILDING THE CENTER POST

If you are not using a lally column, you must build a supporting post beneath where the center beam will rest at the midpoint between the

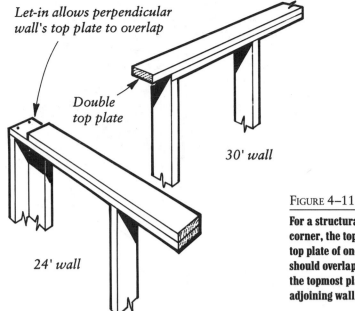

Let-in allows perpendicular wall's top plate to overlap

Double top plate

30' wall

24' wall

FIGURE 4–11

For a structurally strong corner, the topmost top plate of one wall should overlap a let-in on the topmost plate of the adjoining wall.

end walls. This center beam will be identical to the one you built to fit in the center pocket of the end walls. It should support the center beam so the elevation of the top of the center beam is flush with the topmost top plate.

Building the Beam

The center beam will be made out of 2x12s and extend 30 feet. But you can't go out and buy three 30-footers. Instead, you'll make this beam out of four 15 footers and three 10 footers. Once all your walls are up, construct this beam where it will rest, because, believe me, it's going to be heavy and you won't want to lift it. Use temporary A-frames to support it (figure 4–12).

First, eyeball the 2x12s. You will see that they *crown* or *bow* along their length. You want to have the crown up. Turning the crown up is called *crowning*, something we'll do with rafters and ceiling joists as well. Take two of your 15-footers and put them up in the beam pockets so that one 15-footer spans one half of the barn and the other abuts it and spans the other half.

Now place a 10-footer in one of the beam pockets next to a 15-footer. Have your helper hold it flush to the 15-footer while you nail it flush and square. Next, place another 10-footer so it abuts the first 10-footer end-to-end. Rest this second 10-footer on the center post (or midwall), hold it flush and square to the first,

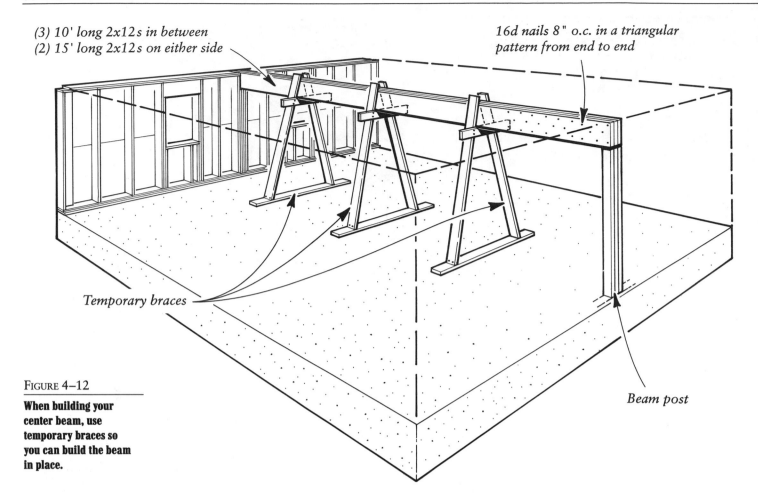

(3) 10' long 2x12s in between
(2) 15' long 2x12s on either side

16d nails 8" o.c. in a triangular pattern from end to end

Temporary braces

Beam post

FIGURE 4–12

When building your center beam, use temporary braces so you can build the beam in place.

and nail it. Now rest your last 10-footer in the beam pocket of the other end wall, hold it flush and square to the beam assembly, and nail it. You now have a structure made of 2x12s that extends the full length of your barn. Finally, put up your remaining two 15-footers end-to-end and nail them in place so that they sandwich the three 10-footers in between. Voilà! One very sturdy center beam is now in place.

CEILING JOISTS

With the beam up, it's time to put up our ceiling joists (you can also call these *floor joists* since they support the second floor decking). How big should those joists be? Design loads for any structure are divided into two categories: *live loads* (people, snow, furniture—that is, movable loads) and *dead loads* (loads that are permanent—such as the weight of flooring, subfloor, and joists). A standard live-load requirement for a building like ours is 40 pounds per square foot; its dead-

load requirement is 10 pounds per square foot. Given these requirements, we must use 2x10 joists for our second floor. Since the span is 12 feet and we are positioning these joists 24 o.c., we have to use a strong wood species. Use only Grade 2 2x10s that are made of Douglas Fir (Larch or Southern), or Grade 2 Western Hemlock. Before you install the ceiling joists, eyeball them along their length and see which way they crown. As with the beam members, you want to install the joists crown up.

When the rafters and ceiling joists are in place, a triangular section of each joist will stick up above the rafters where the latter sit on the top plates. We eventually want to nip off this triangular section above the rafters, but we can't do that until the rafters are placed. (If you read ahead to the rafter section, you'll see that it is possible to put up one rafter on your ridge beam, determine the angle, and then cut all your ceiling joists to that specification, but it's not impossible to make the cuts later, with all the rafters in place.)

Position the ceiling joists directly over the studs, so the building load is carried through the joists, and then through the studs to the bottom plate and sill. As a temporary brace, lay a 2x4 along the top of the joists as you are setting them in place. Place this 2x4 about a foot from the outside wall line and nail it down. This will keep the joists from flopping over as you set and nail them.

You want the joists to overlap each other where they cross the center beam. Though the span is 12 feet, use 14-foot joists and overlap them. Toenail them to the beam with three 8d nails and drive three 16d nails through each lap point.

After you have set the ceiling joists, cut and insert 2x10 *blocking boards* between them to minimize the joists' twisting and warping (figure 4–13).

Then, lay out and nail down plywood on the joists so you have a temporary work surface. You might wish to use *doubleheaded nails* so you can remove them easily when the time comes to put down permanent decking.

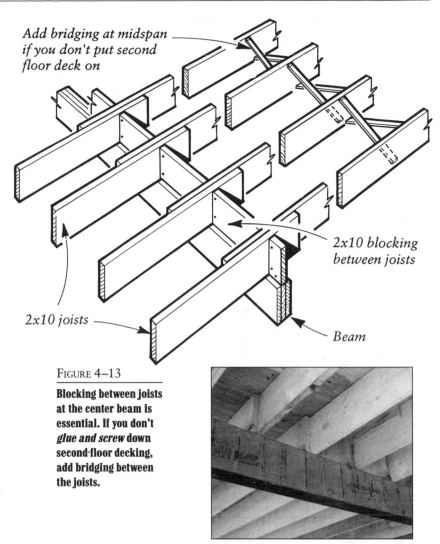

Add bridging at midspan if you don't put second floor deck on

2x10 blocking between joists

2x10 joists

Beam

FIGURE 4–13

Blocking between joists at the center beam is essential. If you don't *glue and screw* down second-floor decking, add bridging between the joists.

Here, the joists are properly overlapped.

RAFTER FRAMING

Rafter framing is the part of construction that scares most people off. There are angles to measure and pitches to figure. But, really, the process is very simple, and you need only a basic knowledge of geometry to understand it. In addition, the roof we are building is simple and straightforward—not *complex,* with adjoining gables, valleys, hips, and jack rafters. We have only one pitch to figure, and one type of rafter to cut.

In a subsequent section in this chapter, we'll look at how to build a shed dormer if you want one for your barn, but for now, let's learn how to frame a simple gable roof.

The end walls will now be referred to as our *gable ends.* The gable rafters will slope up from the top plate of our 30 foot walls and will be parallel with each gable end.

To set our rafters properly, we need to know what *pitch* (also called *slope*) means. A pitch is

a mathematical expression for the angle of the roof line. An 8:12 pitch is a way of saying that the roof rises 8 feet for every 12 feet it travels horizontally (see "Roof Pitch and Headroom: How One Affects the Other"). Since our gable end walls are 24 feet, we can easily predict how high our roof will be with an 8:12 pitch. If we divide the gable end top plate in half, we have two 12-foot sections. Since our roof is an 8:12 pitch, we know that, from the outside edge of the plate, the roof will rise 8 vertical feet by the midpoint of the gable wall's top plate. The theoretical bottom of our ridge beam, therefore, will be 8 feet above the center of the gable wall's top plate. We call this the "theoretical bottom of the ridge beam" because, when the rafters are in place, the bird's-mouth cut (we'll learn about this soon), where the rafter meets the top plate, effectively lowers the ridge beam, making it 7 feet 8 1/2 inches high (that is, 8 feet minus the vertical

PYTHAGOREAN THEOREM

A is the short side.
B is the long side.
C is the hypotenuse.

$$A^2 + B^2 = C^2$$
$$96^2 + 144^2 = C^2$$
$$9216 + 20736 = C^2$$
$$29952 = C^2$$
$$173.07 = C$$

173.07 = 14 feet 5 1/8 inches

cut of the bird's mouth).

If your rafters and ridge beam were made of string, building a roof would be easy. You'd just stretch the string from the top plate to the ridge beam and by magic, you'd have the "rafter" defining the outer edges of your desired 8:12 pitch. But since real rafters have depth and the ridge beam has thickness, we have to custom-cut the rafters so they sit on the top plate and against the ridge beam to form a triangle that has an 8-foot altitude, a 12-foot base, and a 14-foot 5 1/8-inch hypotenuse.

This hypotenuse figure is calculated using the old Pythagorean theorem that says $A^2 + B^2 = C^2$. Since using feet in this calculation would give you a final answer in feet and tenths of feet, it's better to convert the 8-foot and 12-foot dimensions to inches, and then reconvert the answer to feet and inches.

Let's do the calculation: 8 feet = 96 inches. 12 feet = 144 inches. The Pythagorean theorem says 96 x 96 (= 9216) + 144 x 144 (= 20,736). Add these two sums together, and we have the hypotenuse length squared in inches: 29,952.

Roof Pitch & Headroom: How One Affects the Other

FIGURE 4–14

THE PITCH OF YOUR BARN'S ROOF determines the headroom available on the second floor. The barn design presented in this book assumes an 8:12 pitch. For a barn 24 feet wide, that means the bottom of the ridge beam is approximately 8 feet above the walls' top plate. But don't assume you get 8 feet of headroom in your second floor—you don't. Since the floor joists are 2x10s, you have to subtract their dimensions plus any finished flooring to figure your actual ceiling height. It turns out that the actual ceiling height in your second floor at the apex of the gable is about 7 feet above the second-floor decking.

Want more headroom? Increase your roof pitch. Since our barn is 24 feet wide, the first number in the pitch expression (the 8 in 8:12, for example) will always be the number of feet that the bottom of the ridge beam sits above the top plate. If your barn is not 24 feet wide, then you have to calculate this another way, by figuring how far your roof rises in height for every 12 feet it

travels horizontally.

Since an 8:12 pitch doesn't give you an 8-foot ceiling, a 9:12 pitch won't give you a 9-foot ceiling. Again, you have to subtract the height dimension of your ridge beam and the height dimension of your floor joists from that figure. Using 2x10 joists, a 9:12 pitch would give you an 8-foot ceiling. A 10:12 pitch would give you a 9-foot ceiling, and so on.

You can't increase your roof pitch indefinitely. A 12:12 pitch is the high end of most common roofs. Also, a steeper pitch increases the risk of wind shear because there is more vertical surface area to act as a sail. Not only that, but sheathing and shingling such a surface gets a bit precarious.

As for low pitch, in northern climates, you shouldn't go below 8:12 because snow could accumulate on the roof and add a serious load. In southern climates, a low pitch is acceptable. Check your code book to see what pitches are allowable in your area.

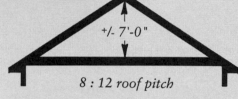

+/- 7'-0"

8 : 12 roof pitch

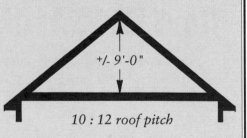

+/- 9'-0"

10 : 12 roof pitch

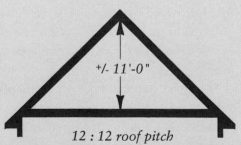

+/- 11'-0"

12 : 12 roof pitch

By increasing the roof pitch, you increase your second floor headroom. An 8:12 pitch on a 24-foot-wide barn with 2x10 rafters and 2x10 ceiling joists will yield approximately 7 feet of headroom. A 10:12 pitch will yield approximately 9 feet, and a 12:12 pitch—a radically-steep pitch—will yield 11 feet.

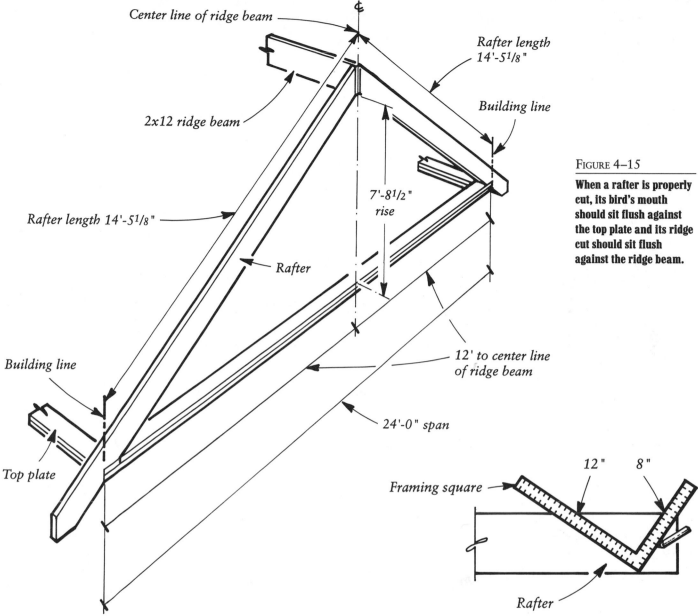

Center line of ridge beam

Rafter length 14'-5⅛"

2x12 ridge beam

Building line

Rafter length 14'-5⅛"

7'-8½" rise

Rafter

Building line

Top plate

12' to center line of ridge beam

24'-0" span

Framing square

12"   8"

Rafter

FIGURE 4–15

When a rafter is properly cut, its bird's mouth should sit flush against the top plate and its ridge cut should sit flush against the ridge beam.

FIGURE 4–16

The roof pitch you seek will determine how you position your framing square on a rafter. Here, the framing square indicates the proper angle for a bird's-mouth cut.

Take the square root of this figure, which is 173.07 inches, and convert it to feet and inches: 14 feet 5 ⅛ inches.

We now have all the crucial basic dimensions. The height of the ridge beam is 7 feet 8 ½ inches from the top plate to the bottom of the ridge beam. The rafter is 14 feet 5 ⅛ inches from its outside top edge at the ridge beam (though we have yet to account for the ridge beam's width in this length) to a line plumb with the top plate of the long wall (figure 4–15).

For several reasons, 14 feet 5 ⅛ inches will not be the actual length of your rafter. First, there is the additional length you want the rafter to overhang the building. Second, since we have figured the rafter length in the abstract, using

lines of a triangle that have no depth, we will have to subtract from that rafter length, at the ridge-beam end, half the thickness of the ridge beam. That way the rafter will sit against the ridge beam so that the rafter's outside top edge will define the 8:12 triangle we want as our roof pitch. To understand this better, let's cut a rafter and actually put it in place.

We'll use our framing square which has two parts: the thicker blade is called the body, and the thinner blade is called the tongue. By laying the framing square on a rafter and lining up the inch markings on the tongue and body, we can define an angle (figure 4–16). The unit rise (in our case 8) is on the tongue; the unit run (in our case 12) is on the body.

FIGURE 4–17

Cutting rafters is a four-step process.
1. Lay out the ridge cut.
2. Back off to account for the width of the ridge beam.
3. Measure the mathematical length of your building line.
4. Cut the bird's mouth.

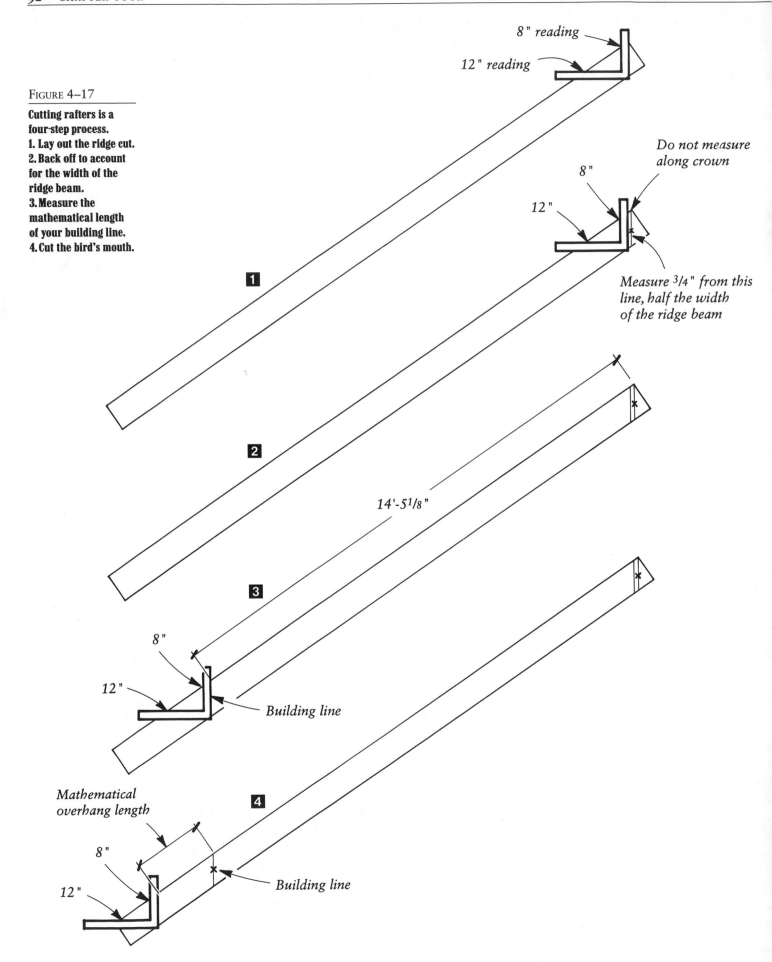

8" reading

12" reading

Do *not* measure along crown

8"

12"

Measure ³/4" from this line, half the width of the ridge beam

1

2

14'-5¹/8"

3

8"

12"

Building line

4

Mathematical overhang length

8"

12"

Building line

Now, let's cut a 2x10 rafter. We'll use a 16-footer, which will give us enough overhang for either a soffit for a vented roof or a simple overhang for an unvented roof (for definition of these roof types, see chapter 2). Eyeball the boards and crown them (crown end up). You don't want the board sagging further under the weight of your roof.

Lay the rafter on sawhorses and place your framing square on it so that the 8-inch mark on the tongue is very close to the end at the top edge of the 2x10. Then position the framing square so that the 12-inch mark on the body touches the edge of the 2x10 (see figure 4–17–1). Draw a line along the tongue.

Since we will be using a 2x12 ridge beam, we need to subtract from this line we just drew a measurement equal to one half the thickness of the ridge beam. Step the framing square back so the next line you draw along the tongue is ³/₄ inches from this first line you drew. *Do not measure ³/₄ inches along the crown edge for this cut.* Measure ³/₄ inches perpendicular to your first line. This new line is where you will actually cut your rafter; we'll call it the *first-cut line.* Cross out the first line you drew so you are not confused when you cut (figure 4–17–2).

Next, along the crown edge measure back from your very first line (the one you just crossed out) 14 feet 5 ¹/₈ inches, the mathematical length of your rafter. Make a mark. Now position your framing square so that its tongue at the 8-inch

point touches this mark and the 12-inch point on the body touches the rafter's edge, just as we have done for the first two cuts. The line drawn along the body will be our *building line.* When you stand the rafter in place, this line will be plumb with the outside walls. We will not cut this line; it is merely a reference, so cross it out (see figure 4–17–3).

Next, along the crown edge, measure the mathematical length of your overhang from the building line. But slow down here for an explanation. The mathematical length of your overhang will not be equal to the distance your overhang will extend from your barn's walls. To figure the actual overhang, first decide how much of one you want. A common overhang is 1 foot 6 inches. That means that the distance from the barn wall to the outside edge of your rafter bottom will be 1 foot 6 inches. If you want that much overhang, you would take the *unit length* of the rafter (that is, the length of the rafter for every foot of horizontal run) for an 8:12 pitch, and multiply it by 1.5 (1 foot 6 inches expressed in decimals). We already know the unit length of an 8:12 roof pitch. It's 14.42. That figure is a precalculated number. In fact, you can read it in the rafter table etched into the body of your framing square, just under the 8-inch mark. So, to obtain a 1-foot 6-inch overhang, we multiply 14.42 by 1.5 and get a product of 21.63 inches. Converting this to feet, we find that the mathematical overhang length along the top edge of

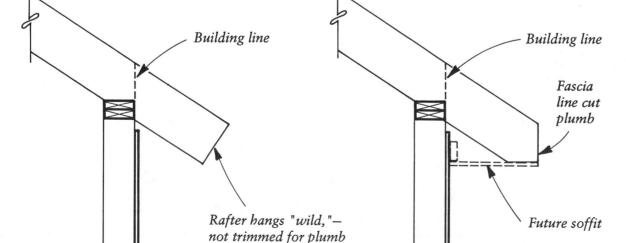

Building line

Rafter hangs "wild,"— not trimmed for plumb but left "square"

Building line

Fascia line cut plumb

Future soffit

FIGURE 4–18

A "plumb cut" (right) versus a "wild" cut (left). If you plan to install fascia (face boards) along the bottom edges of your roof, use plumb cuts on your rafters.

Can I "Platform-Frame" My Barn?

THE FRAMING METHOD OUTLINED IN this chapter positions the rafters at the eaves, on top of the first floor wall's topmost top plate. Since these rafters are positioned flush against the floor joists, you can nail through from both sides to hold the rafters in place. With this design, the floor joists serve a number of purposes. They support the second floor; they hold the walls in place; and they act as *collar ties* that check any spreading in the rafters. A collar tie is any framing-grade board that spans the barn and keeps the rafters from pushing out due to the downward force of the roof's live and dead loads.

In another common method of framing, called *platform framing,* the rafters don't sit on the top plate. They sit on a platform—the second floor decking. With this framing method you deck the entire second floor *before* you put up your rafters. Once the floor joists are completely covered with decking, you nail plates the length of the deck's long sides and onto those you nail the eaves ends of your rafters. Platform framing the roof changes the loading dynamics of your barn because it disallows the floor joists from acting as collar ties. The rafters have little in place to check spreading (figure 4–19). So if you platform-frame your barn's roof, you will have to install collar ties a third of the way down on each rafter. This will compensate for the holding power the joists would have provided.

In a platform-framed barn, you gain headroom by elevating your rafters onto the second-floor deck, and yet you lose that headroom (and then some) with your collar ties. There can be advantages, though. If you plan your roof pitch properly to account for headroom, the collar ties can provide a perfect nailing surface for a second floor ceiling.

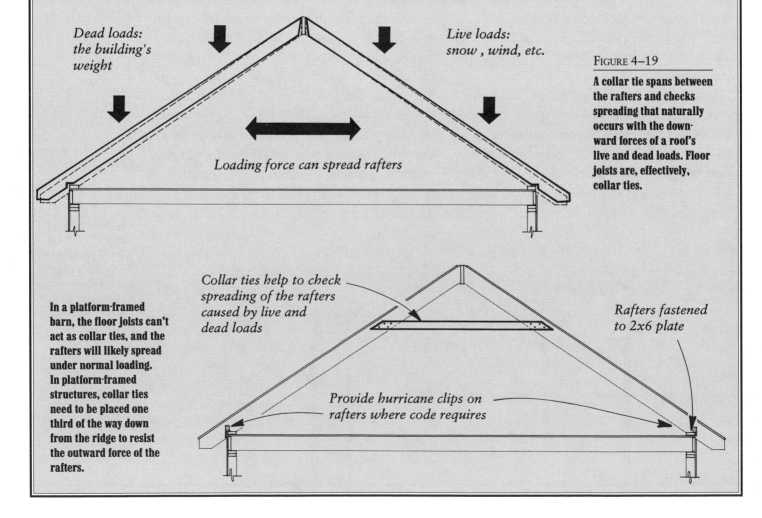

Dead loads: the building's weight

Live loads: snow , wind, etc.

Loading force can spread rafters

FIGURE 4–19

A collar tie spans between the rafters and checks spreading that naturally occurs with the down- ward forces of a roof's live and dead loads. Floor joists are, effectively, collar ties.

Collar ties help to check spreading of the rafters caused by live and dead loads

Rafters fastened to 2x6 plate

Provide hurricane clips on rafters where code requires

In a platform-framed barn, the floor joists can't act as collar ties, and the rafters will likely spread under normal loading. In platform-framed structures, collar ties need to be placed one third of the way down from the ridge to resist the outward force of the rafters.

the rafter should be 1 foot, 9 9/16 inches. That will yield a 1-foot, 6- inch overhang, not including a *fascia,* or face board along its length.

Measure that mathematical overhang length from the building line on your rafter along the crown edge (see figure 4–17–4). Make a mark. Just as we did before, place the 8-inch point of your framing square's tongue on this mark and its 12-inch point on the body along the crown edge. Draw a line along the tongue. This is your *overhang plumb cut,* also called a *fascia line.*

In the end, you will make only two cuts for all the lines we just drew. First we'll cut the angle where the rafter meets the ridge (our first cut line), and second, we'll cut the fascia line.

This last step in calculating overhang length can be skipped entirely if you want the remaining length of your rafter to hang *wild.* This is sometimes called a *square cut* (figure 4–18). The decision about whether to have a plumb or square cut is purely one of aesthetics, though it will affect what kind of soffit you can use.

Cutting the Bird's-Mouth

We have now marked all the necessary lines along the crown edge of the rafter. But we still have some more cuts to make.

If you look at any of the drawings of rafters and top plates in this chapter, you'll see that the rafters are notched to fit the top plates. The type of notch used is called a *bird's-mouth* and it has two lines. The line that marks where the rafter sits flush on the top plate is called the *seat cut,* and the line that runs along the building line is called a *vertical line.* Draw a line 90 degrees to your building line (figure 4–20) and you create the seat cut. How deep should the seat cut be? First, we don't want to cut in and remove more than one third of the 2x10's width. You would think that you could simply divide 9 1/4 (the 2x10's actual width) by 3 and arrive at a figure. Well, don't forget that the board will be sitting at an angle, so its "one third" must be calculated with the rafter in position. In that case, the "width" of the rafter becomes about 11 inches, and our "one third" is actually 3 3/4 inches (figure 4–20).

FIGURE 4–20

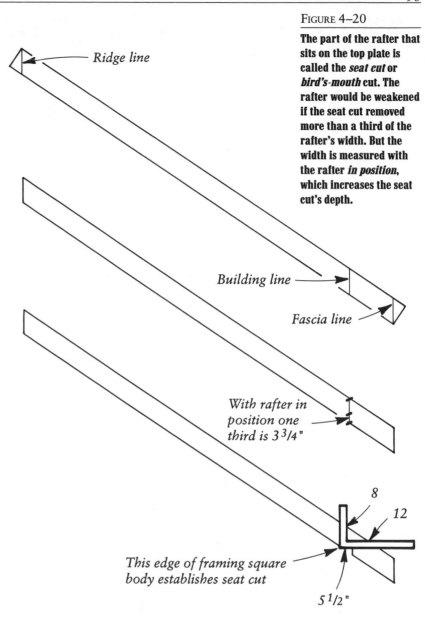

Ridge line

Building line

Fascia line

With rafter in position one third is 3 3/4"

8

12

This edge of framing square body establishes seat cut

5 1/2"

Place your framing square along the crown edge at 12 and 8, just as we have for the other cuts, and slide it so the bottom blade of the body intersects the 3 1/2-inch mark and the building line (figure 4–20). Draw a line. This defines the seat cut. When you cut this with your circular saw, you will have to finish the cut with a hand saw, because your circular saw can only cut into the line so far before it starts into the main section of the rafter.

Now make all your cuts. You will have one complete rafter. You can use this rafter as a pattern master to mark all the rest of them. But before you do that, you should erect the ridge beam and hold the pattern master against it to make sure it fits properly.

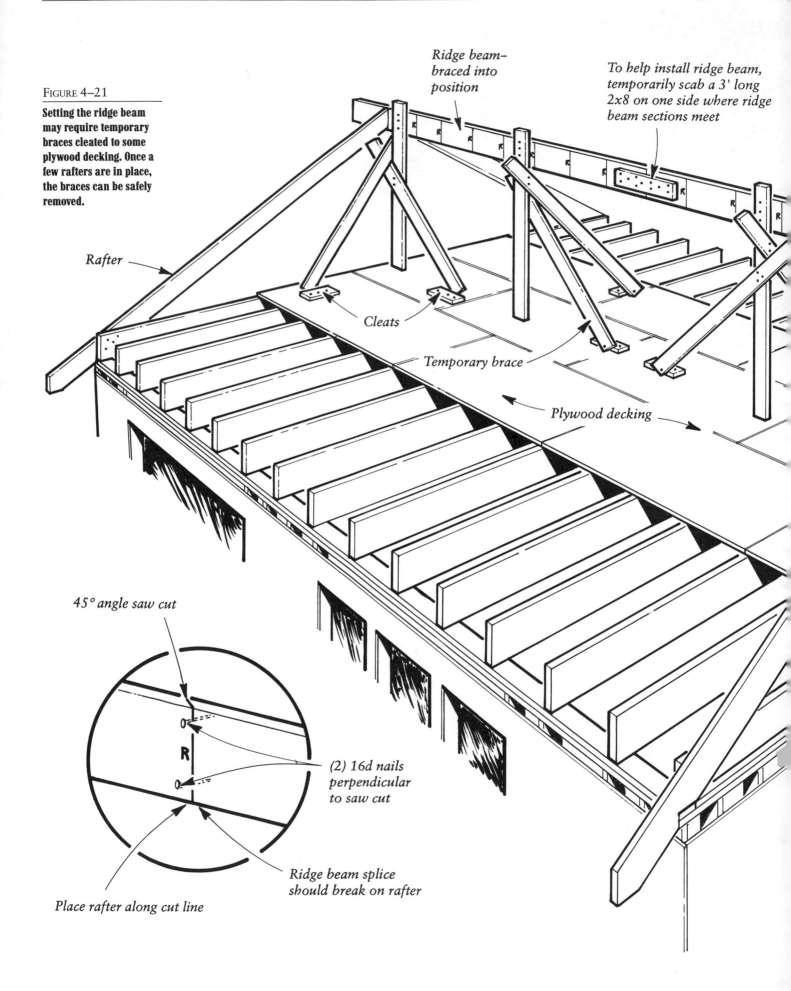

FIGURE 4–21

Setting the ridge beam may require temporary braces cleated to some plywood decking. Once a few rafters are in place, the braces can be safely removed.

Ridge beam–braced into position

To help install ridge beam, temporarily scab a 3' long 2x8 on one side where ridge beam sections meet

Rafter

Cleats

Temporary brace

Plywood decking

45° angle saw cut

R

(2) 16d nails perpendicular to saw cut

Ridge beam splice should break on rafter

Place rafter along cut line

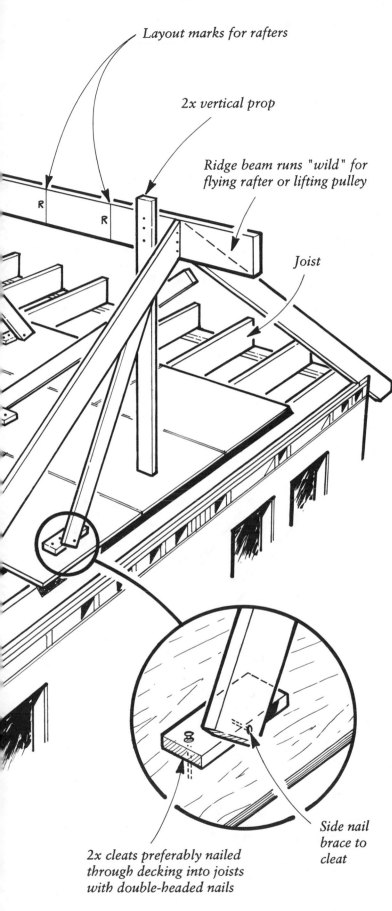

Layout marks for rafters

2x vertical prop

Ridge beam runs "wild" for
flying rafter or lifting pulley

Joist

Side nail
brace to
cleat

2x cleats preferably nailed
through decking into joists
with double-headed nails

Erecting the Ridge Beam

Since our ceiling joists are up in place, you can put some decking down to make a platform. Take a stepladder or some scaffolding and erect a section of the 2x12 ridge beam at least 15 feet long. If you want a *flying rafter* that will overhang the gable ends of the barn, you will have to use a longer 2x12 and cantilever it off the gable end. Even if you don't want a flying rafter, you may want to extend your ridge beam anyway so you can attach a pully to it for hauling material to your second floor (see "Building an Overhang at the Gable Ends"). Support the bottom of the beam 7 feet 8 $\frac{1}{2}$ inches above the topmost top plate. To hold the ridge beam in place, use temporary braces (figure 4–21). Plumb your ridge braces. Once a few rafters are in place, the ridge braces can be removed.

With the ridge beam properly positioned, lay your master rafter in place, making sure the rafter's ridge beam cut is perfectly flush to the ridge beam and that the seat cut sits completely flush on and against the top plate. If everything looks good, you can use this master rafter to mark the others.

But first, cut three more rafters so you can support your ridge beam and remove the braces. Install the rafters at the ends of the ridge. Use 8d nails at the ridge and 16d nails (through a predrilled hole in the bird's-mouth) into the top plate. Once in place, the four rafters should support the ridge beam. Set your next run of rafters 24 o.c. They should sit flush against the ceiling joists at the eaves end. Nail through from both sides so the ceiling joists can act to resist any outward thrust of the rafters. (The object—as with our ceiling joists—is to carry the load from the roof to the slab in a clean vertical line.)

Those of you not building a dormer can cut and set all your rafters now. If you are building a dormer, read ahead to that section, because you have to decide which rafters to leave out.

Since our first section of ridge beam is at least 15 feet long, you must put up a second section of ridge beam 15 feet long (or longer, if you want a gable end overhang). Put up and brace this second 15 foot 2x12 in the same manner as the first. To make sure the ridge is a straight line from end to end—this is crucial—use the string-and-block method we used earlier to line up our wall sections. In addition, make sure the ridge-section joint falls where a rafter will naturally lie. Have the two 15-foot ridge beam sections meet end to end and "join" them with opposing 45-degree mitered angles cut vertically down the length of each. Nail the joined boards together from the top and sides.

GABLE-END STUD WALL

After you have all your rafters set, you need to build a gable-end 2x6 stud wall that will fill in the triangle created by the rafters at the gable ends. These studs will be 24 inches o.c., just like the wall below. Place 2x6s directly above the

Building an Overhang at the Gable Ends

IT DOESN'T TAKE MUCH EXTRA WORK TO add an overhang at the gable ends of your barn. You may want one if you have any kind of a doorway at your gable ends. With an overhang, rain won't drip on you as you stop to open the latch. Plus, an overhang just plain looks good.

There's no need structurally for an overhang. Your barn will stand up just fine with or without it. But here's how you make one if you decide to do so.

When you are erecting your ridge beam, extend it out beyond the end wall's top plate the distance you want your overhang to be. After you have put up all your other gable rafters, cut four more, two for each end of the barn. But wait! On these four extra rafters, don't cut a bird's-mouth; only make ridge beam and fascia board or soffit cuts. Put these extra rafters aside.

Now, one quarter and three quarters of the way down your *end rafters* (the ones directly over the end-wall top plates), notch out for a 2x6 along the crown edge.

Then cut 2x6 *barge rafters* that

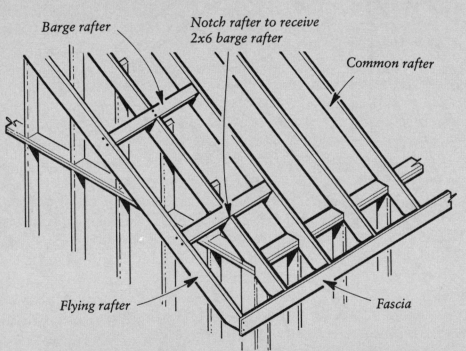

FIGURE 4–22

A flying rafter is usually a full rafter bay extending out from the end of the building. Here, a flying rafter is supported by *barge rafters* halfway down the last true gable rafter. The flying rafter is nailed off at the ridge like any gable rafter and is supported at the eaves end by a fascia board.

Barge rafter

Notch rafter to receive 2x6 barge rafter

Common rafter

Flying rafter

Fascia

will abut your second common rafter, run through the notch in your first rafter, and end up abutting your *flying rafter,* the overhang rafter (figure 4–22).

Put up your flying rafters, nailing them off at the ridge and into the 2x6s that will support it. Then, extend your fascia board so it ends at the flying rafter and nail into it.

In a vented roof, there is no need to extend your soffit panel to cover the eaves underside of the flying rafter, though you may want to do this for looks. For the most part, the flying rafter can just hang there with the underside exposed. There is, of course, no need to vent a flying rafter since there is no source of moist air beneath it.

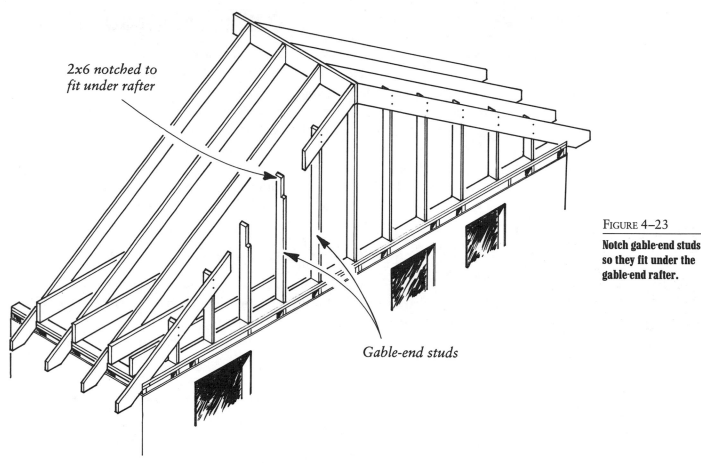

2x6 notched to fit under rafter

Gable-end studs

FIGURE 4–23

Notch gable-end studs so they fit under the gable-end rafter.

studs in the wall below. Hold each 2x6 in place against the rafter, and, using your level to make sure the stud is plumb, mark the cut line by running your pencil across the top and bottom of the rafter where it meets the stud. This is your angle cut line. If your roofline is symmetrical, the studs can be cut in pairs. You will have to notch the tops of the studs to get them to fit snugly against the rafters and flush against the outside of the gable end wall (figure 4–23).

BUILDING A SHED DORMER

A shed dormer adds light and room to a second floor. For those of you who want to finish off your second floor for a living area—now or in the future—a good, long shed dormer is a must. Otherwise, living in your second floor will be like living in a tent: The roof will slope precipitously from a 7-foot, 8 ½-inch-high ceiling, and your living area won't have natural light unless you install skylights in the gable roof or add gable-end windows.

When planning and constructing a shed dormer, refer to figure 4–24. But before you even start on your shed dormer, you must decide the size window(s) you want to put in. When you settle on those dimensions, you can design your shed dormer around them. For construction ease, you should design a shed dormer in width increments of 24 inches, because we are going to fit the dormer in between existing 24 o.c. gable rafters. For example, let's say you want to install two 36 x 36-inch windows in your shed dormer, separated by 2 feet of wall. In that case, you'd have two 3-foot-wide rough openings and 2 feet of wall between them. That would require 8 feet, or four rafter bays.

Next, decide how much wall space you want between the outside corners of the dormer and the windows. Let's say you want 2 feet of wall space to the outside of both windows. Now the total width of the shed dormer is 8 feet (for windows in the dormer's center and the wall space between them) + 2 feet + 2 feet = 12 feet, or 6 rafter bays.

For a dormer this size, you would leave out five common gable rafters and make those to either side of the shed dormer double rafters. Remember, the inside edge of these double gable rafters defines the edge of your shed dormer, because the corner studs of the shed dormer will rest directly on them. In addition, for a dormer this size you may need to double up your entire ridge beam to carry the extra load. Check with a structural engineer if you have doubts about your design.

Begin construction of your shed dormer after you have all your required gable rafters in place. First, build a stud wall that will be the face of the shed dormer. This dormer stud wall is really just a smaller version of the stud walls you built for the first floor. It will include studs, a top plate, and rough openings for the windows. But there are a couple of differences. For one, you build it without the corner studs (you will have to measure across the gable rafters to determine how long your top plate should be; the top plate should extend outwards and be flush with the outside edge of the gable rafters). For another, the dormer should have a triple 2x6 top plate. There's no need for a 2x12 header above the windows because the load carried there is not substantial enough to demand one.

You'll also notice in figure 4–24 that the dormer stud wall has no bottom plate of its own. The dormer wall studs sit on the first floor wall top plate and are nailed off to the ceiling joists. Once you feel comfortable with these differences, erect the wall plumb with the first-floor barn walls below.

After the wall is up, mark your corner studs in place by holding them against the top plate and the rafter. These corner studs won't be full-length because they will intersect the gable rafter as it rises to meet the ridge beam (see figure 4–24). As mentioned earlier, the triple top plate should extend out over the double rafter. If you were to drop a plumb line from the outside edge of your dormer's top plate it would be flush with the outside edge of the double rafters. Also, notice that the dormer's end rafters will sit on the double gable rafter at the ridge beam.

Cutting Shed Dormer Rafters

Once this dormer face stud wall is constructed— *and* checked for square, level, racking, and plumb—you need to cut dormer rafters. Since the dormer rafters carry less load than your main roof, they can be 2x8s. You already know how to cut them. Apply all you learned from cutting gable rafters to cutting dormer rafters. The only difference: the pitch and length have changed.

To find the new pitch, let's take some measurements. First, determine (with plumb bob and tape measure) the distance from the center line of your ridge beam to the outside of your wall. This is your total *run*. Then measure the difference in height from the top of the ridge beam to the top of your dormer wall. This is your total *rise*. If the dormer roof drops 4 feet vertically (from ridge beam to top plate) over the course of 12 horizontal feet (the distance from outside wall to ridge in a 24 foot wide barn) that means that your roof pitch is 4:12. If you are venting the roof, be careful not to make your pitch less than 3.5:12. It's hard to find ridge vents for pitches this low; also, asphalt and fiberglass shingles usually require a 4:12 pitch or greater. With a pitch lower than 4:12, you may be committing yourself to a metal roof. You can see why people who are going to finish off second floor living areas will choose a different overall roof pitch and a higher ridge beam because a 4:12 dormer pitch on an 8:12 roof in a 24-foot wide barn with a ridge beam at 8 feet puts the dormer ceiling height at the outside walls at about 4 feet above the top plate (see "Roof Pitch and Headroom: How One Affects the Other").

Knowing that your pitch is 4:12, and knowing the mathematical rafter length, use your framing square and mark your rafters cuts just as you did for our gable rafters. Calculate your overhang length using the same principles we employed earlier.

Cut enough rafters to place them 24 inches o.c. and install them. Notice in figure 4–24 that the dormer's end rafters do not end at the ridge beam at the same angle as the other dormer rafters. In fact, these rafters lay on top of the double gable rafters. The easiest way to figure

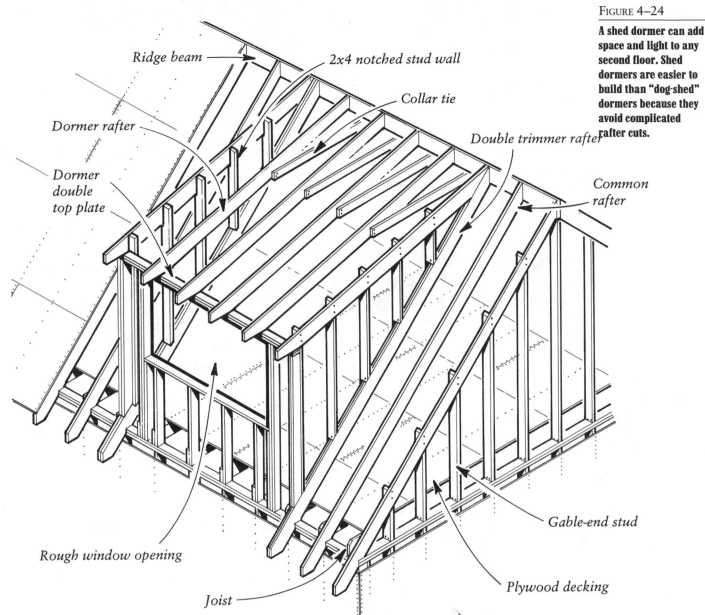

FIGURE 4–24

A shed dormer can add space and light to any second floor. Shed dormers are easier to build than "dog-shed" dormers because they avoid complicated rafter cuts.

Ridge beam

2x4 notched stud wall

Collar tie

Dormer rafter

Double trimmer rafter

Dormer double top plate

Common rafter

Rough window opening

Gable-end stud

Plywood decking

Joist

this cut line is to cut a regular dormer rafter at the 4:12 pitch, then hold it in place against the double gable rafter and mark the angle with your pencil. Cut and install.

Once the dormer rafters are in place, install 2x4 studs that run from the end rafters of the shed dormer to the double gable rafters below. We'll call these *dormer-end wall studs*. Notch the tops of these dormer-end wall studs so they fit snugly against the dormer-end rafters, just as we did for the gable-end wall studs. To determine the angle where the studs sit on the double-gable rafter, plumb them in place and mark them with a pencil.

Finally, install 2x6 blocking between the rafters over the top plate.

Installing Dormer Joists

For structural stability, we need to install *collar ties* or *ceiling joists* (board framing that prevents a roof from sagging or spreading) that run from the dormer rafters across the second floor ceiling to the opposite roof's gable rafters. The easiest way to determine cuts is to mark the joists in place. One at a time, hold the 2x6 joists where they will go, level them, and then draw your cut line using the top of the gable rafter as your guide. Notice that where the joists meet the dormer-end rafters at either end, they will hit the dormer end-wall studs (figure 4–24). To avoid this, take a 2x8 and span at least two stud bays to create a nailing surface for your joist.

For uninsulated, water-shedding roofs, metal panels on purlins are simple to install and cost efficient.

FIGURE 4–25

Use 2x4 purlins, spacing them 2 feet on center.

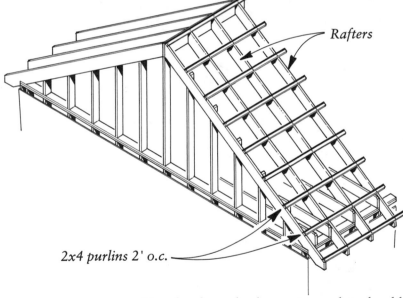

Rafters

2x4 purlins 2' o.c.

How far above the dormer's top plate should the joist sit? Split the distance between the bottom of the ridge beam and the top of the dormer's top plate. If you want to put your joists higher to add more head room in your second floor living area, discuss the issue with an engineer. He or she will likely recommend using fasteners or metal ties where the gable rafters meet the first-story wall's top plate opposite the shed dormer. But you need to give your engineer the specs to have him or her determine the outward thrust that the fasteners/ties must resist.

Should you or shouldn't you?

Constructing a shed dormer at the framing stage really isn't all that difficult, and you'll never regret the extra space and light. So if you're at all inclined to install a dormer in your barn, *do it now.* If you build your barn and then decide to add a dormer, you will encounter lots of extra work and cost, including re-roofing and construction debris disposal, to say nothing of the risk and hassle of opening your barn to weather while you are building.

Sheathing the Roof

There are a number of different kinds of roof materials you can use. The type of roof you choose depends on the desired end use of your building. Read ahead to the roofing section to get a better idea of what kind of roof you want to put on your barn, or go back to chapter 1 to review the differences between vented and unvented roofs.

For those of you who want to install an unvented agricultural metal roof, there's no need to sheathe it. That kind of metal roof can be attached to purlins, which are 2x4s (sometimes 2x3, but 2x4s are sturdier to stand on as you work) nailed perpendicular to your rafters at regular intervals (figure 4–25). Yes, you can put agricultural metal roofing over plywood roof sheathing, but at a higher cost. And you'll need plywood sheathing if you intend to vent your roof.

On your own, research which type of roof material you want to use, and find out what the manufacturer suggests for sheathing (decking) material. Some manufacturers recommend plywood sheathing, some recommend purlins. If purlins are recommended, the manufacturer will indicate the desired spacing of them, 24 inches o.c. being most common.

If you don't know what kind of roof you want, *or* if you want to play it safe, you'll never go wrong installing half-inch plywood over the rafters. Installing these panels is easy, if done safely. It's not a bad idea to use a rope and harness system for all above-ground work. The ground may not seem a long way down, but you can injure yourself seriously even in a short fall.

When sheathing the roof, start from the bottom and install one full row of 4x8 panels horizontally. If there is excess at the gable ends, let it hang "wild" over the edge (for a 30-foot roof, you will have 2 feet of overhang after installing four panels). Later, we'll trim all the overhang at the same time for a good, clean line. Let the bottom edges of these plywood panels overhang ³/₄ inch beyond the end of your rafters and nail the panels to the rafters using 6d galvanized for half-inch and 8d galvanized for ⁵/₈-inch at the same nailing schedule we used for the first-floor wall panels: 6 inches o.c. for perimeter panels and 12 inches o.c. for interior.

Once this first row of panels is secured, nail some temporary horizontal 2x4s over it for footholds or build a roof scaffold (page 120).

On the next row, start with a half panel to stagger the plywood ends and thus avoid their forming a perfect grid (staggering the panels gives more stability).

For those of you building a vented roof, you need to accommodate a ridge vent by not having your roof panels meet at the apex of the gable. Run your panels nearly up to the ridge but leave at least 1 ¹/₂ inches open on either side of it. Moist

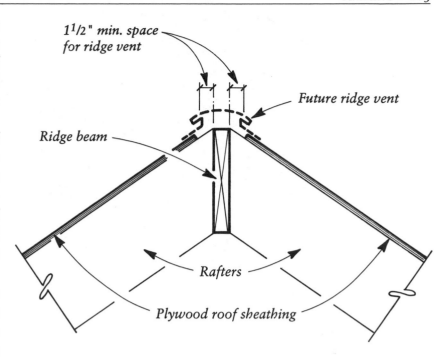

air from our barn will flow up and out through this opening. After we put on our roofing material, we will protect this opening from weather with a ridge vent (figure 4–26).

If you have rafters like the ones we described earlier in this chapter (16 feet 2 ⁵/₈ inches long, including the overhang), you can use four sheets of plywood and have 2 ⁵/₈ inches at the ridge. Many low-profile ridge vents can span that distance, so there may not be any need to put in that extra strip of plywood.

For those of you building an unvented roof, run your plywood right up the rafters and have it meet over the ridge beam. If you have a small gap at the ridge (say, 2 ⁵/₈ inches) fill it with solid wood; don't use a strip of plywood for small spaces—it can splinter and delaminate.

FIGURE 4–26

When sheathing a vented roof, leave a gap at the ridge to allow air to escape from the rafter bays. A ridge vent will cover the ridge beam and span the gaps to either side.

Building a Vented Roof

To build a vented roof, you must create an unrestricted passageway for air to flow from one end of the rafter to the other. Inside our rafter bays, we will be putting batt insulation, but we need to prevent that batting from fluffing up into the air passageway. There are many preventive techniques, including using cardboard baffles. Here's a popular one.

The first step is easier to perform before you sheathe your roof, but it can be done with the

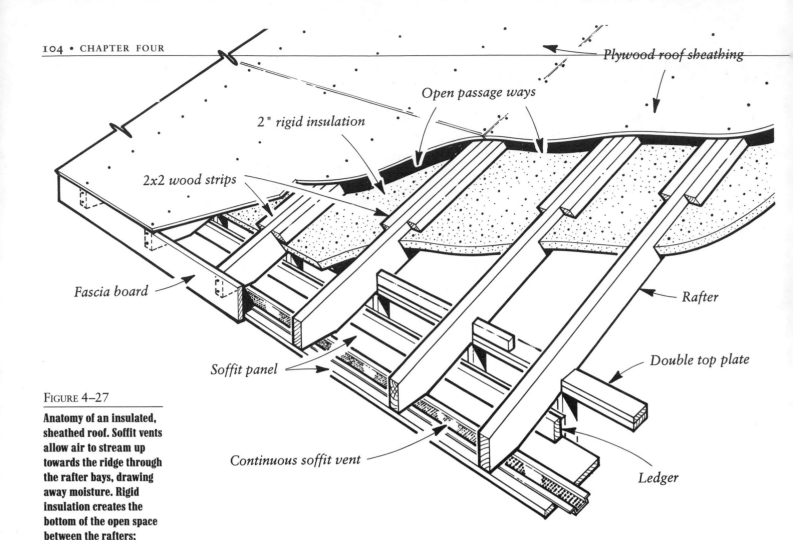

Plywood roof sheathing

Open passage ways

2" rigid insulation

2x2 wood strips

Fascia board

Soffit panel

Continuous soffit vent

Rafter

Double top plate

Ledger

FIGURE 4–27

Anatomy of an insulated, sheathed roof. Soffit vents allow air to stream up towards the ridge through the rafter bays, drawing away moisture. Rigid insulation creates the bottom of the open space between the rafters; plywood sheathing covers the top.

Install soffit vents between strips of ³/₈-inch plywood. Make sure your vent sections break on a rafter so their joints have some backing.

sheathing on. Nail some 2x2 wood strips (you can rip some 2x4s in half) along the rafters an inch below the crown (figure 4–27). When we install our insulation, we will install a piece of 1-inch blueboard against the underside of these 2x2s. This will create a 3-inch passageway, bordered on the underside by blueboard and on top by our roof sheathing. Under the blueboard, we will put our insulation batts, but the blueboard will prevent that batting from fluffing up into the air space.

Along the length of the ridge we will install a ridge vent, which will serve a dual purpose. It will let air out, but, as mentioned, also keep rain and snow from getting in. There are many different kinds of ridge vents. Some come rolled up, others in sections. Most ridge vents are made of polyethylene, and usually installation is obvious. You roll out the vent, cut it to length with snips, and nail it into place with 6d galvanized nails or whatever the manufacturer specifies. (Most of you will eventually be installing *caps* of asphalt shingles on top of the ridge vent.) Be careful not to hammer the ridge vent nails too deep, as this can crush some of the vent space. Since codes require a certain *net free vent area (NFVA),* crushing your vents may put you in noncompliance.

At the other end of the rafter, the eaves end, we have to design a *soffit* that will allow air up into the passageway we created with our 2x2s. Figures 4–27 and 28 suggest two designs, though others can work just as well. In the first suggested design, the principle is to build a soffit panel and *fascia* (face board). The fascia board (typically pine or cedar) forms the face of the soffit, and it is parallel to the building line. The ends of the rafters must be cut plumb to sit flush against the fascia board. The soffit panel is $^3/_8$-inch plywood, and it should run from a 2x4 block (nailed to the sheathing) to the outside edge of your fascia. When you plumb-cut your rafter, be sure to make the cut level for your soffit. The soffit needs to be vented, so you should install a continuous vent strip in this $^3/_8$-inch plywood. Vent strips are available at building supply stores. When you install them, make sure each section breaks on a rafter so it can be secured.

The second suggested soffit vent is much simpler. You don't install a soffit or fascia. Instead, install 2x6 blocks in the rafter bays, between the ceiling joists. (Your sheathing should extend up to cover the blocking.) Between the top of the 2x6 block and the underside of the roof sheathing there will be a gap that will allow air to flow up into your rafter bays. To keep animals out of the rafter bays, staple screening between the roof sheathing and the blocks.

SECOND-FLOOR DECKING

Decking your second floor with $^3/_4$- or $^5/_8$-inch tongue-and-groove plywood will give it a good strong platform, and it won't feel spongy when you walk on it. Go with $^3/_4$ tongue-and-groove if your budget allows. It's a good idea to glue these panels to the joists with an elastomeric

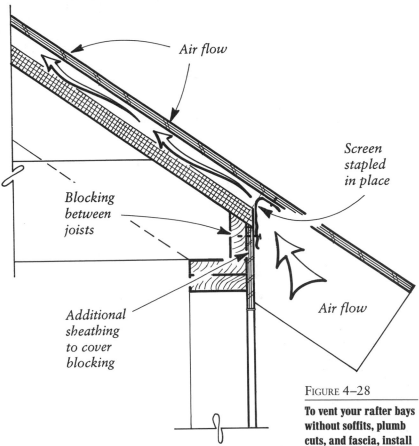

Air flow

Screen stapled in place

Blocking between joists

Additional sheathing to cover blocking

Air flow

FIGURE 4–28

To vent your rafter bays without soffits, plumb cuts, and fascia, install blocks above the topmost top plate and staple screening as shown to keep out bugs, birds, and vermin.

adhesive and screw them down with 1 $^5/_8$-inch wood screws (not drywall screws, though with the same head). This practice is known in the trades as *glue and screw.* When you install the decking, lay it so the long edges of the plywood are at right angles to the joists.

If you are going to finish off your second floor for a living space and you want to put tile or linoleum down in the kitchen or bath area, you will have to lay $^3/_4$-inch plywood beneath the tile or *PTS (plugged and touch-sanded)* decking beneath any vinyl application. You may also need an underlayment such as *plugged plywood* beneath tile or vinyl. *Plugged means that the knotholes and defects in the plywood have been removed and replaced with a "plug" of quality wood.* See what the tile or linoleum manufacturer recommends. If you skip this second floor decking, you will have to install bridging (2x3s nailed in an "X" pattern) between the joists. Bridging will provide the needed stability that, otherwise, plywood decking would provide.

Building a Stair

BUILDING STAIRS IS ONE OF THOSE subjects that could fill an entire book. There are so many types of stairs, and so many design variations, it would take pages and pages to cover every possibility. To make things easy, let's look at one type of stair that can either be roughly built or elegantly finished. It's called a *cleated stairway*.

Preparing the rough opening.

Your stairway needs a destination. It must rise through the second floor joists and deck. Either while you are installing your floor joists, or before you build your actual stairway, you must make an opening in the second floor joists. Where you cut joists out of the way, you must header off the joists that remain and double up the joists to the left and right of the stairway opening. Wherever a header board meets a ceiling joist, nail through the joist and into the header. Also, use a joist hanger to "hang" the header on the joist. Joist hangers are available at any good building supplier.

How big a hole should you create in the floor? The hole's width, of course, will be at least as wide as the stairway itself. Most building codes require that stairways be at least 30 inches wide (commonly, stairways are 33 to 44 inches wide). The length of the hole you create in the ceiling is determined by the headroom required by code between the treads and the first floor ceiling above. Check your code book. Generally, you should allow at least 6 feet 8 inches of headroom between the header opposite where the stair stringer rests and the stair tread directly below it.

The stairway.

Building the stairway itself is very simple. You are going to cut two 2x10 *stringers*—essentially rafters with a plumb cut at the top similar to the ridge-beam cut in your gable rafters. At the bottom, you can square off the stringer, just as we did to accommodate the fascia in our roof rafters.

If you have an 8-foot ceiling, your stringers' vertical rise will be about 8 feet 10 inches (8 feet between the slab and the bottom of the joists, plus the width of the joist and the second-floor ³/₄-inch decking). If you make your stairway an 8:12 pitch, which is about 34 degrees, you are in the right ballpark, because the preferred angle for a stairway is 30 to 35 degrees. So, just as with a gable rafter, calculate the mathematical length of a stringer with a rise of 8 feet 10 inches, or 106 inches.

How to make that calculation?

Commonly, every stair step gains 7 inches in height or rise, so let's divide the 106 figure by 7 and see how many total steps we'll need. It turns out that we need 15.1 steps, each one gaining 7 inches, to lift us 106 inches. We'll round that number to 15.

We also know that each vertical *riser* requires 11 inches of tread or run. Knowing our rise and run (which comprise the altitude and base of a mathematical right triangle) we can figure our hypotenuse, which will give us our stringer length. Using the $A^2 + B^2 = C^2$ formula, we find that A^2 is $15x7^2$, B^2 is $15x11^2$ and together they equal C^2, which is 38,250. Taking the square root of 38,250 (195.58) and dividing that figure by 12 gives us our answer in feet. It turns out that our stringer, from the bottom of the first riser to the back edge of the top tread is 16.3 feet, or about 16 feet 4 inches. To fit the stringer against the joist or stair header, make an 8:12 plumb cut.

But, you ask, what about where the stringer meets the slab? How do you determine that angle? It is the converse angle of your 8:12 plumb cut. The easiest thing to do is to make your plumb cut at one end. But save the cutoff, because you can use that angle to mark the cut at the stringer's slab end. Next, measure out the stringer length, and hold the cutoff scrap in

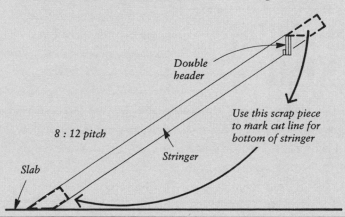

Double header

8 : 12 pitch

Use this scrap piece to mark cut line for bottom of stringer

Stringer

Slab

FIGURE 4–29

The angle of the stringer where it meets the slab is the converse angle of your 8:12 plumb cut. The easiest thing to do is to make your plumb cut, but save the waste cut off. You can use that angle to mark the cut at the stringer's slab end.

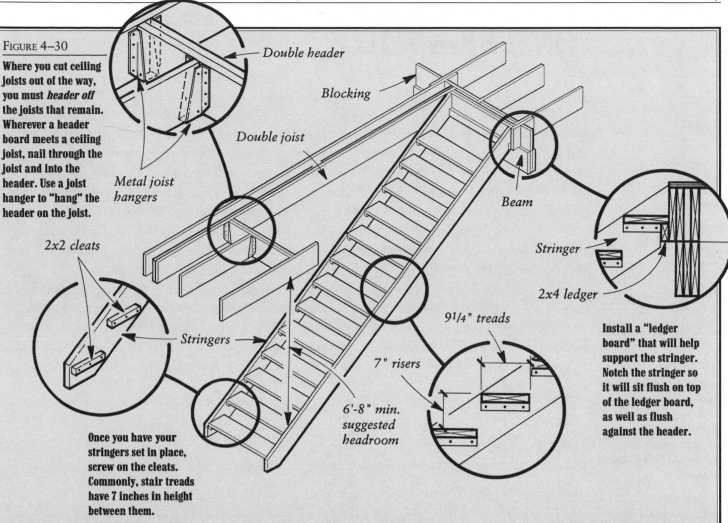

FIGURE 4–30

Where you cut ceiling joists out of the way, you must *header off* the joists that remain. Wherever a header board meets a ceiling joist, nail through the joist and into the header. Use a joist hanger to "hang" the header on the joist.

Double header

Blocking

Double joist

Metal joist hangers

Beam

2x2 cleats

Stringer

Stringers

2x4 ledger

9¼" treads

7" risers

6'-8" min. suggested headroom

Once you have your stringers set in place, screw on the cleats. Commonly, stair treads have 7 inches in height between them.

Install a "ledger board" that will help support the stringer. Notch the stringer so it will sit flush on top of the ledger board, as well as flush against the header.

place to mark your cut line.

Once you have your stringers chosen and cut, prepare the header that the stringer will rest against by nailing up a horizontal 2x4 ledger board where it will support the stringer. Then notch the stringer so it will sit on top of the ledger board, as well as flush against the header. Then, install the stringers.

Setting the cleats.

Once you have your stringers set in place, it's time to screw on the cleats. As mentioned, stair treads (the part of the stair you step on) commonly rise in increments of 7 inches.

In measuring our stringer and

dividing by 7, we found that we needed 15.1 treads, which we rounded to 15 because we won't notice that missing .1 tread spread over 15 stairs.

To set your cleats, you need to know the thickness of your tread. Set your first cleat so the top of the *first tread* is 7 inches above the finished floor (subtract the thickness of any finished flooring now!), and set subsequent cleats 7 inches above the top of the cleat below.

For cleats, use good-quality wood, such as 2x2 clear stock and glue and screw them in place with steel wood screws. For rough utility stairs, quality 2x4s as cleats will do just fine. You can also use steel angle brackets designed just for this

purpose. Whatever material you use, make sure you install them level. You may want to draw in all your cleat marks ahead of time with a level once your stringers are installed. Then, glue and screw the cleats into the stringer.

Screwing down your treads.

With the cleats in place, you can screw down your tread boards. The only thing to watch for is that you pick a good-quality lumber that won't bow under the weight of people climbing the stairs. Choose knot-free 2x12s.

Want to get fancy? Run the tread boards through a router and give them a rounded bullnosing before installing them.

INTERIOR WALLS

If you are finishing off this second floor, you'll want to build walls to partition the area. Interior partition walls are not load bearing, so you can frame them using 2x4s and single plates top and bottom. One exception is a wall you will surely want to build if you are finishing off your interior space, the *knee wall*. This wall extends from your rafters to your second floor deck (figure 4–31). Since the knee wall will face onto cold air, you'll want to build it with 2x6s so you can add the required insulation. Exactly where you put the knee wall depends on how much headroom you want where the knee wall meets the rafters and how much attic crawl space you want behind the knee wall. When installing the knee wall—which, later, will probably be covered with

sheetrock—you'll want to build in some access doors so you can get to your attic crawl space.

The knee wall you build will need a top plate, but since the top plate will be parallel with the rafters, you need to install blocking that creates a nailing surface for your ceiling's sheetrock. Figure 4–31 shows a good blocking method.

Construct any other interior walls that you want out of 2x4s. It's a good idea to work from a floor plan, which should have actual dimensions for your second floor area. Before you start, you may want to lay out your walls and snap chalk lines where the bottom plates will sit, just to predict any later problems.

Interior walls are built using the same basic principles as our other walls, only they aren't load bearing, so they don't require headers. Read ahead to chapter 8, "Fitting Out the Interior," for more specific details.

FIGURE 4–31

For finished second floors, knee walls make convenient partitions, but they need to be blocked properly to provide a nailing surface for sheetrock.

2x6 blocking in between rafter bays for sheetrock nailing

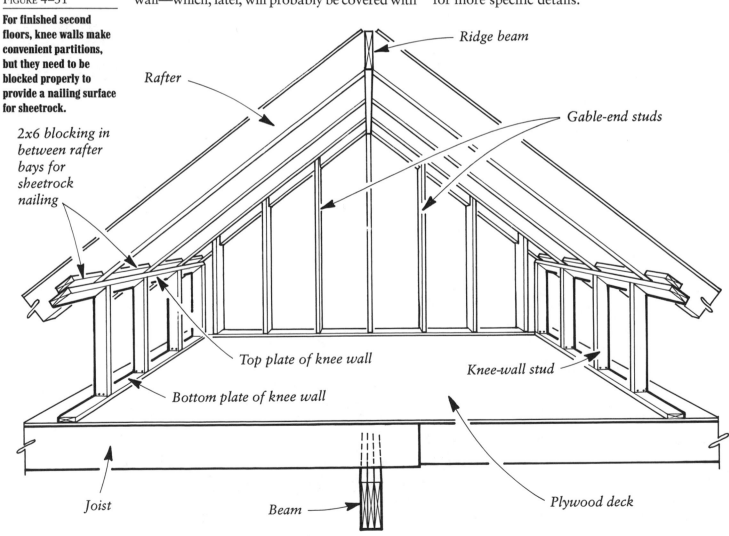

Rafter

Ridge beam

Gable-end studs

Top plate of knee wall

Knee-wall stud

Bottom plate of knee wall

Joist

Beam

Plywood deck

WINDOWS AND DOORS

The type of windows you use will depend on your barn's use, the size of your budget, and how good you are with your hammer, nails, and saw. If you intend to use your barn for storage and animals, or as a workshop, you might want to build windows yourself or use salvaged or refurbished units. If you plan on finishing off your second floor, and/or you want to heat the place, you'll want tighter windows, probably new ones.

The choice of doors varies widely too. You could simply build plywood doors with 2x4 frames and mount them on hinges, or you could go upscale and buy a pre-hung insulated oak door. It all depends on how you'll use your barn. A finished-off second floor will probably demand a weathertight, lockable door. Downstairs, you may want to install a sliding barn door, or double doors that open out, or just a few oversized pedestrian doors so that gardening tools and workshop projects can be easily moved in and out.

Let's take a look at how to install different kinds of windows and doors. From there, the choice is up to you.

Windows

There are two categories of windows: *pre-hung* and *non-pre-hung*. Within those categories are *double-hung* (over/under windows where both glass units slide up and down), *sliding* (windows that slide from side to side), *awning* (windows that open to the top like a hatch), *casement* (windows that crank open), or *picture* (windows that don't open at all).

Pre-hung windows come entirely prebuilt, with *jamb* (the wood frame that contains the sash), *sash* (the framework that holds the windows), and *casing* (trim pieces attached to the walls that frame a window or door) all sent to you as one unit. After your rough opening is prepared with *building felt* (tar paper) or house wrap (such as Tyvek® or Typar®), you pop the unit in place, leveling and plumbing it with shims.

Then you nail the casings to the sheathing, and the jambs to the jack studs, header, and rough sill. Pre-hung windows are simple to install; their drawback is cost: easily $150 a unit.

Recycled pre-hung windows are windows that have been discarded with the jambs still intact, encasing the sash. Often, you just have to replace some glass and pull any old nails out of the jamb. After you install the window, you trim it out with new casings, and you're done, much happier for the money you've saved.

Nervous about your carpentry skills? Go with pre-hung windows. Their installation is easy—in fact, hard to botch. If you want to save money, go with recycled windows if you can find them, or install a piece of glass in a sash and jamb of your own making. What have you got to lose? The worst you can do is improve your carpentry skills while saving some money. And if you don't like what you build, you can always get out your credit card and dial an 800 number. Ah, the American way!

Preparing the Rough Opening

No matter what kind of window you will use, on all your rough openings, take 15-pound building felt (tar paper) cut into 12-inch-wide strips and install it around the window opening so the felt folds over from the inside of the sill to the sheathing. As mentioned, a popular alternative to tar paper is house wrap (Tyvek®, Typar®). Staple the felt or house wrap to the rough sill and jack studs (see photo, page 110). Where pieces meet, overlap them at least 3 inches with each other. Along the sides, make sure the pieces overlap so they don't catch water, the upper piece overlapping the lower.

Also, just before installing a pre-hung window, apply a bead of caulk to the sheathing where the casing will press flush against it. That helps reduce air infiltration.

Pre-Hung Window Installation

To install a pre-hung window, you'll need 10 or 12 good-quality shims. Pine or cedar shingles, sold as shims in the lumberyard and cheaper than

TIP

WEDGES CUT ACROSS THE GRAIN CAN BE USED TO SHIM WINDOW SILLS. CUTTING OFF THE EXCESS WITH A CHISEL IS EASY.

Before installing pre-hung windows, prepare the rough opening with roofing felt, or, as shown here, house wrap.

actual shingles, make great shims; they're the perfect shape, and you can easily cut or break off the excess once they're in place. Start your installation by inserting your pre-hung window into a rough opening that's been prepared with building felt. Place at least eight shims around the corners of the window between the jamb and the rough opening (jack studs to the left and right, header above, and rough sill below). This is probably a two-person job. If the window is large, place shims in the middle of the jambs as well. You'll find that you have to work the shims from the inside of the building because the casing or flange blocks access from the outside.

Place a level on the pre-hung window's sill. Adjust the shims until the window is level. Then, drive a single 6d or 8d casing nail in the bottom right casing. Nail the casing to the sheathing.

Next, check the window for plumb. Place your level vertically and adjust the shims until the window is plumb. When it is, drive two nails in the casing, one in the left and one in the right top corner. Nail the casing to the sheathing. Your window should now be plumb and level. Double-

check it, because we're about to nail it permanently in place. To do this, use 6d or 8d finish nails, driving them through the jamb into the jack studs. Ideally, you want to nail through your shims, so they stay in place.

Pre-Hung Door Installation

Pre-hung doors are installed much the same way as pre-hung windows. You set the jamb in the rough opening, level and plumb it with the shims, taking care each time not to nail through the casing until the frame has been double-checked for level and plumb. Once the door jamb is set in place, nail through the jamb into the jack studs to either side and the header above.

One thing to watch for is the *doorsill*. Door-sills are usually made of a hardwood, like oak, to endure the rigors of foot traffic. Be aware that the height of your doorsill on the inside of the door must account for any flooring material you are putting down. If the sill is too high, you'll find yourself stubbing your toe as you walk through.

Recycling Windows and Building a Jamb for a Piece of Glass

You may find you'll have to build your own jamb. Most recycled windows you get will just be the sash and whatever unbroken glass remains. Building a jamb is rather easy. All you need is the proper lumber and some basic carpentry skills.

Of course, you'll have to have planned for your recycled windows when you framed for your rough openings. At this point, then, all you have to do is build a jamb into the rough opening. (Incidentally, this is the same process you would use if you want to box a glass pane to make your own simple window.)

Construct the sill out of a 2x10 so it will span the 2x6 wall, the width of the sheathing, and the width of whatever you are putting on the inside walls—say, sheetrock or plywood—and yet still be wide enough so it will overhang the outer wall and drip water away from the building. Even if you are leaving your inside walls bare, use a 2x10 and don't worry about it overhanging slightly inside. Bevel the outside of the sill so it sheds rainwater. For the side jamb and head of the jamb, use $^5/_4$ x 8-inch #2 pine (it is usually 1 $^1/_8$ inches thick and easier to work with than full 2x8s).

Assemble your jamb by first nailing together the jamb head and side jamb pieces with 6d or 8d finishing nails (figure 4–32). Slide this unit in and insert shims around the three jamb pieces just as you did with the pre-hung window. Next, fit your windowsill piece in between the side-jamb pieces, supporting it with shims as well. You may want to have precut a notch (called an *ear*) on the outer underside of the sill so it creates a drip edge an inch or so out from the wall (figure 4–32).

Level, plumb, and square your jamb pieces. But before you set the jambs with nails into the header, rough sill, and jack studs, see if the window you intend to use actually fits. You may have bowed some of the jamb pieces with the shims. If the window fits, remove it and nail in your jamb, jacks, and sill.

Before nailing them into position, check and double-check windows for level.

Shim windows so they sit plumb and level in the rough openings.

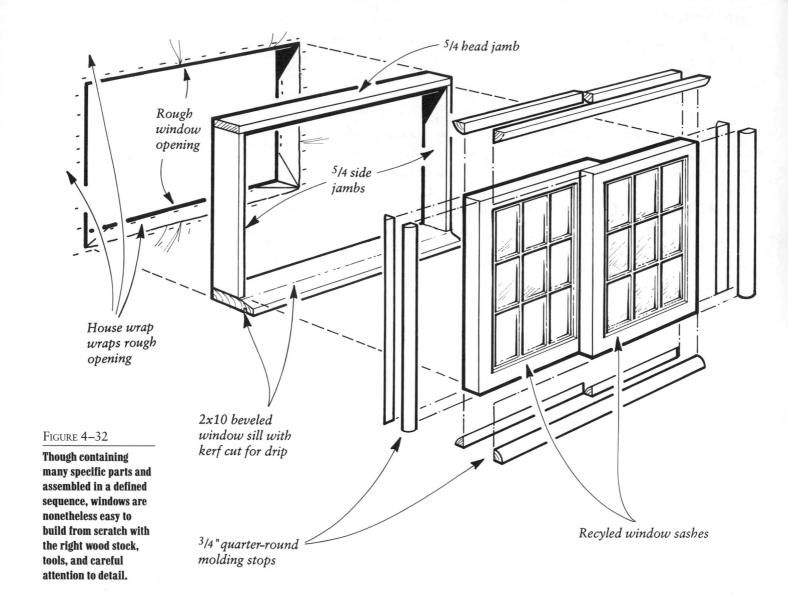

5/4 head jamb

Rough
window
opening

5/4 side
jambs

House wrap
wraps rough
opening

FIGURE 4–32

**Though containing
many specific parts and
assembled in a defined
sequence, windows are
nonetheless easy to
build from scratch with
the right wood stock,
tools, and careful
attention to detail.**

2x10 beveled
window sill with
kerf cut for drip

3/4" quarter-round
molding stops

Recyled window sashes

With some molding stock, build a *stop* all the way around the jamb. Place your window (or glass) in the frame and push it up against the stop. Then box the window or glass in place by nailing in another set of stops (figure 4–33).

Building a Door Jamb

Building a door jamb for a salvaged door or a door that's not pre-hung is very much like building a window jamb. The jamb described here is not for large barn doors nor for industrial type doors, but for pedestrian doors that will close

and latch or lock. More on those larger doors in the next section.

Use good, sturdy pine stock for the door jamb because it will be carrying the door's weight on it. For a 2x6 wall, use 5/4 x 8s for the side and head jambs. Construct the three-piece side-jamb/head-jamb unit just as we did for the windows and slip it into place in the rough opening for your door. For shims, use full cedar shingles, making sure to place one set of shims 7 inches down from the jamb head and one set 11 inches up from the slab. Reason: This is where your hinges will be set and you want to establish a

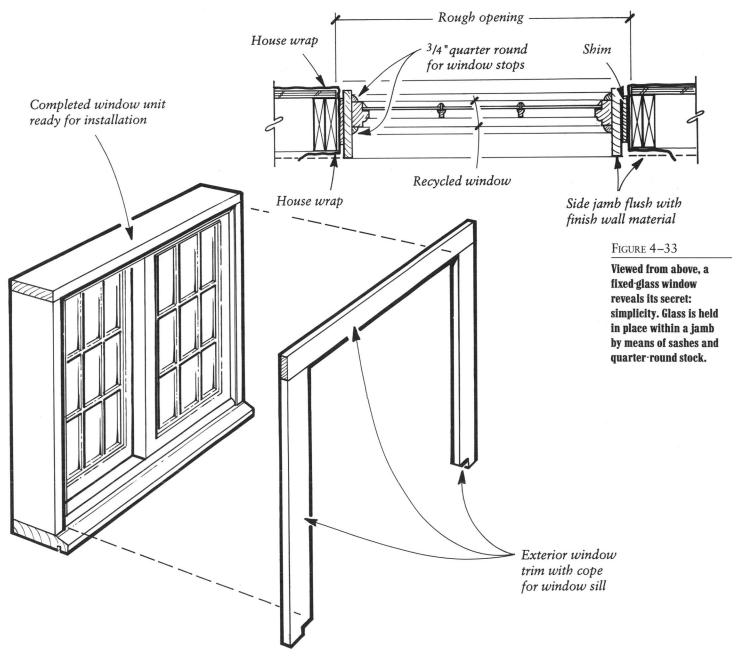

Completed window unit ready for installation

Rough opening

House wrap

3/4" quarter round for window stops

Shim

House wrap

Recycled window

Side jamb flush with finish wall material

FIGURE 4–33

Viewed from above, a fixed-glass window reveals its secret: simplicity. Glass is held in place within a jamb by means of sashes and quarter-round stock.

Exterior window trim with cope for window sill

firm base for them. If the door is heavy, you'll want a third hinge, so put shims in at the center line between the 7-inch mark up top and the 11-inch mark down below (figure 4–34).

Once you have the side jamb and head jamb in place and shimmed, place your framing square in the top corners of the jamb to check for square. Adjust the shims as required. Plumb your side jambs and level your head jamb.

Once you've done that, mark and cut a board that fits snugly between the side jambs an inch below the head jamb. This is a spacer board. Once it is cut, it represents the desired width of the jamb. Slide it down the length of your door, and check to make sure the jamb width is the same correct width all the way down.

Let the spacer board sit at the bottom, between the side jambs. Tap your shims so the side jambs snug up on the spacer board. When you have the right width, check for plumb and nail through your shims at the 11-inch mark. Then move the spacer board up and do the same at the mid-shim mark. Again, tap your shim to get the width just right, then nail through the shims into the jack stud. Next, do the same at the 7-inch shim. Be careful not to drive a nail right where your hinges will be set. You don't want a nail in the way of a future hinge screw.

Hanging the Door

Once your jamb is in place, you can hang your door. To do this, place the door in the jamb and shim it into place so it sits exactly where you want it to be. Make sure there is correct clearance between the top of the door and the head jamb. Measure down 7 inches and mark the top

of your upper hinge with a razor knife on both the side jamb and the door. Then measure up from the bottom 11 inches and mark for your lower hinge. If there is a middle hinge, mark for that, too, exactly halfway between the top and bottom hinges.

Remove the door. If you can take your hinge apart by removing the pin, do so. In any event, place the appropriate hinge-half against the razor mark on the side jamb or door. Make sure it is square and plumb. Scribe around it with a

FIGURE 4–34

For doors, only set hinges where the jamb is backed by shims.

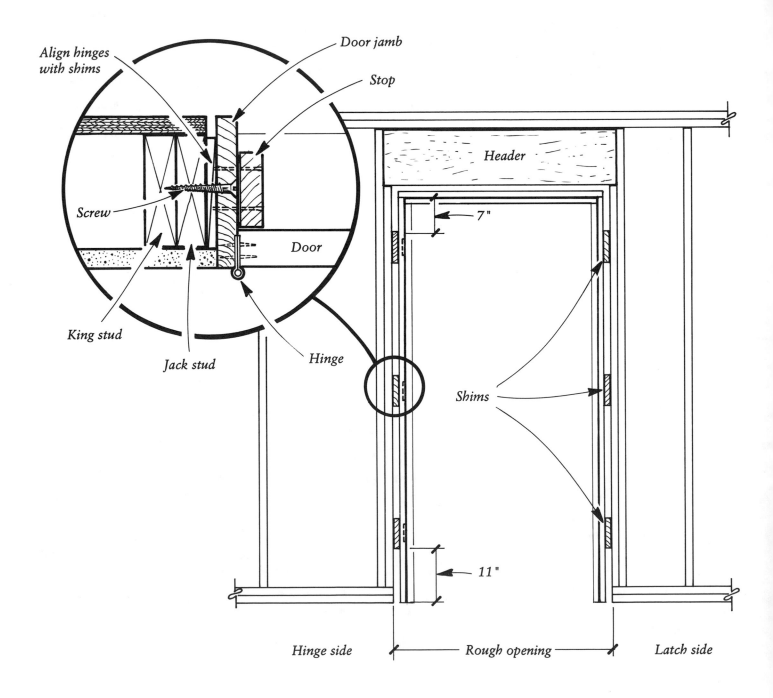

razor knife.

Next, hold the hinge against the door and then against the jamb to determine how much to cut out of this scribed square so the hinge will sit flush with the surface of the wood. Trace the hinge to get this depth on the wood.

With a sharp chisel, score and scribe the square you've marked with your razor and slowly chip out the wood for both the door and jamb. Then set the hinge halves and screw them in place. Once they are set, you can hang your door on them, dropping the pin in the hinge.

If you haven't already, install some doorstops so the door has something to stop against once it's in place and closed. Then slowly close the door and see if it needs to be planed anywhere.

You can adjust the hinges' side jamb clearance by slipping thin slivers of wood behind the jamb hinge plate. By putting the sliver on one side of the hinge or the other, you can increase or decrease the clearance between the door and jamb on the hinge side.

FIGURE 4–35

Making doors requires careful assembly of quality lumber stock, using glue, screws, and clamps. Shown here, a variety of traditional barn-door patterns and assembly methods.

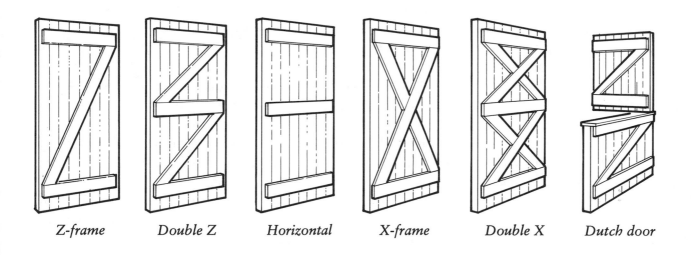

Z-frame   *Double Z*   *Horizontal*   *X-frame*   *Double X*   *Dutch door*

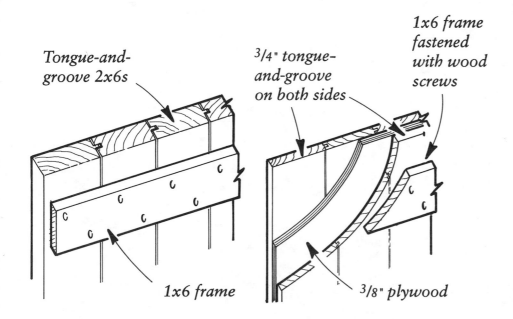

Tongue-and-groove 2x6s

3/4" tongue-and-groove on both sides

1x6 frame fastened with wood screws

1x6 frame

3/8" plywood

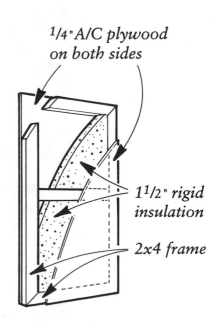

1/4" A/C plywood on both sides

1 1/2" rigid insulation

2x4 frame

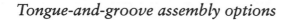

Tongue-and-groove assembly options   *Basic insulated door*

Once the door is in place, install hardware as directed by the manufacturer.

Building Larger Doors

You can build doors of your own design using plywood and 2x4s or barn board. Use your imagination. Figure 4–35 shows you a few designs. When constructing these doors, you may want to embellish them by assembling the wood in a creative design or using interesting hinges and latches.

When installing a large door, you must build the jamb big and strong enough to handle the door's weight and the hinges' size. For doors large enough to drive cars or tractors through, you may want to add an extra *king stud* while you are framing. This will give you more of a surface to screw your hinges to, and it will add substance to the jamb. Building up the jamb is not necessary if you are installing a sliding barn door. The rail and wheel mechanism you buy for it should come with installation specs; all you've got to do is follow them. Incidentally, sliding barn doors are great in areas that receive a lot of snow because swinging doors eventually get snowed or iced in.

STEP BACK AND ADMIRE

When visiting building sites, you may have noticed that some builders place an evergreen or tamarack branch at the highest point of the building once it is up, as a gesture to safety and good luck. You may want to practice that tradition. Wait until your ridge beam is up and be careful on the ladder! Once you complete the steps in this chapter, all your planning and hard work have really come to substantial fruition. Where once there was bare ground, now there is a structure you can rightfully call a barn. With a little research to help you along the way, it has sprung from your imagination and been built with the hands and labor of you and your helpers. Good work.

In the subsequent chapters we'll look at how to finish the other essentials: a roof, the siding, power, plumbing, and an interior if you have planned a living area in your barn. For now, though, it may be time to haul out a few lounge chairs, call a few friends, and sit back and admire what you've built so far.

Roof purlins installed on these rafters will support a metal roof. Notice that the rough opening for the gable-end second-story window needs no header because it carries no building load.

SILL

12-foot 2x8s:

_____ PER-FOOT COST X _____ TOTAL FEET = _____

10-foot 2x8s:

_____ PER-FOOT COST X _____ TOTAL FEET = _____

FIRST-FLOOR WALLS

2x6 pre-cuts:

_____ PER PRECUT COST X _____ TOTAL QUANTITY = _____

2x12 header:

_____ PER-FOOT COST X _____ TOTAL FEET = _____

**½-inch plywood
for headers:**

_____ PER-SHEET COST X _____ TOTAL SHEETS = _____

2x6 top plates:

_____ PER-FOOT COST X _____ TOTAL FEET = _____

2x6 sills:

_____ PER-FOOT COST X _____ TOTAL FEET = _____

BRACING MATERIALS

2x4 braces:

_____ PER-FOOT COST X _____ TOTAL FEET = _____

2x4 stakes:

_____ PER-FOOT COST X _____ TOTAL FEET = _____

String:

_____ PER-ROLL COST X _____ TOTAL ROLLS = _____

2x6s for blocking:

_____ PER-FOOT COST X _____ TOTAL FEET = _____

2x4 for level extender:

_____ PER-FOOT COST X _____ TOTAL FEET = _____

SUPPORTING MID BEAM

Midwall post 2x10s:

_____ PER-FOOT COST X _____ TOTAL FEET = _____

**2x6s for partition wall
(optional):**

_____ PER-FOOT COST X _____ TOTAL FEET = _____

**Partition wall sheathing
(optional):**

_____ PER-SHEET COST X _____ TOTAL SHEETS = _____

2x10s for mid beam:

_____ PER-FOOT COST X _____ TOTAL FEET = _____

CEILING JOISTS

2x10s for ceiling joists:

_____ PER-FOOT COST X _____ TOTAL FEET = _____

**2x10s for ceiling joists
blocks:**

_____ PER-FOOT COST X _____ TOTAL FEET = _____

2x4 temporary support:

_____ PER-FOOT COST X _____ TOTAL FEET = _____

RIDGE BEAM AND GABLE RAFTERS

2x12 ridge beam:

_____ PER-FOOT COST X _____ TOTAL FEET = _____

2x10 rafters:

_____ PER-FOOT COST X _____ TOTAL FEET = _____

FRAMING COSTS

WORKSHEET

RIDGE BEAM AND GABLE RAFTERS (CONTINUED)

2x4s for temporary ridge support: _____ PER-FOOT COST X _____ TOTAL FEET = _____

GABLE END WALLS

2x6s: _____ PER-FOOT COST X _____ TOTAL FEET = _____

SHED DORMER

2x6 studs: _____ PER-FOOT COST X _____ TOTAL FEET = _____

2x8 rafters: _____ PER-FOOT COST X _____ TOTAL FEET = _____

2x4 side-wall studs: _____ PER-FOOT COST X _____ TOTAL FEET = _____

2x8 collar ties: _____ PER-FOOT COST X _____ TOTAL FEET = _____

2x10 (additional wood for double gable rafters): _____ PER-FOOT COST X _____ TOTAL FEET = _____

WALL SHEATHING

½-inch plywood: _____ PER-SHEET COST X _____ TOTAL SHEETS = _____

ROOF SHEATHING

½-inch plywood: _____ PER-SHEET COST X _____ TOTAL SHEETS = _____

DECKING

⅝-inch plywood: _____ PER-SHEET COST X _____ TOTAL SHEETS = _____

Screws: _____ PER-POUND COST X _____ TOTAL POUNDS = _____

Glue: _____ PER-GALLON COST X _____ TOTAL GALLONS = _____

SOFFIT

■ OPTION 1

Plywood fascia board: _____ PER-FOOT COST X _____ TOTAL FEET = _____

1x8 soffit panel: _____ PER-FOOT COST X _____ TOTAL FEET = _____

Soffit vent screen: _____ PER-SQ. FOOT COST X _____ TOTAL FEET = _____

2x4 wall ledger: _____ PER-FOOT COST X _____ TOTAL FEET = _____

■ OPTION 2

2x6 blocking: _____ PER-FOOT COST X _____ TOTAL FEET = _____

Extra sheathing: _____ PER-SHEET COST X _____ TOTAL FEET = _____

Screening: _____ PER-SQ. FOOT COST X _____ TOTAL FEET = _____

WORKSHEET

FRAMING COSTS

KNEE WALL

2x6s: ________ PER-FOOT COST X ________ TOTAL FEET = ________

FLYING RAFTER

2x10s: ________ PER-FOOT COST X ________ TOTAL FEET = ________

2x6 barge rafters: ________ PER-FOOT COST X ________ TOTAL FEET = ________

DOORS AND WINDOWS

5/4 pine side and head jambs: ________ PER-FOOT COST X ________ TOTAL FEET = ________

Quarter-round or trim: ________ PER-FOOT COST X ________ TOTAL FEET = ________

Trim for stops: ________ PER-FOOT COST X ________ TOTAL FEET = ________

Building felt: ________ PER-ROLL COST X ________ TOTAL ROLLS = ________

Hinges: ________ PER-UNIT COST X ________ TOTAL UNITS = ________

Hardware: ________ PER-UNIT COST X ________ TOTAL UNITS = ________

Caulk: ________ PER-UNIT COST X ________ TOTAL UNITS = ________

Shims: ________ PER-PACKAGE COST X ________ TOTAL PACKAGES = ________

Pre-hung windows: ________ PER-UNIT COST X ________ TOTAL UNITS = ________

Pre-hung doors: ________ PER-UNIT COST X ________ TOTAL UNITS = ________

Salvaged doors: ________ PER-UNIT COST X ________ TOTAL UNITS = ________

Salvaged windows: ________ PER-UNIT COST X ________ TOTAL UNITS = ________

STAIRS

2x10 stringers: ________ PER-FOOT COST X ________ TOTAL FEET = ________

Joist hangers for header: ________ PER-UNIT COST X ________ TOTAL UNITS = ________

Ledger board: ________ PER-FOOT COST X ________ TOTAL FEET = ________

Cleats: ________ PER-FOOT COST X ________ TOTAL FEET = ________

Treads: ________ PER-FOOT COST X ________ TOTAL FEET = ________

2x10s for rough-opening headers: ________ PER-FOOT COST X ________ TOTAL FEET = ________

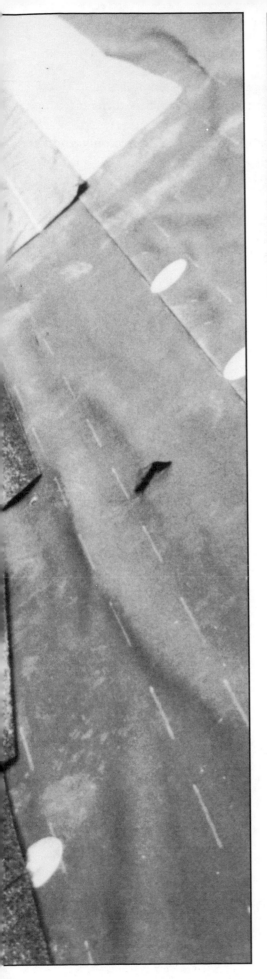

5 Roofing

There are many different types of roofing materials that are perfectly acceptable and can adequately serve a multipurpose barn. The choice of which kind to use depends on your budget and how you want your barn to look. An asphalt-shingle roof is extremely functional, and though it doesn't add much charm, its installation is straightforward, it's trouble free for a roof that needs a ridge vent, and it's economical. On the other hand, a metal roof (either standing seam or agricultural panel) can look dazzling: it has a classic, traditional look, and you can get it in colors like fire engine red or forest green. A cedar-shingle roof can give a charming country cottage look, but its installation is tricky and not really something the first-time barn builder should tackle alone.

In this chapter, we'll look at how to put on an agricultural metal roof and an asphalt shingle roof. We'll also look briefly at standing-seam roofs. If you'd like to put on a roof type not mentioned here—slate, cedar shingle, or others—you should refer to a text dealing specifically with their installations. We've chosen metal and asphalt-shingle roofs for our barn because they're economical, look good, and are relatively easy to install. A metal roof is an especially good choice for an uninsulated barn that doesn't need roof venting. Asphalt shingles lay up easily, particularly on a barn like ours that doesn't have a complex roof with hips and valleys to account for. Also, asphalt-shingle roofs are easy to replace when they wear out 10 to 15 years or so down the line.

If you plan on shingling your barn's roof, first lay roofing felt over the plywood sheathing and install a removable roof scaffold to ease shingle installation.

METAL ROOFS

There are a number of types of metal roofs, but two popular types are *standing seam roofs* and *agricultural-style panels,* or *ag panels* (figure 5–1). Within each category there are different thicknesses, coatings, and finishes. Here's a general overview of some options:

Most metal panels are made of steel and then coated or dipped in a protective coating at a very high temperature that permanently bonds the coating to the steel. There are three basic types of coatings—zinc, aluminum, and aluminum-zinc alloys—and each is different from paint.

Zinc-coated panels are commonly known as *galvanized* panels. They come with ratings, like G-60 or G-90, which designate the weight of the coating per square foot of panel. The higher the number, the thicker the coating. Over a period of years, a zinc coating will slowly oxidize as it sacrifices itself to protect the steel panel from rust. Zinc coatings are desirable because they are relatively inexpensive and the zinc is minimally water soluble and can actu-

FIGURE 5–1

Metal-roof options include standing seam and agricultural ("ag") panels. Ag-panel installation requires standard tools and basic skills. Standing-seam roofs are more challenging; they require special crimping tools that take practice to master.

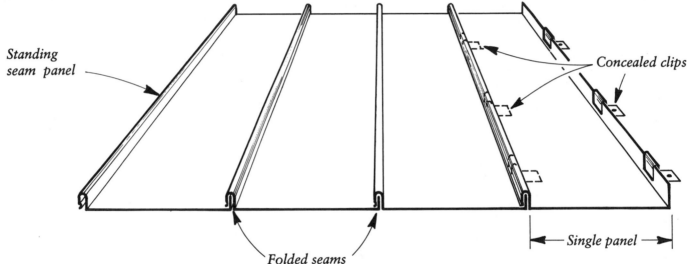

Standing seam panel

Concealed clips

Folded seams

Single panel

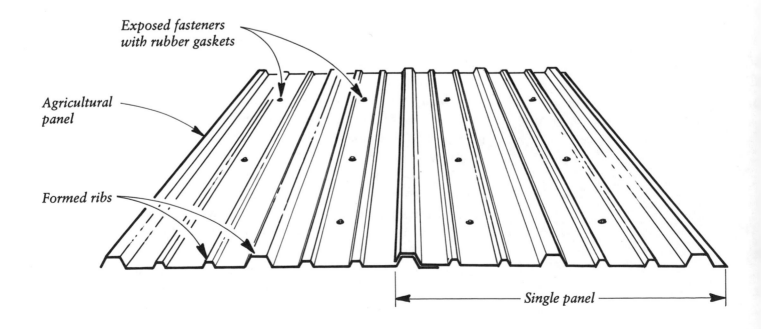

Exposed fasteners with rubber gaskets

Agricultural panel

Formed ribs

Single panel

ally wash down and "heal" places on the panel where the coating has been scratched or worn away. Galvanized panels with appropriately thick zinc coatings can last as long as 30 years in dry conditions. Even in the worst conditions (wet, with lots of snow and ice build-up on a moderately-sloped roof), they will probably last over five years before some other type of protective coating need be applied.

Next there are panels with aluminum coatings. These are commonly called *aluminized panels*. The aluminum coating offers a durable barrier that protects the steel panels. Their coatings can easily last 20 years, but they don't heal the way zinc panels do.

Recognizing this, manufacturers have mixed the two alloys to create a third type of coating: *aluminum-zinc alloy*. This offers the healing capacity of zinc with the superior protection of aluminum.

Different manufacturers have also added small amounts of copper, nickel, lead, tin, and chromium to the coatings to give different kinds of added protection. For example, the popular *terne* roofs contain 80 percent lead and 20 percent tin. But as with most building material, you get what you pay for: Specialty coatings that offer greater protection will cost you more.

When you select a metal panel type for your barn, pick the one with the thickest coating of the best alloy that your budget allows.

You can install these panels either *bare* (unpainted), or with a *factory finish* (a coat of paint applied at the factory). If you like the look of a bare panel roof—and it can be very attractive—then, bare panel is really the maintenance-free way to go. If you go with factory-finished panels, and the factory uses good-quality paint (applied in controlled conditions and often baked on), you'll get a few years of maintenance-free use out of them. Still, factory-finished panels will eventually need a paint job some years down the line.

Still want factory-finished panels? Then ask beforehand what kind of paint they're finished with and see if there are options. Most manufacturers offer two or more grades of paint. The least expensive and shortest lasting is *polyester*

resin. The next best is *silicon-modified polyester resin* (it adds about 12 cents per square foot to the cost), and the very best is *fluoropolymer resin* (it adds about 25 cents per square foot to the cost). As for color, light color is better than dark; it's cooler and will add to the life of your roof. Which color is best? As a rule, the closer a color is to its primary one, the more rapidly it will fade.

If you buy bare panels and paint them yourself, you will commit yourself to a serious and regular maintenance task for years to come. It's almost impossible to find a paint that will last more than three or four years, given the toll the sun takes on panels that can have a surface temperature of 80 degrees Fahrenheit *above* the air temperature. You can paint the panels yourself but do you really want to?

Metal-Roof Installation

Before we actually get into metal-roof installation, we need to make a distinction between *watertight* and *water-shedding* roofs. If your barn need not be entirely watertight and can stand an occasional drip or some windblown rain from under the eaves or where panels meet, then you want a water-shedding roof. On the other hand, if you have a finished ceiling inside, or insulation in the rafter bays, or anything else that shouldn't get wet, you want a watertight roof.

Of the two metal roofs available to us—standing seam and ag panel—ag panel is the easiest to install by yourself. Standing seam roofs take some real practice and special tools to install. They are not for novice builders and typically require an experienced subcontractor to install. But ag panels can be properly nailed or screwed on with some careful reading of instructions on your part. For our barn, we'll focus on ag panels as our metal roof of choice.

Ag panels can be used to create water-shedding *or* watertight roofs. Typically, water-shedding roofs are ag panels over purlins. Watertight roofs consist of ag panels sealed at the edges and laid on plywood sheathing covered with building felt (tar paper). However, you can

TIP

UNLESS YOU ARE EXPERIENCED WITH THEM, AVOID INSTALLING STANDING SEAM ROOF PANELS YOURSELF. THEY TYPICALLY REQUIRE SPECIAL TOOLS AND AN EXPERIENCED SUBCONTRACTOR TO INSTALL.

build a watertight roof over purlins *or* plywood. We'll see how these installation techniques differ later in this chapter.

Nail choice is important.

When installing ag panels (or *any* metal roof) for water-shedding or watertight properties, you can't use any old nail or screw. Since the coating on ag panels is subject to galvanic action, certain metals will quickly corrode the panels if they come in direct contact. Zinc and aluminum are on the *anodic* end of the galvanic scale. Metals like graphite and copper are on the *cathodic* end of the scale. When cathodic and anodic metals come in contact with each other, corrosion occurs. If you have galvanized (anodic) panels, use anodic metal nails. The manufacturer will recommend a nail type for your panel that will avoid any chance of corrosion. But common sense should tell you to use nails that are made of the same metal as your panels. For a galvanized panel, use galvanized nails. And don't let any cathodic metal come in contact with that galvanized panel. For ag panels, use galvanized *ring-shank* or *ringlock* nails, or galvanized steel screws. Both come with neoprene gaskets at their heads. The gasket seals out the water where the nail or screw head meets the panel as you drive it in. These types of screws or nails will not cause corrosion and thereby will help preserve your panels.

While we're on the subject, note that even the mark of a graphite pencil will start to corrode your panels. Use only a felt marker or crayon for marking your cut lines. And avoid copper gutters or copper flashing. Copper should come nowhere near the anodic metal roof panels. Even rain dripping from a copper gutter can cause corrosion.

Installing ag panels for a water-shedding roof.

It's best and easiest to put water-shedding ag panels over 2x4 purlins. Some people use 1x3 purlins, but 2x4s are better for two reasons. First, they add needed cross bracing to the rafters. Second, 2x4s are sturdy enough to stand and crawl on when you're installing panels. That's not always the case with flimsier 1x3s,

especially over 24-inch o.c. rafters!

In most cases, the purlins' spacing must correspond to what the manufacturer recommends for the panels you purchase. Check the manufacturer's specs to see what the required purlin spacing is for your roof panels. Since the thickness of your panel is rated for a certain span, a thicker panel will require fewer purlins because it can safely span a greater distance. For instance, galvanized steel, 26 gauge panels are popular and economical; 26 gauge (.22 inches thick) can span purlins placed 24 inches apart. The panel manufacturer will supply a chart for the purlin spacing. Do not guess at it. If need be, call the manufacturer, ask what the recommended purlin spacing is, and stick to it. If the panels come with a warranty —and many do—it's probably dependent on proper purlin spacing; improper installation can void it.

Panels come in lengths from 4 to 30 feet and widths from 2 to 3 feet, though they are purchased by the *square* which typically covers 100 square feet of roof.

There can be quite a bit of thermal movement in panels, as they expand and contract in response to temperature swings over the course of a day. You'll want to do all you can to reduce this thermal movement because it can loosen screws and nails and cause leaking. One way to reduce the movement is to use short panels, say, two or three per row rather than one from eaves to ridge.

Before installing the panels, first nail your 2x4 purlins to your rafters, spacing them as required. Nail the purlins flush to the outside of the gable end rafters. Don't end any purlins midway between rafters. All purlins should end on top of rafters.

Start installing your panels at a gable end, not in the middle of the roof. When you lay your first panel at the gable end, you'll see a gap between the panel and rafter caused by the purlin. You can cover over this gap with a *gable-end starter/finisher,* a piece of metal bent at 90 degrees and designed to fit at the gable ends of a roof, under the first (or last) panels (figure 5–2). Gable trim pieces are available from the panel manufacturer. For water-shedding roofs,

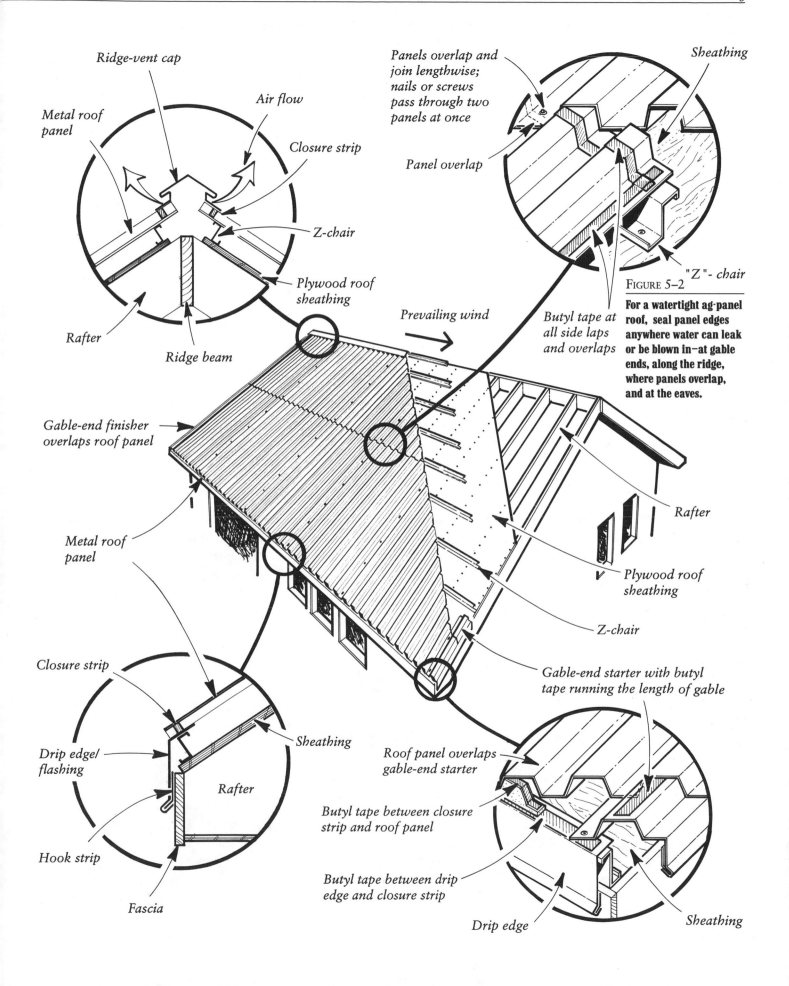

Ridge-vent cap

Air flow

Metal roof panel

Closure strip

Z-chair

Plywood roof sheathing

Rafter

Ridge beam

Panels overlap and join lengthwise; nails or screws pass through two panels at once

Sheathing

Panel overlap

"Z"- chair

FIGURE 5–2

For a watertight ag-panel roof, seal panel edges anywhere water can leak or be blown in—at gable ends, along the ridge, where panels overlap, and at the eaves.

Prevailing wind

Butyl tape at all side laps and overlaps

Gable-end finisher overlaps roof panel

Rafter

Plywood roof sheathing

Metal roof panel

Z-chair

Gable-end starter with butyl tape running the length of gable

Closure strip

Sheathing

Drip edge/ flashing

Rafter

Roof panel overlaps gable-end starter

Hook strip

Butyl tape between closure strip and roof panel

Fascia

Butyl tape between drip edge and closure strip

Drip edge

Sheathing

you may feel you don't need this trim piece. Watertight roofs, however, do need them.

Notice that overlapping roof panels present an edge for wind to get under. When you install the panels, arrange them so the prevailing wind will not catch under the panel to lift it and drive in rain and snow (figure 5–2).

When installing the panels, place your first at an eaves' end. Let the panel extend out over the eaves about 3 inches to create a drip edge. From there, work upwards until the row is completed at the ridge.

Where panels meet lengthwise, screws or nails will go through two panels at once (figure 5–2), so don't put in all your screws or nails for your first row. Note where adjacent panels will meet lengthwise and figure that the row of screws or nails at this overlap will hold two panels at once.

Nail or screw through the panels into the purlins. Use the nailing schedule recommended by the manufacturers. Be careful not to overdrive the nails, since that can dent the metal and deform the nails' gaskets. Still, you should drive them firmly enough to seal the gasket against the panel's top.

If your panel is not pre-drilled, you may be tempted to drive nails through the higher part of the panel (let's call it the *hill,* as opposed to the *valley,* which sits flush on the purlin.) Nail only in the valley. You get the benefit of the entire nail holding the panel to the purlin, and

it decreases the possibility of leakage (figure 5–2). Nailing at the hill leaves a large part of the nail exposed above the wood, reducing the nail's holding power and increasing the risk of the panel blowing off. Give your panels all the holding power you can. Be a valley nailer!

Finish off the ridge with a *ridge cap,* also available from the manufacturer. The ridge cap is simply bolted on over the ag panels.

Installing ag panels for a watertight roof.

Ag panels make an attractive roof on any structure, whether an agricultural building or a residential home. Increasingly, ag-panels are being used on residential structures and ag-panel manufacturers have developed ways to seal the ag panels completely against the weather. If you want to make a watertight ag-panel roof for your barn, you'll have to seal the panels in a prescribed way using proprietary products.

Watertight ag-panel roofs can be installed over plywood sheathing or purlins, but for best results use plywood. Once again, thermal movement can be a problem but is preventable in two ways. As with our water-shedding roof, you can use shorter panels. And you can install your ag panels on Z-shaped metal purlins (minimum 22 gauge) that serve as "chairs" on which the panels sit (figure 5–3). The chairs, screwed to the sheathing, rock back and forth as the panels flex in the heat and cold, but the screws attaching everything aren't loosened.

FIGURE 5–3

For ag-panel roofs, z-shaped "chairs" flex during thermal movement and reduce the stress on nails or screws holding panels to the plywood or purlins.

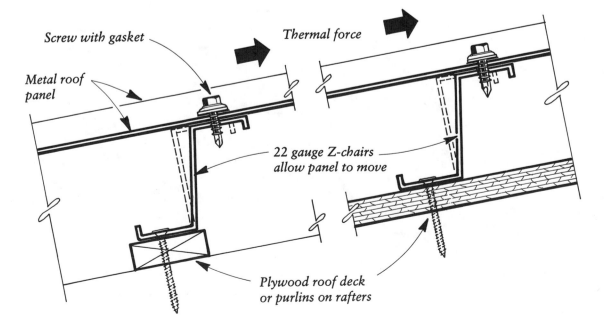

Screw with gasket

Thermal force

Metal roof panel

22 gauge Z-chairs allow panel to move

Plywood roof deck or purlins on rafters

As for sealing the panels against weather to make the roof watertight: If you think about it, there are only four places where water can penetrate our barn's roof. It can be blown up under the eaves, in at the gable ends, in at the ridge, and anywhere the panels overlap. (Water can enter where exhaust stacks from the plumbing and heating penetrate the roof, but as we'll see, those openings can be sealed with special boots and collars.)

For our watertight roof, we want the panels to overlap as they did for the water-shedding roof, but now we'll seal the overlap with butyl tape or a specially designed sealant (figure 5–2). Which should we use? I prefer butyl tape because it lasts longer, especially if it's properly installed and kept out of the ultraviolet rays of the sun. The pumpable sealants are 30 percent solvent that evaporates over time, drying out the adhesive. When you install the butyl tape, be sure to cut it with a razor knife because pulling it—like pulling taffy—stretches the tape and compromises its sealing ability. Also, when setting a panel, position it first, then drop it on the tape because once the two come in contact with each other, positioning the panel further is nearly impossible.

Figure 5–2 shows the details for sealing with butyl tape where panels meet. The tape prevents water or snow from being blown in where panels meet lengthwise or where they overlap at mid-roof.

As for the eaves' ends where water can be blown up under the ag panel, seal them with a *closure strip*, a rubber gasket shaped to fit under the ag panel's profile and block out air and water (figure 5–2.)

At the gable ends, seal the gable starter/finisher piece with butyl tape.

You may also have to run a stack exhaust or an insulated fireplace chimney up through an ag panel. Here, too, the ag panel's odd shape presents a sealing problem. You can obtain a special rubber *boot jack* that slips down over your pipe, then seal the boot jack to the ag panel with a moldable aluminum *compression ring* that screws into place (figure 5–4). These products are available from ITW Buildex, Dynamic

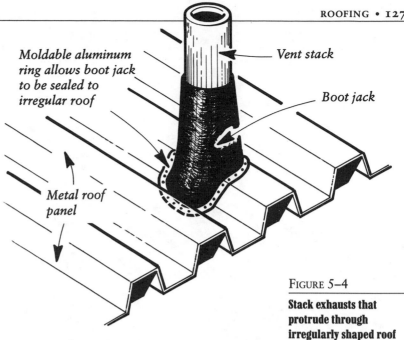

Moldable aluminum ring allows boot jack to be sealed to irregular roof

Vent stack

Boot jack

Metal roof panel

FIGURE 5–4

Stack exhausts that protrude through irregularly shaped roof panels can be sealed with a "boot" held in place by a malleable aluminum ring.

Fasteners, Atlas Bolt and Screw Company, and East Coast Fasteners and Closures, or where you buy your panels.

Your watertight roof requires sealing where the ridge cap meets the roof panels. Some manufacturers make ridge caps whose profiles fit right over the hill-and-valley profile of the ag panels. But if the ridge cap doesn't have such a profile, you'll have to install a closure plug like the one at the eaves to seal up the ridge gaps.

Let's say you want to put a ridge cap on an insulated, vented metal roof. Where does the moisture from your eaves go? You have to allow for the moisture streaming up the underside of your sheathing to escape. The Metal Roof Advisory Group in Colorado Springs suggests that, with the approval of your code official, you combine a standard low-profile roof vent beneath a ridge cap that you would not seal with a closure plug. The ridge cap covers the low-profile ridge vent and lies on top of the ag panels. The low-profile ridge vent keeps the weather out of the ridge opening, and the proper-size ridge cap extends down far enough over the low-profile ridge vent to keep weather from being blown between the ridge vent and the top of the ag panel. This is a tricky installation. If your code official approves it, you'll have to install the low-profile ridge vent at your ridge before installing your panels and then abut your roof panels to that vent. The ridge cap would then cover the ridge vent with the expressed

Here, the crimped seam on a standing-seam roof, formed where two panels have been joined.

cap over closure-plugged panels.

The type of roof easiest to vent at the ridge is an asphalt shingle roof, *which is what I recommend for vented roofs*. Installing such a roof is covered later in this chapter.

Standing-Seam Roofs

Standing-seam roofs are attractive and durable. The roof gets its name from its panels' shape—flat except at the edges where the metal turns up at a 90 degree angle. It is these "standing" sections that are joined in a seam between panels. Hence, "standing seam."

In principle, standing-seam roofs are laid the same way as ag-panel roofs but with one difference: where adjacent panels meet, their seams are joined with special tools that crimp the panels' edges and bend them together in a two-step process.

Standing-seam roofs can be sealed not only with crimping but with solder and various types of cleats. The panels themselves can be made of any number of materials, including stainless steel, copper, T-C-Z (tin, copper, zinc) alloy, terne, and copper-bearing steel. Typically, the widths of the panels vary from 14 to 25 inches, and panels are available in lengths from 4 feet to over 50 feet.

Unless you know how to put on a standing-seam roof and have the appropriate tools, you may want to hire a subcontractor to do the job. To prepare for the subcontractor, you need only lay 15-pound building felt on your roof sheathing. Or, if you are using purlins, install the purlins at the panels' required spacing.

ASPHALT AND FIBERGLASS SHINGLE ROOFING

Asphalt and the newer fiberglass shingles are the most common roofing material for residential structures. They are durable, relatively maintenance free, and easy to install. In addi-

purpose of covering where the ridge vent meets your roof panel.

If your code official says yes, you may be able to install a simple ridge cap without a low-profile ridge vent beneath it. That depends on whether in doing so you maintain your code-required net free venting area and if it will keep the weather out. Figure 5–2 shows a suggested ridge detail using a standard ridge cap for venting. If you find that you can't vent your ridge as part of a watertight ag-panel roof system, you may be able to vent your barn with gable-eaves vents, typically placed high up under the flying rafters. If you can satisfy the code-required "net free venting area" with gable-eaves vents, you can seal your ridge using a closure plug without regard for venting moisture.

As you can see, watertight ag panels on vented roofs present something of a problem at the ridge. So check with your ag-panel manufacturer to see if they make a ridge cap that can either be properly vented or fits over a low-profile ridge vent. Again, with the approval of your code official, you may be able to adapt a low-profile vent to an ag-panel cap at the ridge.

In the end, if you want ag panels on an insulated roof, you may have to research a non-vented roof design called a *cold roof*. A properly-designed cold roof doesn't need a ridge vent, and you could put your ag-panel ridge

tion, they come in a variety of colors and styles. If you use good-quality shingles and install them properly, the roof can last 20 years. On vented roofs, asphalt or fiberglass shingles best accommodate ridge vents but can be used just as easily on unvented roofs.

Asphalt and fiberglass (glass, for short) shingles can only be installed on sheathed roofs where plywood is covered with 15-pound roofing felt. You cannot install asphalt or glass shingles over purlins.

Once your sheathing is installed, but before you put on your roofing felt, nail a *drip edge* around the edge of the roof, including along the roof sheathing at the gable ends. Use the same wide-headed galvanized roofing nails you will use for installing the shingles themselves. This drip edge will be covered by the roof felt and by the shingles, which cover everything (figure 5–5).

With the drip edge in place, cover the sheathing with 15-pound building felt and, where sheets of roofing felt meet, overlap them at least 4 inches. Use the lines on the felt to keep each row parallel. Roofing felt protects the sheathing from weather until the shingles are in place, and it provides added protection once the shingles are on. Also, the felt protects the shingles from possibly being degraded by wood resins in the sheathing—an infrequent problem.

Estimating Quantity and Installing the Shingles

A package of shingles is called a *bundle*. Three bundles make a square, which is 100 square feet. Shingles come in different *weights*. Commonly, 235-pound shingles are used on barns and residences. This weight means that a square of shingles weighs 235 pounds and each bundle weighs about 78 pounds (though you'll swear they weigh more once you start hauling them up to the roof).

Estimating how many bundles you will need is rather simple. Measure your roof, length by width, and multiply those dimensions to arrive at square feet. Divide square feet by 100 to determine how many squares you will need and

add 5 percent so you'll have enough for starter shingles and ridge caps. Then, for every square you'll need, order three bundles.

To install asphalt or glass shingles, first open a bundle and cut a few in half lengthwise so the tabs are discarded and the tar paper section is intact. You will put down a *course* (or row) of these half shingles at the eaves end to cover beneath where your first full shingle tabs let weather through. This course goes on top of the roofing felt (tar paper) and beneath the first course of full shingles. The starter strip should be ¼ inch back from the drip edge. (The actual first course will extend about ¼ inch over the drip edge.) Now, install a few of these half shingles—they should be at least 9 inches wide—at the eaves end of the roof, using 1 ¼-inch galvanized roofing nails with a wide, flat head (figure 5–6). Install the half-shingles so the tab ends face the ridge; that way you get a nice, clean factory line at the eaves. (If you don't cut the tabs off—and some roofers don't—you will install an upside-down shingle along the eaves, tabs facing uphill toward the ridge.) Put four nails in each of these shingles.

Then, covering the starter row, install full shingles for your first real course (figure 6–8). For the second course, you have to make sure the tab lines stagger. Otherwise there will be leaks. So, for the first shingle of your second course, trim off 6 inches. If you remove 6 inches, the remaining shingle is 30 inches wide. Use that as your starter shingle. Then, for the third course, use a shingle that has 12 inches cut off, making it 24 inches wide (figure 5–6). Keep trimming an *additional* 6 inches off each shingle until you start a course with a 6-inch shingle. The course above that one should start again with a full shingle. Start the process again, removing 6 inches from the next starter shingle, and so on.

Want a few roofer's tips? When cutting the shingles, cut from the back; you won't dull the knife as quickly. To ensure a good seal between the roof shingles and the drip edge, some roofers draw a bead of plastic cement with a caulk gun to the latter's lower edge. (Make sure the plastic cement you choose is compatible with

TIP

TO ESTIMATE HOW MANY SQUARES OF SHINGLES YOU WILL NEED, MEASURE YOUR ROOF, LENGTH BY WIDTH, AND MULTIPLY THOSE DIMENSIONS TO ARRIVE AT SQUARE FEET. DIVIDE SQUARE FEET BY 100 TO DETERMINE HOW MANY SQUARES YOU WILL NEED. ADD 5 PERCENT FOR STARTER ROWS AND THE RIDGE CAP. REMEMBER: THREE BUNDLES MAKE A SQUARE, WHICH IS 100 SQUARE FEET.

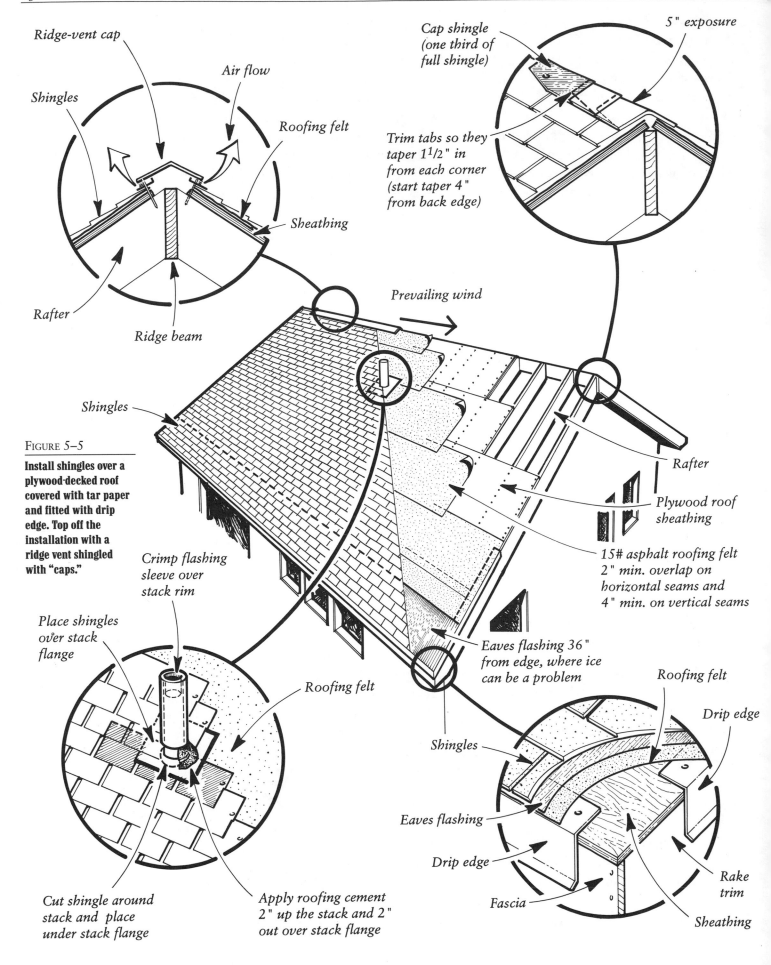

Ridge-vent cap

Air flow

Shingles

Roofing felt

Sheathing

Rafter

Ridge beam

Cap shingle
(one third of
full shingle)

5" exposure

Trim tabs so they
taper 1 1/2" in
from each corner
(start taper 4"
from back edge)

Prevailing wind

Shingles

FIGURE 5–5

**Install shingles over a
plywood-decked roof
covered with tar paper
and fitted with drip
edge. Top off the
installation with a
ridge vent shingled
with "caps."**

Rafter

Plywood roof
sheathing

15# asphalt roofing felt
2" min. overlap on
horizontal seams and
4" min. on vertical seams

Eaves flashing 36"
from edge, where ice
can be a problem

Crimp flashing
sleeve over
stack rim

Place shingles
over stack
flange

Roofing felt

Roofing felt

Drip edge

Shingles

Eaves flashing

Drip edge

Rake
trim

Fascia

Sheathing

Cut shingle around
stack and place
under stack flange

Apply roofing cement
2" up the stack and 2"
out over stack flange

shingles; some plastic cements will "eat" asphalt or glass shingles.) For safety's sake, you may want to install *roofing jacks* as you go. These are brackets with a special metal flange at the head that can be nailed under existing shingles without damaging them. The brackets are designed to hold planks you can work from. The jacks should be set up 4 feet o.c., and you should drive the nails that hold the jacks through the roof sheathing and into the roof rafters. Use heavy, galvanized nails (you might want to use double-headed ones). Once you have some planks set on the jacks, you can establish a work station for holding bundles and cutting shingles.

As mentioned, use four nails per full shingle, driving the nails above the line marking where the next course of shingles will sit so the nails won't show. This is called *blind nailing*.

It's best *not* to start a course and nail it up all the way across the roof. Rather, start a course, nail on four or five shingles, and then start another course. Nail on three or four shingles, and then work in a diagonal pattern that sweeps across and up the roof (figure 5–6). Every eight courses or so, snap a chalk line to keep the courses straight horizontally.

Shingling the Ridge

At the ridge, if your roof is unvented, simply lay the last course, no matter how far it protrudes over the peak. When you've nailed the row, bend the excess over and nail it down on the other side of the roof. Then, nail some caps (12-inch-long pieces of shingle) along the ridge. Caps should be trimmed at one end so they taper 1 ½ inches in from both sides. This tapered, thinner end is where you nail (figure 5–5). When you install your caps, start at the side opposite the prevailing wind, so it doesn't blow under and lift them. Subsequent caps should cover all but 5 inches of the cap beneath it, and all should be blind-nailed except the last one (figure 5–5). For the last cap, use just the pebbly mineral portion of a shingle, putting roofing cement over the exposed nailheads to seal them against the weather.

If your roof is vented, roof right up to the top of the plywood, installing your ridge vent over the shingles (figure 5–5). Different ridge vents have different installation idiosyncrasies, so be careful. Installing the ridge vent improperly, or crushing the venting area by overnailing

FIGURE 5–6

To ensure that roof tabs are staggered, row for row, you must trim the starter shingle for each row accordingly.

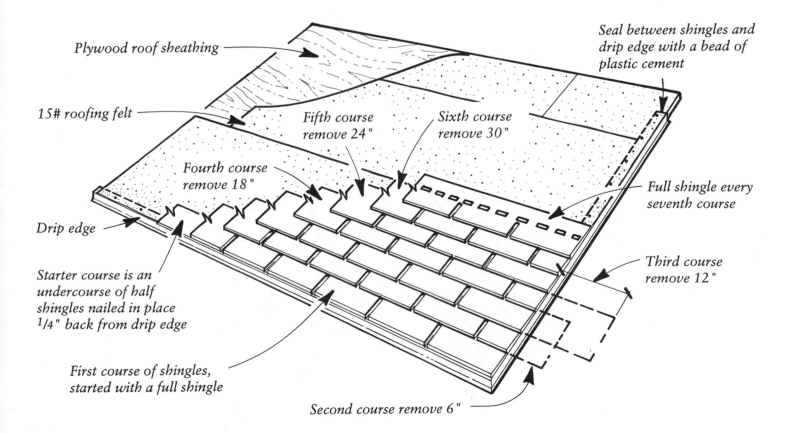

Plywood roof sheathing

15# roofing felt

Drip edge

Starter course is an undercourse of half shingles nailed in place 1/4" back from drip edge

First course of shingles, started with a full shingle

Fourth course remove 18"

Fifth course remove 24"

Sixth course remove 30"

Second course remove 6"

Seal between shingles and drip edge with a bead of plastic cement

Full shingle every seventh course

Third course remove 12"

it, can put you in noncompliance with code. Do your vent installation only after reading the manufacturer's instructions. With the vent in place, cap as you would for an unvented roof, using 12-inch tapered shingles.

Flashing

If you build a shed dormer, you have to *flash* it where the roof and wall meet. Be sure not to use a flashing material like copper that will

FIGURE 5–7

Install flashing along any point where a vertical wall meets your roof. Shingles go on top of flashing. Roofing felt goes beneath it.

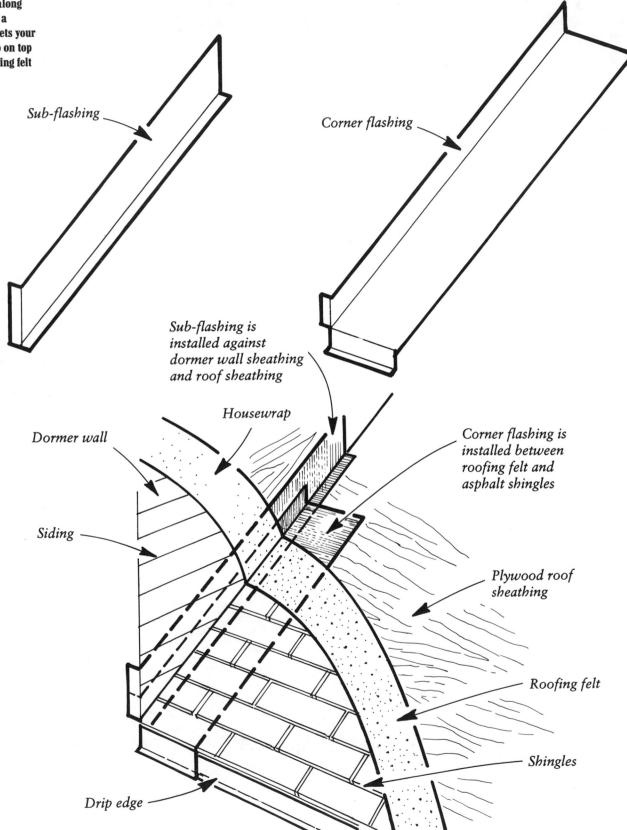

Sub-flashing

Corner flashing

Sub-flashing is installed against dormer wall sheathing and roof sheathing

Housewrap

Dormer wall

Corner flashing is installed between roofing felt and asphalt shingles

Siding

Plywood roof sheathing

Roofing felt

Shingles

Drip edge

cause a corrosive galvanic reaction if you are using metal panels. That would be disastrous, and you would feel the leaky effects very quickly. Flash over the tar paper at junctions of roof and wall before you lay down any metal roof panels, or shingles, and before putting on any siding. The roof panels will lay over the flashing, as will the shingles. Siding will be nailed over the flashing as well. Figure 5–7 shows suggested flashing details.

WORKSHEET: ROOFING COSTS

ASPHALT OR FIBERGLASS ROOFS

Asphalt roofing: _____ PER-SQUARE COST X _____ TOTAL SQUARES = _____

Roofing cement: _____ PER-TUBE COST X _____ TOTAL TUBES = _____

Nails: _____ PER-POUND COST X _____ TOTAL POUNDS = _____

Drip edge: _____ PER-FOOT COST X _____ TOTAL FEET = _____

Ridge vent: _____ PER-FOOT COST X _____ TOTAL FEET = _____

Roofing felt (tar paper): _____ PER-ROLL COST X _____ TOTAL ROLLS = _____

AG-PANEL ROOFS

Ag panels: _____ PER-PANEL COST X _____ TOTAL PANELS = _____

Finishing piece for gable end: _____ PER-UNIT COST X _____ TOTAL NEEDED = _____

Eaves closure strip: _____ PER-UNIT COST X _____ TOTAL UNITS = _____

Ridge vent: _____ PER-FOOT COST X _____ TOTAL FEET = _____

Ridge vent cap: _____ PER-FOOT COST X _____ TOTAL FEET = _____

Ridge vent closure strip: _____ PER-FOOT COST X _____ TOTAL FEET = _____

Boot jack: _____ PER-UNIT COST X _____ TOTAL UNITS = _____

Screws with gaskets: _____ PER-POUND COST X _____ TOTAL POUNDS = _____

Z-chairs (for plywood): _____ PER-UNIT COST X _____ TOTAL UNITS = _____

Butyl tape: _____ PER-ROLL COST X _____ TOTAL ROLLS = _____

Purlin 2x4s: _____ PER-UNIT COST X _____ TOTAL UNITS = _____

Roofing felt (tar paper): _____ PER-ROLL COST X _____ TOTAL ROLLS = _____

DORMER

Flashing (aluminum or copper): _____ PER-FOOT COST X _____ TOTAL FEET = _____

6 Siding

Of all your barn's components, siding is the face you put forward to the world and the one you'll be looking at for a long time to come. There are many types of siding, some expensive, some economical, some easy to install, some not so easy. When making a choice, you may want to go with a more attractive siding that takes a little extra installation effort rather than opt for something easy and cheap. After all, you'll quickly forget the cost and labor involved in installing siding you like, but you'll always regret installing a cheaper siding that you never really cared for.

What kind of siding should you choose? If you're willing to put in the time learning to install the siding properly, you should pick a quality siding that looks good on your barn. Keep the surrounding structures in mind when making your choice. If your house is a Federal style, with wide corner boards and bevel clapboarding, you may not want a log-cabin finish on your barn. On the other hand, if your house is board-and-batten, you probably don't want to over-dress the barn with beveled clapboards.

When in doubt, the best idea is to side your barn with the same kind of materials used on surrounding houses or structures or take a drive and see how others have combined siding styles in attractive ways. In some parts of New England, for example, many barns have two sidings: cedar shingles on three sides and bevel clapboarding on the side adjacent to the house.

Carefully cut any siding so it fits snug around drip edge and butts square and tight against window casings.

Rabbeted edge

Profile dictates
minimum lap

Use 8d nails

T & G drop

Profile dictates
required lap

Use 6d nails
for T & G profile

Board-on-board

Recommended
1" lap

Use 10d nails

Plain bevel

1" min. lap

Use 6d nails

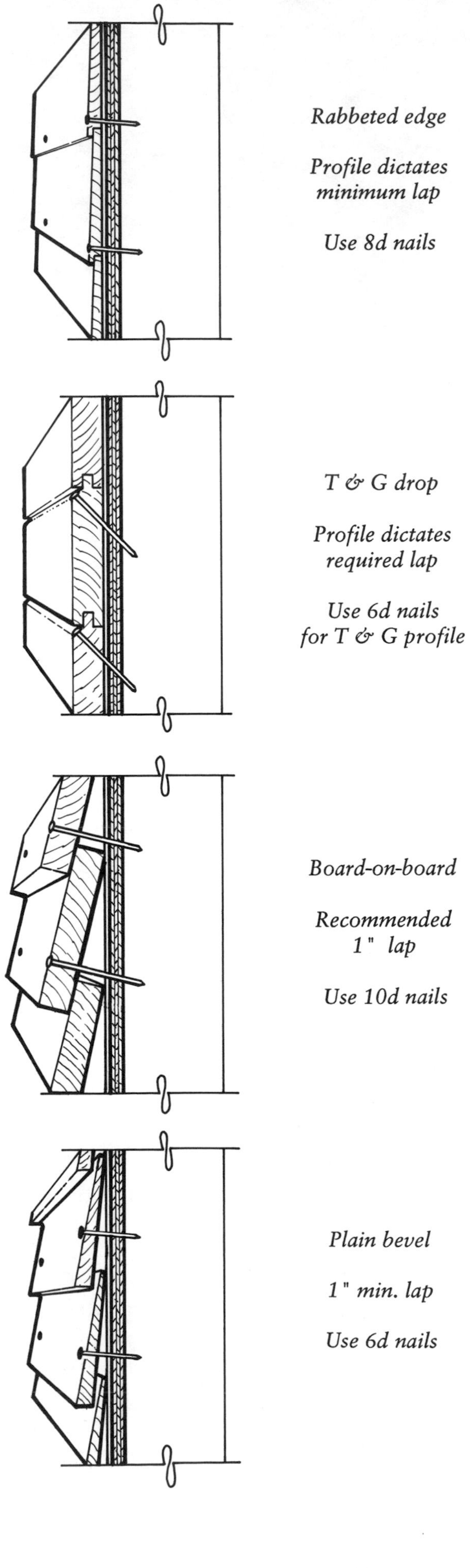

FIGURE 6–1

As these pages show,
there are a number of
different horizontal
siding types, each with
a distinct look and
nailing pattern.

In other locales, Victorian or Federal farmhouses with bevel clapboard siding can look beautiful beside a barn with weathered vertical boards.

To make your choice a more informed one, let's look at a few types of siding and the labor involved in installing them.

SIDING TYPES

There are at least a dozen different types of horizontal siding, at least five different types of vertical siding, and a wide range of panel sidings, from textured plywood to a variety of metal panels. For our barn, we'll focus on one type of horizontal siding, called *plain beveled clapboards*. Before we get into their installation specifics, let's look at some other horizontal siding choices. Most of these are relatively simple to install and if you choose to use them, you can use this overview as a general guide to their installation.

Figure 6–1 shows a number of different types of horizontal siding, with their recommended lap distances and nail types. As you can see, each siding type has a distinctive profile and nailing schedule. Sometimes the profile of the siding board dictates how far the boards will overlap (for example, the log cabin or rabbeted-edge siding), and sometimes you have to create that overlap yourself (plain bevel siding, clapboards, cedar shingles). A few general rules concerning horizontal siding: First, though some contractors overlap horizontal siding as much as 2 inches, you should overlap it only half that much. A 1-inch overlap is widely recommended as adequate. Second, never nail through two layers of siding at once—a rule that applies to both horizontal and vertical siding. For example, you should never nail through the overlap, driving your nail through two siding boards one on top of the other. Why? Well, when the siding shrinks, as it always does (mostly across its width), double-nailed boards will split because they can't move freely. By contrast, single-nailed boards are freer to expand and contract, reducing the risk of their splitting.

The majority of horizontal sidings should be nailed over sheathing that is covered with a house wrap. The plywood (or chipboard) sheathing and the framing members underneath provide an adequate nailing surface, but every nail must go through the sheathing and into solid wood (studs).

Avoid *electrogalvanized nails*. Reason: Their protective coats can crack open when hammered and the nail will start to rust. Instead, use 1 1/2-inch *hot-dipped galvanized nails* or, if you're choking on money, *shanked stainless steel nails*. These nails won't rust and won't leave streaks down your siding.

Take a look at the illustrations and captions to see if one of these sidings strikes your fancy. All offer adequate protection for your barn.

SIDING AND INSULATION

All horizontal sidings can go on either an insulated or uninsulated building. You can choose insulation independent of your siding choice so long as you install the siding over sheathing and nail it properly through the sheathing and into the studs beneath. (The one exception is horizontal barnboard, which can be installed over an unsheathed wall.)

Whether you insulate your barn or not, staple a *house wrap* such as Tyvek® or Typar® on the outside of the sheathing before installing your siding boards. House wraps accomplish three purposes: (1) They slow air infiltration, (2) they "breathe," allowing moisture to escape, and (3) they protect against moisture seeping under the sheathing. Some builders prefer to use building paper instead of modern house wraps because house wrap cannot absorb moisture that forms, whereas building paper offers some absorption, however minimal. The choice is yours, though for the money, I prefer house wrap.

You may see tar paper used on the walls of older buildings. Tar paper is not a good choice, given today's other house-wrap options, as it traps moisture that can cause rotting.

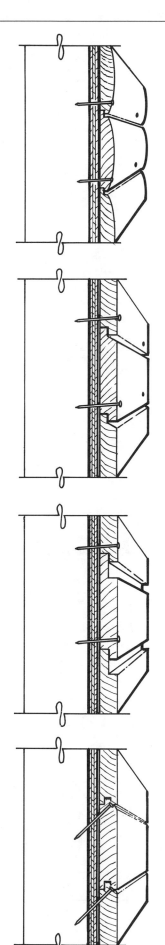

Log cabin

Profile dictates minimum lap

Use 10d nails

Shiplap

Profile dictates required lap

Use 8d nails for shiplap

Channel rustic

Profile dictates 1/2" lap

Use 8d nails

Tongue and groove

Profile dictates required lap

Use 6d nails

Before installing any kind of siding over sheathing, you should cover the sheathing either with building paper, or, as shown here, house wrap.

INSTALLING BEVEL CLAPBOARDS

When choosing your clapboards, you have to pick a grade. The best *standard clear-grade siding* used for premium work is *clear-vg-all-heart, western red cedar.* (VG stands for *vertical grain.*)

You may want to save money by buying a lesser grade. *Grades A, B,* and *rustic* western red cedar or spruce are all perfectly good siding choices (I like Grade B spruce installed rough side out for both its performance and its price). All these sidings are dried to 15 percent moisture content, with most pieces at 12 percent. (This drier wood doesn't crack and split because it is nearly stabilized before you apply it.) Next step down the line is *standard knotty grade,* dried to a 19 percent moisture content. *Select knotty* and *quality knotty* have a "fine knotty appearance" according to the Western Wood Product Association. You can see these grades at your lumberyard, which, incidentally, might not use the same terminology but should have examples of each of these grades. If you're going to paint the barn, and you're not all that concerned about it having a fine, smooth siding surface, be aware that paint holds best on rough surfaces. (More about painting later in this chapter.)

How wide a clapboard should you buy? Most beveled siding comes in widths of 4, 5, and 6 inches. Once it is milled, the 4-inch becomes 3 1/2, the 5, 4 1/2, and the 6, 5 1/2 inches wide. What width boards you choose is a matter both of looks and the amount of work you want to do. If you choose wider clapboards, you get a wider reveal (the part exposed to the elements) and you end up using fewer clapboards. For tight-rowed clapboards close together, choose a narrower board, but know you'll use more of them and work longer to apply them. One width of clapboard offers no more protection than another, but when making your choice, be sure it is one inch wider than the reveal because you'll be overlapping it an inch each row.

The butt end of all the clapboards (the wider part at the base of the board) is typically a half-inch thick. (Eight- and 10-inch boards are 5/8 inch thick at the butt). The other end usually tapers to 3/16-inch thick. The wood is best cut with a chop saw or a hand saw. Each gives good, clean lines and consistent angles. Cutting the clapboards with a circular saw will leave the cut edges ratty, and at the tip ends, the circular saw will really rattle the board, making it hard to cut accurately.

Priming and Back Priming

Before you start to install the siding, it's a good idea to prime your siding boards ahead of time, front *and* back to control moisture infiltration. Priming only the front face of the siding board will allow more moisture to enter the back of the board than the front, leading to *cupping* (lateral warping). Also, it's easier to paint the boards before you install them, saving yourself from the task when the siding is on. Set up some sawhorses and lay your siding boards out for painting. If you really want a superb paint finish, run a palm sander over the face of the siding before painting. Then prime it, and then run your sander again. More on painting in chapter 9.

Installing a Drip Edge

A DRIP EDGE CAN BE FASHIONED on a table saw out of 2x stock. The purpose of the drip edge is to shunt water away from the window. By running a kerf line on the underside of the drip edge, you keep water from simply running down and under the drip edge and back into the window casing. The drip edge should be flashed, and the flashing should run over the drip edge and beneath the siding boards as shown.

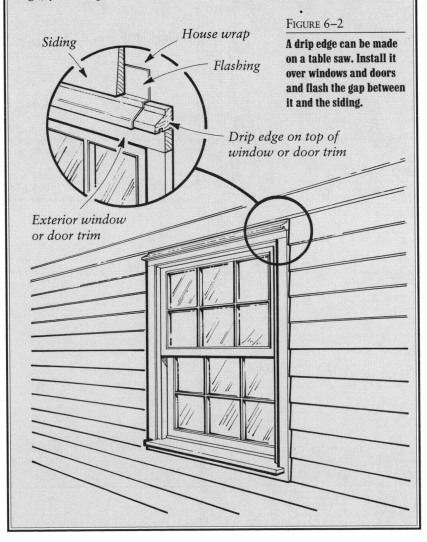

FIGURE 6–2

A drip edge can be made on a table saw. Install it over windows and doors and flash the gap between it and the siding.

Siding *House wrap* *Flashing* *Drip edge on top of window or door trim* *Exterior window or door trim*

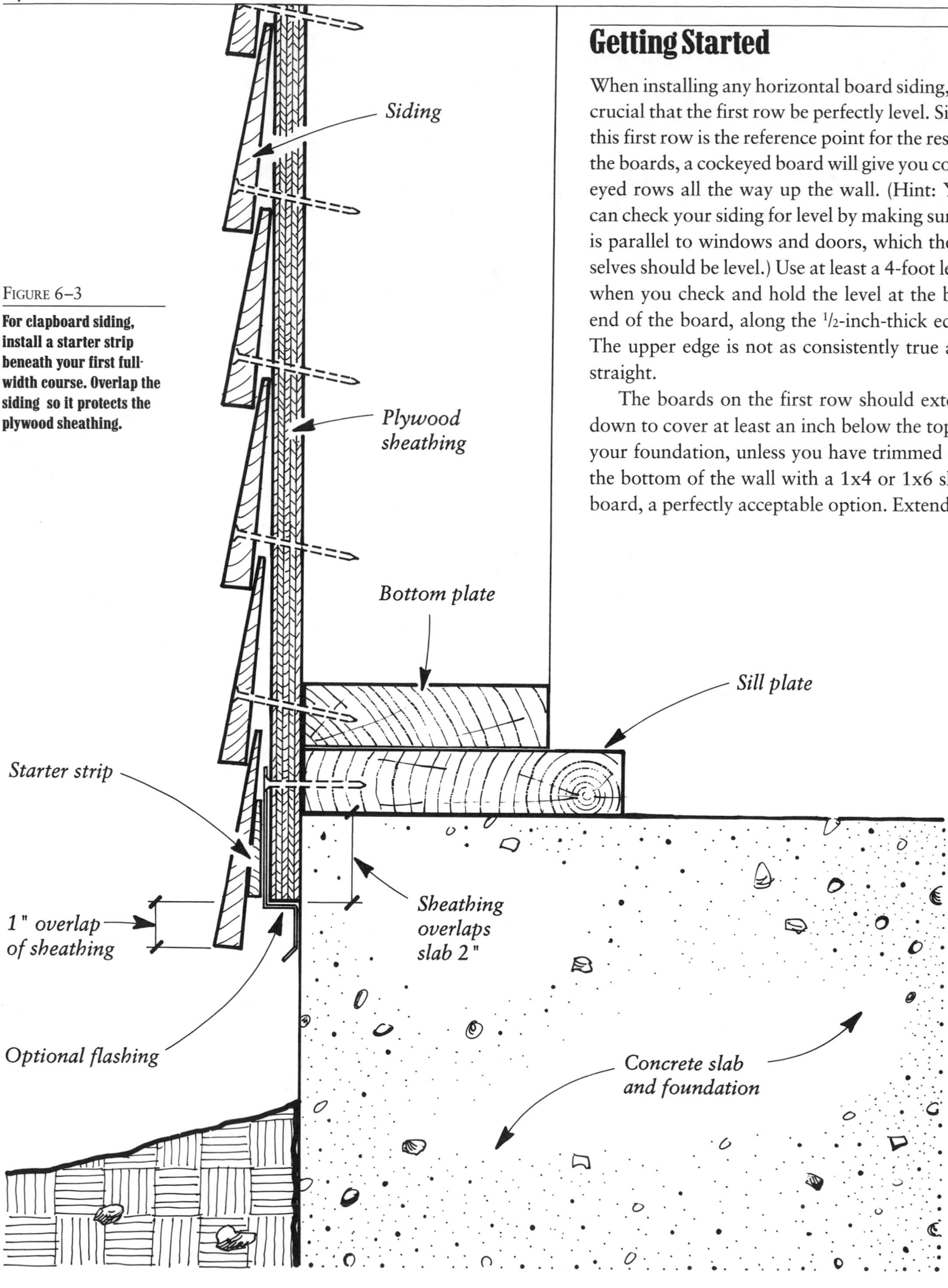

FIGURE 6–3

For clapboard siding, install a starter strip beneath your first full-width course. Overlap the siding so it protects the plywood sheathing.

Siding

Plywood sheathing

Bottom plate

Sill plate

Starter strip

1" overlap of sheathing

Sheathing overlaps slab 2"

Optional flashing

Concrete slab and foundation

Getting Started

When installing any horizontal board siding, it's crucial that the first row be perfectly level. Since this first row is the reference point for the rest of the boards, a cockeyed board will give you cockeyed rows all the way up the wall. (Hint: You can check your siding for level by making sure it is parallel to windows and doors, which themselves should be level.) Use at least a 4-foot level when you check and hold the level at the butt end of the board, along the ½-inch-thick edge. The upper edge is not as consistently true and straight.

The boards on the first row should extend down to cover at least an inch below the top of your foundation, unless you have trimmed out the bottom of the wall with a 1x4 or 1x6 skirt board, a perfectly acceptable option. Extending the first row of clapboards or the skirt board an inch below the foundation helps shed rain away from the foundation wall.

Installed properly, all bevel siding angles outward, since each course rests on the course below it. Since the first row of boards has no row beneath it to force it to angle out, you must install a starter strip beneath this first row. The starter strip should be as thick as the bevel siding at about mid-point (see figure 6–3).

For your next row, the bevel siding should overlap the row beneath it by an inch. Once you establish your overlap, you will find that the distance between the bottom of one row and the bottom of the row beneath it is the same for each and every row. Thus, you can cut a block of wood to use as a guide to help you set the siding (see figure 6–4). When you hold this block in place and run it along your board, it will set the board at the right overlap. (Duct-tape this block guide to your hammer shank for quick and easy access.)

When nailing your siding, use 6d galvanized or stainless steel siding nails. You want the nails to penetrate at least 1 1/2 inches into solid wood, so drive them so they penetrate through the sheathing and into the stud members of the wall. Don't nail randomly; line the nails up with studs. Locate each nail in the lower third of the siding board but *don't drive it through the undercourse row* beneath the board you are nailing.

Since the design of some clapboards leaves a natural cavity behind them once they are installed, hitting the wood with heavy hammer blows can split it. Avoid smacking the boards too hard with your hammer when you are driving home your nails and don't overdrive nails—that can cause splitting, too.

When Siding Meets a Corner

When you come to the corners of your building, you want your clapboards to butt into corner boards, which you must install beforehand. Otherwise you will have to miter your clapboards with 45-degree angles so they fit clapboards from the opposing wall tightly. Those miters aren't easy to do, and even a small margin of error will leave places for weather infiltration. Corner boards to the rescue! Corner boards look good, provide a solid vertical surface for the clapboards to butt into, plus they're a snap to install. Page 142 shows a detail for an outside corner. When installing your own use 5/4x3-inch spruce or red cedar stock or bigger; the stock shown here is 5/4x6. (Don't use less than 5/4 thickness stock; otherwise the clapboard butts may protrude beyond the corner board—an aesthetic no-no.) You may find that your outside corners look better with wide corner boards. Make them as wide as you want. There is nothing to stop you from using even 12-inch-wide corner boards if you think they look good. If you're at a loss for what to choose, 5/4x4 is a nice corner board dimension.

To make sure your clapboards butt the corner board snugly, you may want to make a *cutting guide*. Figure 6–5 shows a wooden guide

FIGURE 6–4

When installing clapboards, use a homemade block to maintain a consistent width between rows.

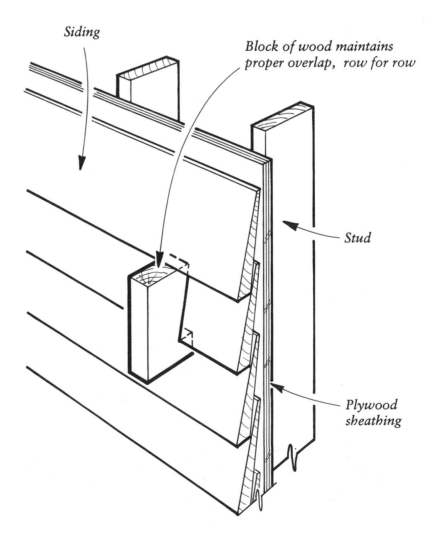

Siding

Block of wood maintains proper overlap, row for row

Stud

Plywood sheathing

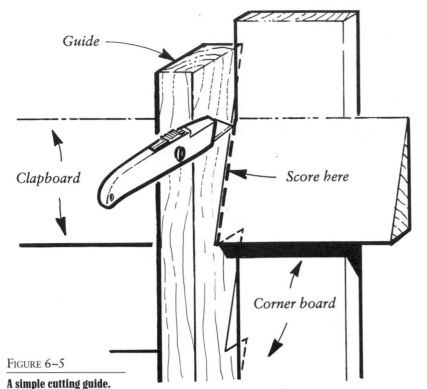

Guide

Clapboard

Score here

Corner board

FIGURE 6–5

A simple cutting guide.

will be your cut line.

Before you start to side your gable ends, you'll want to nail trim along your rake board, which the siding can butt into. Use the same ⁵/₄ x 4 stock that you used in your corners for the rake trim. As you install clapboards up into the gable of your barn, you'll find you are cutting your siding boards at the same angle as the rake trim piece they butt into. If you are using a chop saw, you can simply set the angle on the saw and chop away, or for a very tight fit, fashion a multi-angled cutting guide.

Where the horizontal siding meets a window or door casing, try to align the bottom of one course of siding with the top of the casing. This takes planning. To see where the siding will end when it gets to the casing top, measure the distance from 1 inch below your wall (where the butt end of the first row of siding will sit) to the top of the casing. Divide that figure by the amount of reveal per row. Is your answer a whole number? If so, go ahead and apply your siding. If the answer is not a whole number, adjust each row of siding incrementally so the bottom of the clapboard and the top of the casing line up.

Where the top of the window (or door) casing and the siding meet, you should install a drip edge to shed water away from the window.

you can make to ensure a good fit at the corner boards. Fashion this guide from a nice piece of clear pine. When you are about to cut a clapboard to butt against the corner board, trap the board beneath this guide. Then run the guide flush up against the corner board. Score the clapboard with your utility knife or a pencil by running it along the outside edge of the guide. That

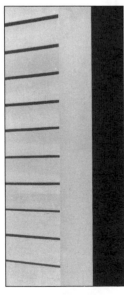

Butt siding into corner boards. Corner boards not only look good, they seal corners where sheathing meets.

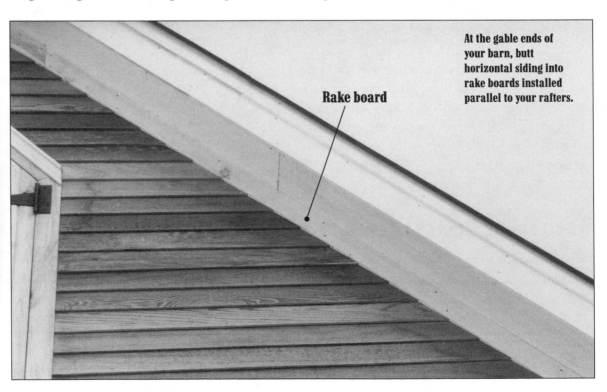

Rake board

At the gable ends of your barn, butt horizontal siding into rake boards installed parallel to your rafters.

VERTICAL SIDING

Vertical board sidings are very popular with barn builders because their installation is relatively easy, and inexpensive, rough-sawn green lumber can be used. Keep in mind, too, that vertical board siding does not *require* sheathing beneath it, unless the structure is insulated. If you have an insulated barn and you want vertical siding, you will be installing it over sheathing.

On the other hand, if your barn is uninsulated and you're not going to use sheathing beneath your vertical board siding, you have to have made some adjustments *early on* in your framing. In the framing process described in chapter 4, sheathing is what we depended on for making our walls square. Also, sheathing braces the walls against racking once the walls are erected. Obviously, without sheathing you'll have to find some other way to test your walls for square, prevent racking, and add permanent diagonal bracing to the walls once they're erected. *This is not optional.* If you intend to put vertical siding over unsheathed walls you must install diagonal bracing. Typically, this bracing is made of 1x4s laid flat, running corner to corner in each wall section. Either cut the bracing into the studs so it is flush with the inside edge of them (essential if you are applying a wall covering inside like sheetrock or tongue-and-groove pine), or nail it on top of the stud's inside face. The diagonal brace should be nailed off to each stud it crosses. It can also be used to prevent walls from racking before they are erected, although you should also test walls for square by measuring

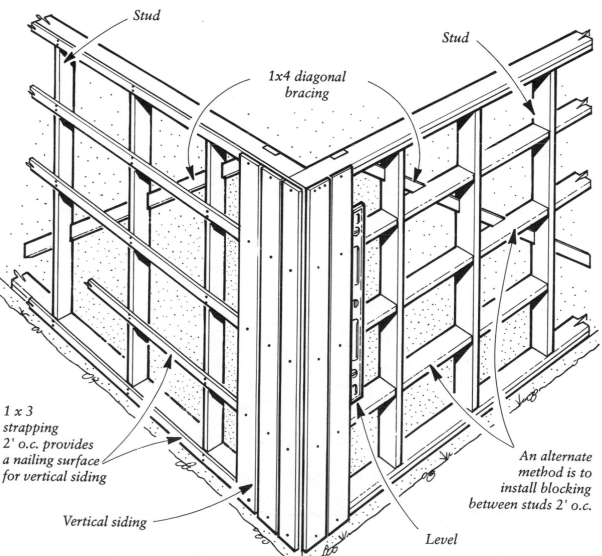

Stud

Stud

1x4 diagonal bracing

1 x 3 strapping 2' o.c. provides a nailing surface for vertical siding

Vertical siding

Level

An alternate method is to install blocking between studs 2' o.c.

FIGURE 6–6

To provide a horizontal nailing surface for vertical siding, install strapping across the top of your barn's studs or nail blocks within the stud bays.

Weathered vertical siding gives a traditional look to any barn. It is an economical choice and easy to install.

each across opposite corners—the measurement method we used for checking our foundation's squareness.

If you do install vertical siding without sheathing beneath it, you also need to install either *horizontal blocking* every 2 feet between studs or *strapping* every 2 feet on the outside of the studs. Strapping or blocking provides a horizontal nailing surface for the vertical siding. Without it, you can't nail the siding with the proper nailing schedule. So, either cut 2x6 blocks and put them in each stud bay every 2 feet on center, or, easier, nail 1x3 strapping every 2 feet on center horizontally to the outside of your studs (figures 6–6).

For board-and-batten, batten-on-board, and board-on-board vertical siding, you can use rough-sawn native lumber. When installing vertical boards (or battens) and covering them with battens (or boards), overlap them a half inch. Don't worry about shrinkage because even the greenest boards would have to shrink radically (more than a half inch at *each* edge) to expose

any gap.

Vertical boards for traditional rough-sawn barn siding come as wide as 12 inches, in lengths 8 feet and over (at 2-foot increments).

For any board-and-batten, batten-and-board, or board-on-board sidings, start the installation at one corner of your barn. Use a 4-foot level to make sure each board is plumb before you nail it. Don't depend on an exisiting board to be the guide for plumb. Rough-sawn boards are terrible plumb guides. Use your level for each board.

The most popular vertical siding choice is board-and-batten. You nail on boards, then cover the gaps between them with a strip of wood (the batten). When installing the boards, space them a half inch apart. Drive a nail through the center of the board at the location of each horizontal framing member (strapping or blocking) and 2 feet on center along studs. The nails you use—typically 10d galvanized—should penetrate 1 1/2 inches into solid wood. Attach 1 1/2-inch-wide battens to cover the gaps between boards, overlapping each board a half inch and center-nailing the batten every 2 feet.

For vertical board-on-board siding, apply these same nailing principles, overlapping the boards at least a half inch. (Note that for board-on-board siding, you nail the outer boards through to the framing member but not through the underlapped siding board. Note, too, that nailing too close to the edge may split the boards—something you should avoid.)

If your nails are splitting your boards more often than you like, do two things: First, make sure you are using the smallest allowable nail for the job (typically 10d), and secondly, dull each nail by setting the head against a solid surface and tapping the sharp point a few times with your hammer.

With either board-and-batten system, nail into the center of the batten and the board unless the latter are wider than 6 inches—those you must double nail. With board-on-board, over-

FIGURE 6–7

Traditional vertical batten-on-board siding is an excellent, economical barn covering.

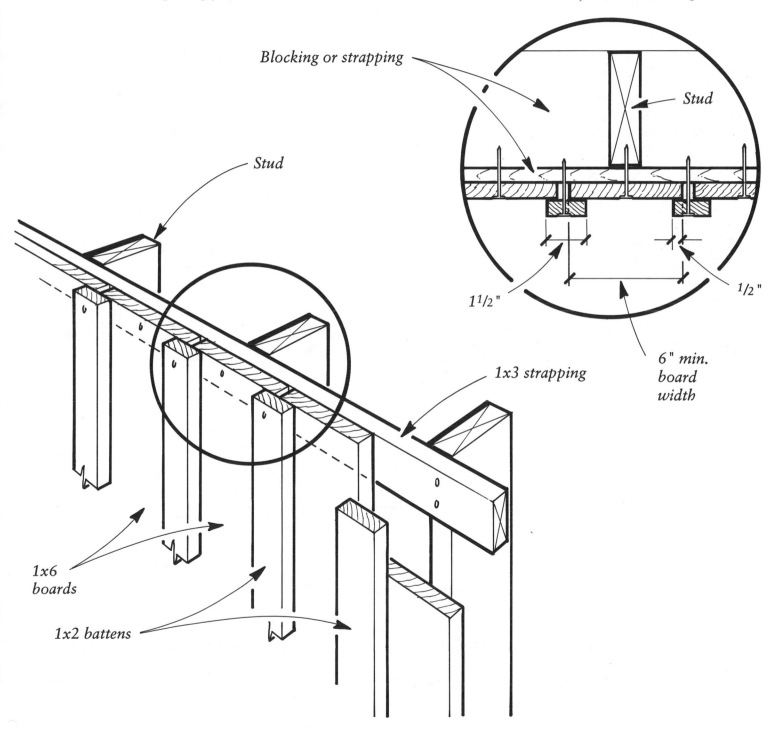

Blocking or strapping

Stud

Stud

1¹/₂ "

¹/₂ "

6" *min. board width*

1x3 strapping

1x6 boards

1x2 battens

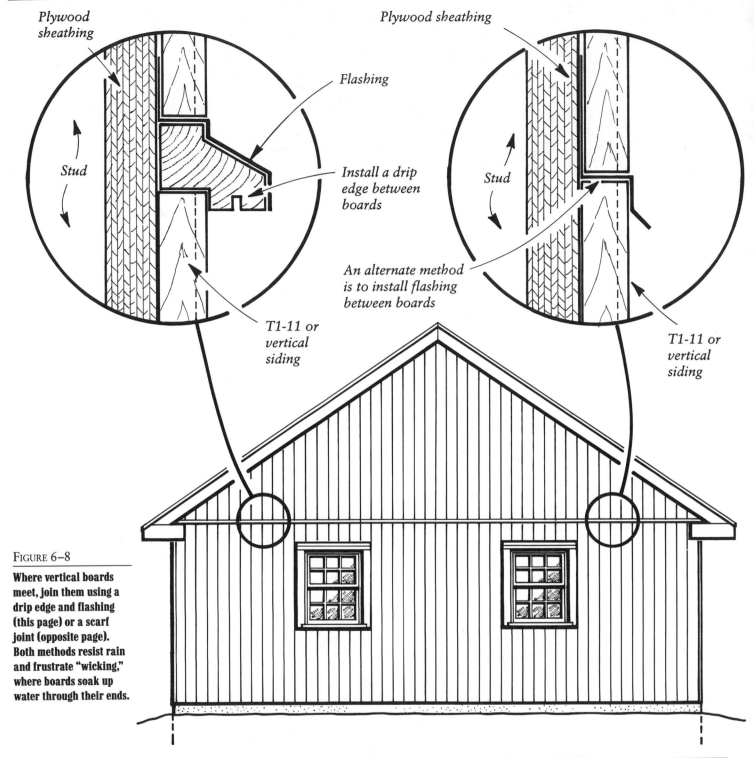

Plywood sheathing

Plywood sheathing

Flashing

Stud

Install a drip edge between boards

An alternate method is to install flashing between boards

Stud

T1-11 or vertical siding

T1-11 or vertical siding

FIGURE 6–8

Where vertical boards meet, join them using a drip edge and flashing (this page) or a scarf joint (opposite page). Both methods resist rain and frustrate "wicking," where boards soak up water through their ends.

lap the boards and nail as close to the edge of the board as you are able, without splitting the boards or nailing though the one beneath.

If you choose tongue-and-groove or shiplap vertical siding, set the boards against your wall with a $1/8$-inch expansion clearance between boards and drive your nails through the boards at least $1\,1/2$ inches from the edge of the overlap and 2 inches away from the underlap.

Joining Vertical Boards

When you side the gable ends of your barn with vertical boards, you'll need to create a butt joint where two boards meet end to end, to prevent water infiltration there. You have three options for joining vertical siding boards. You can install a drip edge or you can flash the joint or you can cut opposing 45-degree angles where the

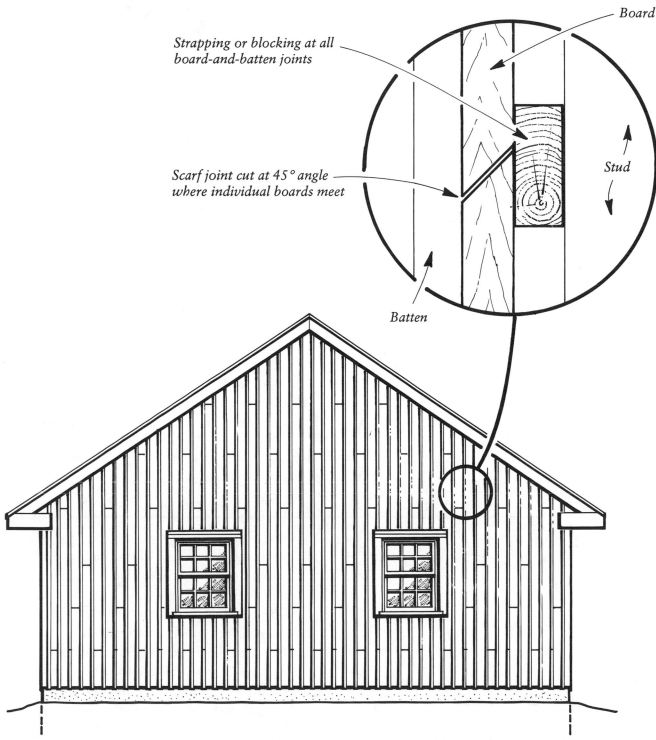

Strapping or blocking at all
board-and-batten joints

Board

Scarf joint cut at 45° angle
where individual boards meet

Stud

Batten

boards meet (make sure the outermost 45-de-gree angle slopes downward so rain won't flow behind your siding—figure 6–8).

Joining opposing 45-degree angles into what is called a *scarf joint* is the easiest option. You don't have to worry about all the rows of boards being the same length (as you do with the flashing or the drip edge) because you can scarf each individual butt joint wherever it occurs, *as long as there is a stud or blocking beneath the joint.* Scarf joints don't have to line up horizontally all the way across the wall; they can happen randomly with boards of nearly any length.

It is essential that you use one of these methods to prevent water from getting to the ends of the boards. Without protection, *wicking* will occur—water will be sucked up by the board ends and the wood will quickly degrade.

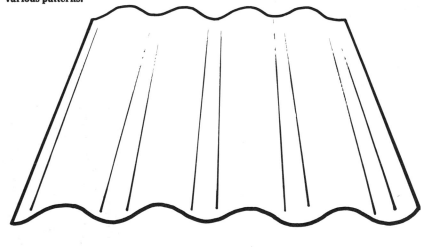

FIGURE 6–9

Though it won't win your barn any beauty prizes, metal panel siding is economical, easy to install, and available in various patterns.

Box rib

Corrugated

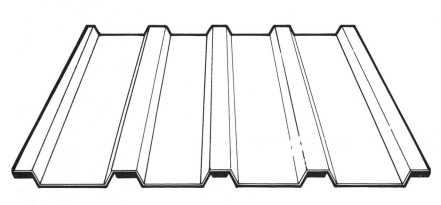

Bold rib

PANEL SIDING

Plywood panel sidings are popular for both barns and homes because they are easy to install, economical, and can be used in place of sheathing. Metal-panel siding, on the other hand, is easy to install and maintain, but it dents easily, the dents are difficult to remove, and thus, many people who have animals (or teenagers) avoid it.

Let's look at plywood panel siding first. If you want to install it, you may be able to do so at the framing stage because some types of plywood sidings can serve double duty as sheathing *and* siding. But you must use high-shear, rack-resistant panels that are at least a half-inch thick, and sometimes as thick as 5/8 inch.

If you want to install panel siding over sheathing covered in house wrap, you can go with a thinner siding panel, say, 3/8 inch. When you install the panels, stagger their seams so they don't line up with the sheathing's seams beneath.

Plywood-panel siding comes in a number of textures. T1-11 siding is very popular, because it has grooves cut in its face every 8 inches to imitate a rough-sawn lumber surface. Check out the different textures at your lumberyard.

Typically, plywood panels come in 4x8-foot sheets, though you can special-order longer lengths. (But are they awkward to handle!) Before you install any panels, prime the edges with paint or preservative to seal the edges so water isn't as likely to delaminate the plywood.

Install the panels long seams up, leaving a 1/8-inch gap between panels to allow for expansion and contraction due to temperature and water. There is no need for blocking beneath the panels, but do adhere to this nailing schedule: With 6d galvanized siding nails (8d for 5/8-inch panels), nail every 6 inches on center around the perimeter of the panel, and every 12 inches on center in the interior of the panel. The nails should drive through the panel, the sheathing beneath it, and into the studs. In addition, as you nail you want to move across the panel and "zip it up," starting at one side and slowly closing the gap between the panel and the barn's frame. Here's how you do it: Once you've positioned a panel and checked it for plumb, tack all four corners. Then, fully nail the seam where the panel meets the one already in place, using the full nailing schedule. Now remove the tacks at the two other corners and work across the panel, nailing off the interior studs, then the panel's far seam.

You'll find the work goes quickly because each panel covers a lot of square feet. Where butt joints occur between panels, flash the joint or install drip edge just as you would with vertical boards. Forget using scarf joints: They won't work with plywood siding.

Metal panels such as corrugated aluminum or galvanized steel typically are available in 8-foot sheets, 32 to 38 inches wide. You install them with ringlock or ring-shanked nails with gaskets at their heads (the same types we used for installing ag panels on the roof) or with hex-head screws. Joints where vertical panels meet present no sealing problem because you overlap the upper panel over the lower panel. Panels can be cut with a circular saw fitted with a metal cutting blade available at any good building supply store. As you might guess, cutting these panels creates shards, sparks, and noise. You may be able to rent quieter, safer electric-powered metal shears for cutting, but whatever you use, be sure to protect your skin, eyes, and ears.

IT LOOKS LIKE A BARN!

What was recently a plywood-covered wood-stick box is now a nice-looking barn. The structure doesn't look quite so unfinished once the siding is on. Oh, there's still lots to do! In the following chapters we'll look at wiring, plumbing, and finishing out the interior. But in the meantime, you can look out the window of your house and see a barn that looks far more finished than not.

WORKSHEET — SIDING COSTS

SIDING MATERIALS

House wrap:
_____ PER-ROLL COST X _____ TOTAL ROLLS = _____

Siding boards:
_____ PER-FOOT COST X _____ TOTAL FEET = _____

Drip-edge stock:
_____ PER-ROLL COST X _____ TOTAL ROLLS = _____

Corner-board stock:
_____ PER-FOOT COST X _____ TOTAL FEET = _____

Gable-end trim (rake board):
_____ PER-FOOT COST X _____ TOTAL FEET = _____

Hot-dipped galvanized nails:
_____ PER-POUND COST X _____ TOTAL POUNDS = _____

Strapping (if required):
_____ PER-FOOT COST X _____ TOTAL FEET = _____

Blocking (if required):
_____ PER-FOOT COST X _____ TOTAL FEET = _____

Aluminum flashing (if required):
_____ PER-ROLL COST X _____ TOTAL ROLLS = _____

METAL PANELS

Metal panels:
_____ PER-UNIT COST X _____ TOTAL UNITS = _____

Screws or nails with gaskets:
_____ PER-POUND COST X _____ TOTAL POUNDS = _____

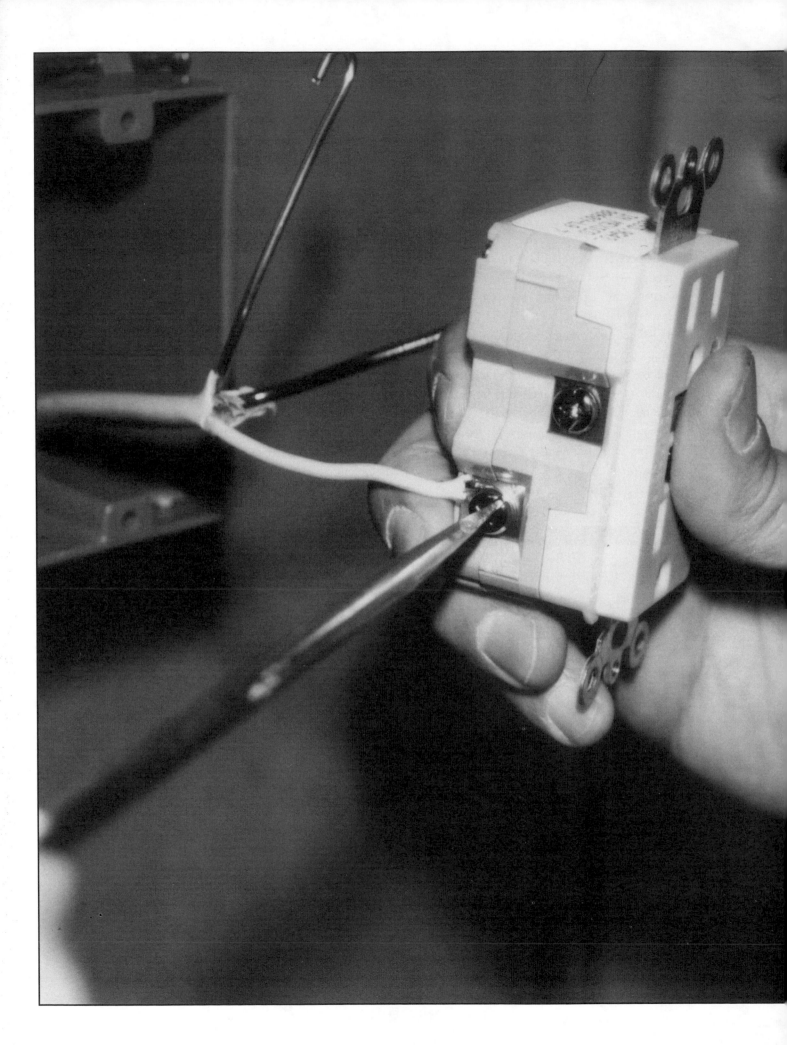

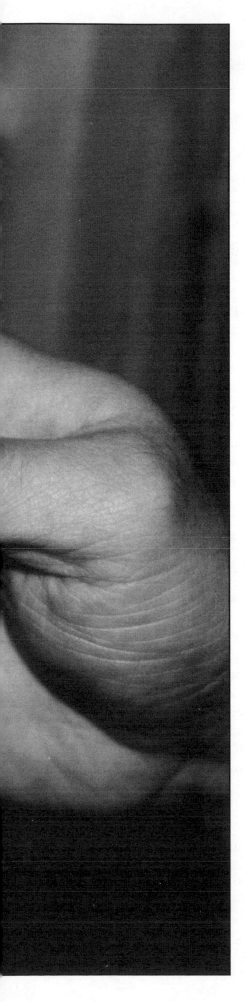

7 Wiring, Plumbing, and Heating

N ow that your barn is framed, roofed, and sided, it's time to consider the basic utilities you want for it, as well as the best means of installing them. If you've thought the project through from the beginning, you ought to have a good, general idea of how you want your barn wired, plumbed, and heated. If you plan on doing any of the work yourself, this chapter will help lead you through what you need to know—or need to ask if you plan on hiring experts.

WIRING

There is nothing so mysterious about wiring that can't be figured out with a little study and careful attention to detail. One reason wiring scares so many people is that electricity can be dangerous and a simple mistake can have severe consequences. You can alleviate that fear by understanding the basics of wiring and circuitry. In the first part of this chapter, we'll look at some wiring basics and outline some of the choices you'll have to make when designing a wiring system for your barn.

Don't be intimidated by wiring. It's easy to learn and satisfying to do. Just be sure you have your work properly inspected.

Many towns and cities will not allow you to do your own wiring unless you are a certified licensed electrician. Some towns allow you to do part of the job (for example, all the wiring except for the breaker-panel hookups), and then submit it to an inspector. But often, an electrician is required to do everything. Check with your local building or electrical inspector to make sure what you plan to do is legal. Take no chances. When in doubt, have an electrician do the work.

No matter who wires your barn, all the systems must adhere without exception to the *National Electrical Code (NEC)* or your state's adaptation of that Code. In fact, your state or region may have adopted the NEC into a local code book, or distilled the NEC book into a "residential" code. If you can use a distilled version of the NEC book, your life will be made simpler and you won't have to wade through the volumes of often complex NEC regulations that are written for industrial application.

After you determine who can do what parts of the wiring, call your local utility and find out where along your electrical service the utility ownership ends. Jurisdiction varies from utility to utility. Sometimes their ownership ends at the service drop and sometimes at the meter. In any event, all wiring beyond the point of utility ownership is your responsibility.

Basic Information

The majority of electrical services installed on residential homes deliver 120/240 volts of electricity. This service can be distributed as 240 or as 120 volts, in separate, discrete circuits. In its 240 form, it can power your heavy-duty appliances such as dryers, water heaters, and electric stoves. In its 120 form, it can power the standard household convenience circuits (what you plug your television or electric lights into). Some people might say, "I'm not sure if my house has 240." For the most part, every house does; it's a matter of wiring it one way for 120 and another for 240.

Usually, a 200-amp circuit service (an *amp* is a measure of the quantity of current flowing

in a wire) will power a three-bedroom house and a small barn if the barn isn't loaded with appliances or electrical tools. If you want to run power to your barn from your house, you may be able to do so without upgrading the house's service. But if your barn will have lots of demand (heavy power tools, motors, appliances, pumps, and so on), you may have to upgrade your main house's service or install a sub-panel at the house to supply the code-required circuits and amps to the barn. When you decide what your barn's demand will be, consult with your electrician and find out (1) how much power you need, and (2) what power you have available.

If you can piggyback onto the house's circuits, you'll probably have to run a supply line from the house to the barn. If you can, run this line underground. It's safer—you won't have to worry about loaded trucks snagging the wire or ice weighing it down and breaking it—and not having the lines strung from pole to house is aesthetically more pleasing. Check your NEC code concerning underground power lines. You'll likely be required to run *UF underground feeder cable*. But you can't just dig a shallow trench, lay down some cable, and backfill everything. You may have to run a conduit, and you'll surely have to trench at least 24 inches deep and add either dirt or gravel to the bottom of the trench to protect the cable from being crushed or broken by heavy traffic. Do whatever your code requires and don't cut corners.

If you plan on finishing off a second floor for an apartment, there are a couple of reasons for getting a new service to the barn directly from the power pole and with its own meter. First, you'll probably be installing some appliances in the second story of the barn, and you may not want all that power being drawn from the house (the circuit may be inadequate and require upgrading). Second, an independent meter lets you bill for the apartment's power separately—a handy thing if the apartment will be a rental unit.

An independent apartment upstairs and a workshop downstairs may warrant a new independent service with two meters, one for each floor. Or, you may want a new metered service for an upstairs apartment, with your downstairs

---

WIRES AND AMPERAGE

Always use wire appropriately rated to deliver the required amperage to your circuits. For example:

size	amps
#10 wire *can carry up to* **30**	
#12 wire *can carry up to* **20**	
#14 wire *can carry up to* **15**	

Remember: higher-numbered wires are thinner and, therefore, can carry fewer amps than thicker, lower-numbered wires.

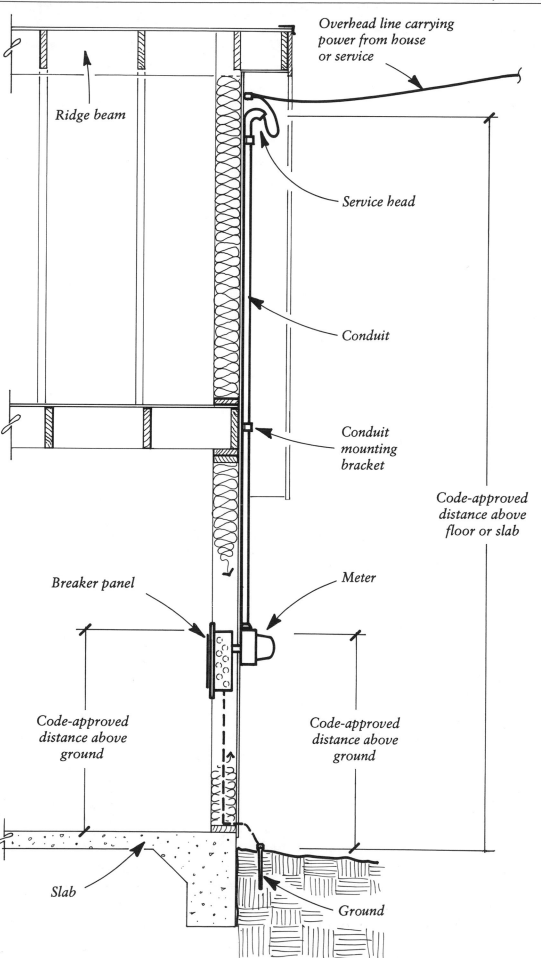

Overhead line carrying power from house or service

Ridge beam

Service head

Conduit

Conduit mounting bracket

Code-approved distance above floor or slab

Breaker panel

Meter

Code-approved distance above ground

Code-approved distance above ground

Slab

Ground

FIGURE 7–1

You may want a new electrical service with an independent meter for your barn. If so, be sure to find out where the power company's ownership and responsibility end and yours begin.

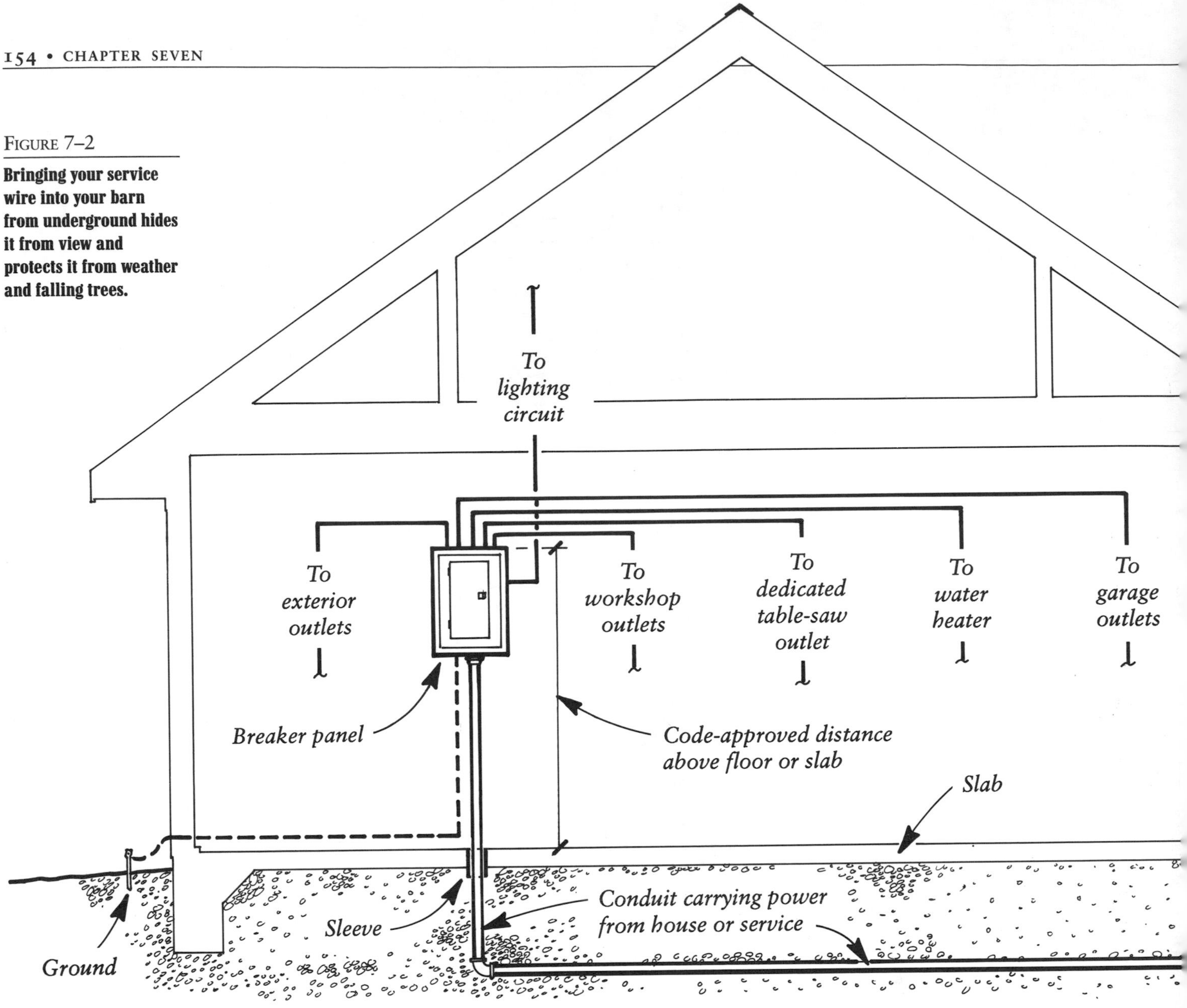

FIGURE 7–2

Bringing your service wire into your barn from underground hides it from view and protects it from weather and falling trees.

To lighting circuit

To exterior outlets

Breaker panel

To workshop outlets

To dedicated table-saw outlet

To water heater

To garage outlets

Code-approved distance above floor or slab

Slab

Sleeve

Conduit carrying power from house or service

Ground

drawing its power from the house. You should be able to mix and match your options as required. Whatever you do, first think it through (figures 7–1 and 7–2).

How Many Circuits and How Many Amps Do I Need?

Whether you run your barn's power from your house or independent of it, you must appraise how much power you'll need and how many circuits that power will course through. Since power is measured in *volts, amps,* and *watts,* (which are volts x amps), each circuit needs a voltage and amperage designation. Typically, household circuits are 120 volts, 15 amps. But higher amperage may be required for circuits servicing machines that draw more amps (like big table saws or electric pumps). If more amps are needed for certain functions, wire that circuit with heavier wire rated for the required amps.

All electrical wire is rated for how many amps it can safely deliver. For instance, a number 10 wire can carry 30 amps, a number 12 wire can carry 20 amps, and a number 14 wire can carry 15 amps. The lower the number on the wire, the thicker it is and the more amps it can carry. *Be sure you use a wire appropriately rated to deliver the required amps to your circuits.* If not, the overload in the wire is dissipated in the form of heat which can start a fire. Never, never use a

because too many things would draw power and the wire would have to be very thick to meet the electrical demand. In most households, we solve this problem by increasing the number of circuits, thereby reducing the power demand on each.

The electrical code has already calculated circuit/demand ratios. Here is a list of the circuits that the National Electric Code requires. Whether you have simply a workshop and storage barn, or a barn with a finished apartment or living area, these rules apply.

For lighting circuits, calculate the barn's square footage along its *outside* walls and plan on supplying 3 watts of lighting per square foot. How many circuits should you have? As a general rule, the code recommends that you take the total square feet of the building and divide by 500 to get the total number of circuits required. A 1,000-square-foot structure, for instance, requires two lighting circuits (1,000 ÷ 500 = 2). Our 24 x 30- foot barn has 720 square feet *per floor*, or 1,440 square feet total. Divide by 500, and we get 2.88, or three circuits required for lighting. With no second floor, the square footage requires 1.44 lighting circuits, so you'd install two.

No part of your barn can be more than 6 horizontal feet from an outlet. An outlet must be in any wall space 2 feet or more in width, and you must have a GFCI outlet outdoors that is properly protected by a gasketed box. Outlets, sometimes called convenience outlets, are typically installed 14 inches from the floor, and they can be on the same circuits as your lighting (except in the kitchen). Those circuits must have a minimum 15 amp capability.

Any kitchen/dining area requires a minimum of two 120 volt/20 amp circuits. One of these circuits will run the appliances—typically just the refrigerator—and one will run the outlets in the kitchen. (All kitchen outlets within 6 feet of a water faucet must be GFCI-type.) Both circuits must have outlets actually in the kitchen, and the outlets on the non-refrigerator circuit must occur at least every 4 feet along counter space 12 inches or wider. Also, an independent circuit is required for any lighting for that room (though

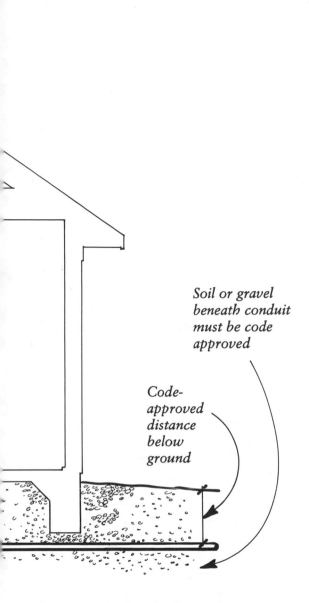

Soil or gravel beneath conduit must be code approved

Code-approved distance below ground

low-amp wire for a high-amp function. You will pay for your mistake—dearly!

Ask most electricians their wire of choice and you'll find that most favor number 12 wire, also known as 12–2 because it provides two wires for circuiting purposes. In a moment we'll cover common amp demands of household appliances. But first, let's look at circuits.

A *circuit* is really just an extended loop of wire through which power runs; "hanging" on that loop are the items that demand power (lights, TV, VCR, stereo, refrigerator, and so on). A *circuit breaker* guards each loop from either delivering a damaging amount of power or from short circuiting due to crossed wires. You can't run your household on one big loop (circuit)

this lighting circuit can branch to other rooms). An electric range may require its own individual 3-wire, 240-volt, 40-amp circuit (check the manufacturer's specs).

If you are going to install anything more than a basic kitchen, you'll need one circuit for the refrigerator, one for the microwave and garbage disposal, one for the dishwasher, and one for the range. Here's a tip for when you install your kitchen outlets. Don't hook all the outlets in a row to the same circuit. Instead, run two circuits, and alternate each outlet: the first to circuit one, the second to circuit two, the third to circuit one, the fourth to circuit two. That way, outlets that are next to each other will be on different circuits and there is less chance of the breaker tripping when you are running a blender, toaster, and coffee grinder all at the same time, as can happen around mealtime.

In the laundry area, a washer and dryer require their own circuits. The dryer needs its own dedicated circuit that isn't shared by any other appliance or outlet. Typically, a dryer needs a 240-volt, 30-amp circuit and a washer needs its own 120-volt, 15-amp circuit. Electric water heaters draw 20 amps, sometimes 30. Check the rating on the water heater and supply service accordingly.

For the bathroom, you need at least one outlet by the sink and it needs to be protected by a ground fault circuit interrupter (GFCI). To reiterate its purpose, this is a device that constantly monitors the electric current, detects power leakage, and shuts the power off before it can do damage. Leakage, or *ground fault,* happens when someone comes in contact with a live wire by touching it, or by using an appliance that has a faulty casing that becomes electrified, or by dropping an electrical appliance in water.

For a barn workshop, you may have equipment that draws lots of amps, such as table saws and drill presses. You need to estimate how many amps you'll use and in consultation with your electrician or electrical inspector, decide how many circuits you'll need to serve the shop, and at what amp rating. You may want a dedicated circuit for some machinery and a second circuit to serve outlets for your other tools. You have

an opportunity at the planning stages to install as many outlets as you want, so if your barn includes a workshop, design it for convenience, with enough outlets to serve your needs. Typically, two 20-amp circuits will fill the bill.

Wiring Basics

Let's assume that your locality's code allows you to do your own wiring. Here are a few basics. Most of the wiring you do will be with *Romex* cable. This is in a class of cable designated *NM* for *non-metallic,* describing the sheathing, which is plastic. You'll run this cable from your breaker panel to your outlets and light fixtures. It's available in sizes from number 14 to number 2. For most applications you'll find yourself using number 12 cable. When you buy it—in 50- or 100-foot rolls—ask for *12-2 Romex* (again, the 2 designation refers to the number of wires in the cable available for circuit use).

Let's say you want to run cable from your breaker box up through the floor or through your walls so you can install outlets. There is a code-approved procedure for running cable, designed to protect it against damage. Here are some basics that apply to running all NM cable: When drilling through studs or joists, the cable must be at least 1 ¼ inches from the outer edge of the wooden member. Typically, you drill a ⁵⁄₈-inch hole for the cable to pass through. (If you're doing the electrical work, invest in a ⁵⁄₈-inch auger bit at least 6 inches long.) As you run the cable, you have to staple it in place. There are specific *U nails* (sometimes called *cable staples*) you use to attach cable to the framing members, and they must be nailed at least every 4 ½ feet between boxes, and at least 12 inches from the box or fitting.

At a junction box or outlet box, the wire should protrude into the box and the outer plastic shield should be intact at least ¼ inch above the connector that holds the wire in the box. Never run Romex along the outside of a stud and never sandwich the Romex between a stud and a piece of sheetrock or siding. Always run your Romex in between the stud bays.

In some cases a cable may have to pass within

TIP

WHEN INSTALLING KITCHEN OUTLETS, DON'T HOOK ALL THE OUTLETS IN A ROW TO THE SAME CIRCUIT. REASON: RUNNING TWO OR MORE APPLIANCES SIMULTANEOUSLY ON THAT CIRCUIT INCREASES THE LIKELIHOOD OF TRIPPING THE BREAKER. INSTEAD, RUN TWO CIRCUITS AND ALTERNATE OUTLETS ON EACH.

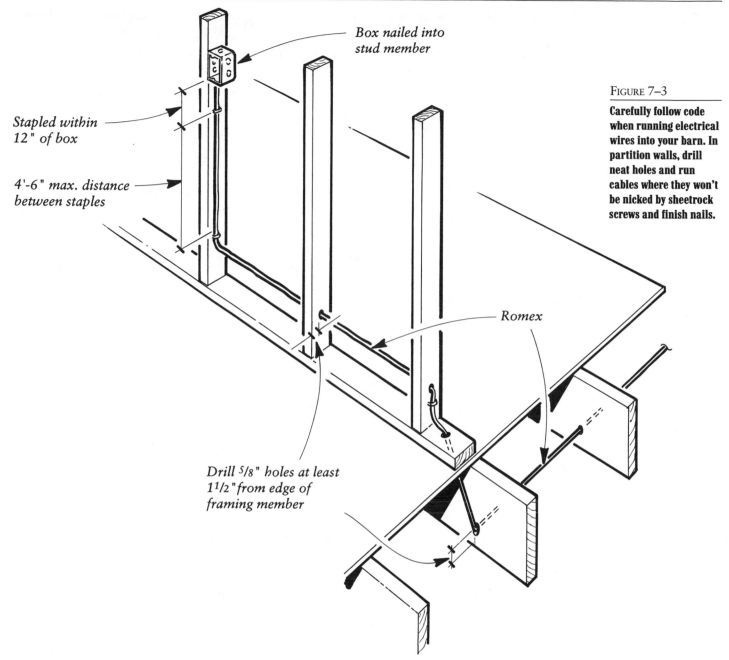

Box nailed into stud member

Stapled within 12" of box

4'-6" max. distance between staples

Romex

Drill 5/8" holes at least 1 1/2" from edge of framing member

FIGURE 7–3

Carefully follow code when running electrical wires into your barn. In partition walls, drill neat holes and run cables where they won't be nicked by sheetrock screws and finish nails.

1 ¼ inches from the inside edge of the stud. In this case you must install *metal shields* so that when your sheetrock screws penetrate the stud, they don't also penetrate the cable. These shields, which you can buy at most electrical supply stores, are usually ¹⁄₁₆-inch steel and are worth the slight installation effort. A builder I know once had to tear out twelve recessed lighting fixtures and all their wiring just to locate a short circuit. After four hours of labor he found the problem: The sheetrockers had screwed into one of the cables!

You'll run Romex cable at the proper amp rating for all your interior outlets and fixtures.

(*Outlets* are mounted on rectangular boxes, and *fixtures* are mounted on round or hexagonal boxes.) You attach Romex to outlets and fixtures in basically the same way.

First, you have to have a good *mechanical* connection where the wire is screwed down to the outlet or fixture. Some outlets and switches now allow you to strip back a half-inch of insulation and stick it into a hole in the back of the outlet or the side of the switch. That saves you the trouble of bending the wire and tightening the screw, but be advised that disengaging this wire is difficult if you ever want to change the outlet. In any event, without a good, sound me-

Lineman's pliers, wire strippers, needle-nose pliers, and a screwdriver are essential tools for most wiring jobs.

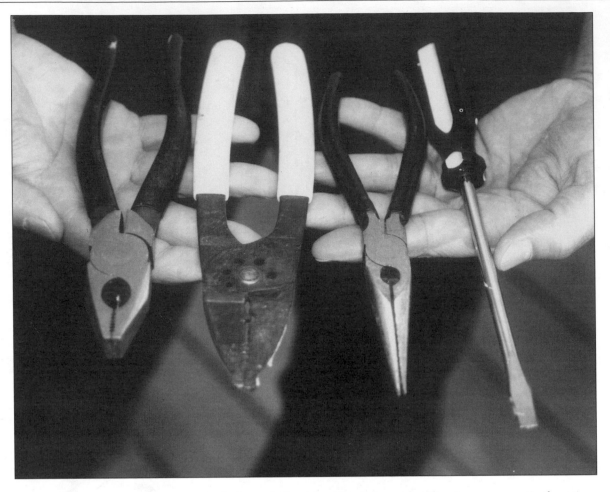

chanical connection—either via the hole and clip or with screws all tight and wire bent and wrapped properly around screw terminals—your wiring job will be potentially unsafe. To prepare your wires for making connections, one tool is invaluable: a pair of lineman's pliers. These pliers are versatile because they can cut most wires and their nose is perfect for bending the individual strands of Romex to fit around outlet and fixture screws (more in a moment).

Do all your wiring—outlet placement, fixture placement, and switch installation—before you hook up any circuits to the breaker box. With all your circuits done, you can safely hook them up all at once at the breaker box and you'll never have to guess which circuit is hot and which isn't.

Let's look at a connection and see how best to make it. When you run your Romex into a box, you'll strip back the outer plastic shield to reveal three wires within. One is black, one white, and one is bare copper (the ground). Whether you are wiring a fixture or an outlet

(we'll get into specifics in a moment), the wires must fit beneath the screws that hold them in a certain, prescribed way. The wiring photos here show how to bend and attach individual strands to a screw, whether that screw is part of a fixture or an outlet. As you can see, the ends of the Romex strands are bent so they curl tightly around the screw in the clockwise direction. *The wire must be flat!* Don't rely on the screw to flatten the wire for you. If need be, clamp the wire with your lineman's pliers and flatten it manually. When attaching the wires to the fixtures or to outlets, the white wire always connects to the silver screws and the black wire always connects to the gold-colored brass screws. This is essential to keep straight in your mind because the black wire is the *hot* wire carrying power from the breaker box, and the white wire is the neutral wire carrying power back to the breaker box. The white wire is continuous through the circuits and only the black wire is interrupted by a switch. Mixing them up can cause havoc.

Installing an Outlet

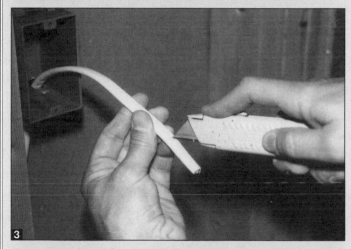

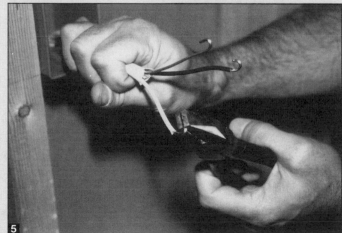

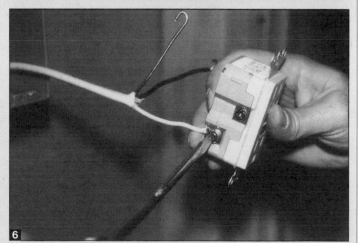

1. When setting electrical boxes, account for the thickness of any wall covering. Set the box forward of the stud so its cover plate will be flush with the finished wall.

2. Nail the protruding box in place so it is square to the stud.

3. Bring your Romex cable into the box and use a razor knife to strip back some of the plastic jacket.

4. Using wire strippers, strip about $3/8$ inches of plastic off the black and white strands.

5. Curl the exposed wire with the nose of your lineman's pliers so the curl just fits beneath a fixture screw.

6. Fit the curled wire beneath the fixture's screw so it wraps clockwise— the same direction the screw will turn as you tighten it.

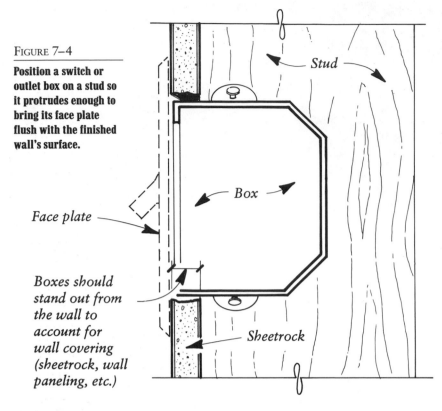

FIGURE 7–4

Position a switch or outlet box on a stud so it protrudes enough to bring its face plate flush with the finished wall's surface.

Stud

Box

Face plate

Boxes should stand out from the wall to account for wall covering (sheetrock, wall paneling, etc.)

Sheetrock

Romex cables entering a metal box—whether for a fixture or an outlet—need to be held in place with individual cable clamps. Romex cables entering modern plastic boxes (now available everywhere) don't need clamps; when the Romex is inserted into the box a plastic tongue holds the Romex in place. The tongue makes a one-way valve: more cable can be pulled in, but can't be pulled out.

The cable clamps for metal boxes are two-piece circular fittings. You insert the male end through the box, and then screw on the female end until it is snug. To snug these connectors tightly, place your screwdriver on one of the jagged edges of the female end and whack the screw driver with your lineman's pliers.

The cable clamp fits into a *knockout*—a hole in the box made by knocking out a coin-sized piece of metal. You knock out this slug with a screwdriver to make room for cable clamps. With the clamps in place, you secure the Romex by tightening a pair of screws at the base of the clamp.

Boxes themselves are secured to studs by nailing through tabs on the top and bottom of the box or by screwing through the interior of

the box into a framing member. Many boxes come with nails already sitting in the tabs. You just hold the box up to the stud and nail away. When nailing switch boxes and outlet boxes into place, set the boxes so they protrude beyond the stud and so that their *face plates* will be flush with the interior wall surface. Simply account for the thickness of whatever you are putting on your interior walls (sheetrock, tongue-and-groove pine, interior paneling) before you secure your boxes to the studs (figure 7–4).

Once your boxes are in place and you've run your wires into them, you may end up joining some wires with *wire nuts*. The photo sequence, on page 162, shows how this is done. Notice that the wires are twirled together in the same direction the wire nut will turn as it tightens. Twirl the wires with your lineman's pliers, making sure you use a wire nut rated to accommodate the number of wires you are joining. A too-small wire nut will leave some unprotected bare wire at its base, and that's dangerous.

To join wires properly, first strip back about $^3/_8$ inch of insulation and place the wires to be joined at 90 degrees to each other. Grab both wires with your lineman's pliers and twirl them clockwise. You may want to clip off the ends of the wires once they are twirled together so they are the same length. Now place your wire nut over these twirled wires and screw it until it is tight. Don't overscrew the wire nut—just until it is snug.

The bare copper wire is your ground wire. Typically, this wire is grounded to the chassis of the outlet or junction box. This ground wire will in turn carry the grounded connection to the service panel, which is grounded to a rod driven into the earth. Figures 7–2 and 9 show how this grounding system works, from the chassis of an outlet box, all the way down through the service box to the grounding rod.

Designing Circuits

Now that we've covered the mechanical basics concerning how to join wires and how to secure Romex cable strands to screws in fixtures and outlets, let's take a look at how to design a basic

Installing a Metal Electrical Box

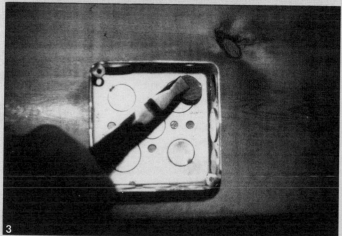

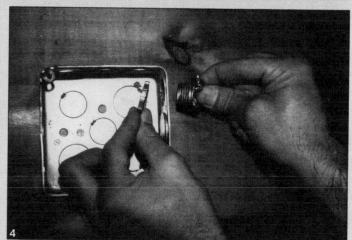

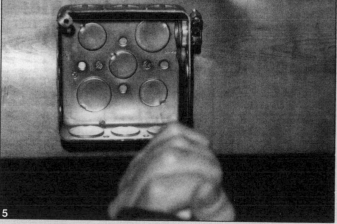

1. Set the box in place with nails.

2. Use a screwdriver to bash in the knockout where a wire will enter.

3. Yank the knockout free with your lineman's pliers.

4. Set your Romex connector in place through the knockout.

5. Tighten the collar and snug it up by tapping it with a screwdriver.

6. Insert the Romex through the connector and tighten the clamp screws to hold it in place.

Connecting Wires in a Junction Box

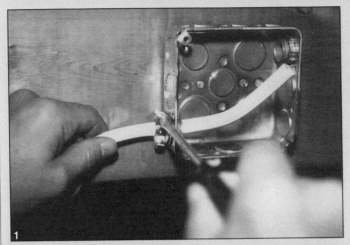

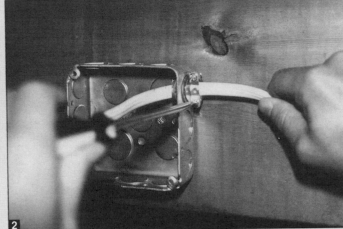

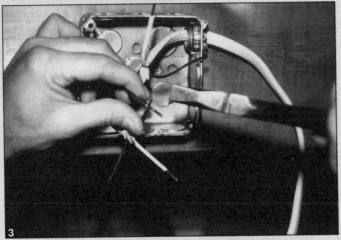

1. Clamps hold your Romex in place.
2. Tighten the screws so the clamp is snug to the Romex, but not so tight that the clamp tears the Romex jacket.

3. Strip the wires you will connect. Cross matching wires at 90-degree angles to each other.

4. Clamp the wires with your lineman's pliers and twirl the wires clockwise—the same direction your wire nut will turn. Twist the

appropriate-size wire nut over the wires with your fingers. Don't tighten the wire nut with pliers or other tools—you might crack it.

FIGURE 7–5

In a dedicated circuit, as shown here, only one outlet is served by a circuit breaker. A good electrical connection first needs a good mechanical connection, so make sure all wires are properly stripped and firmly, neatly attached.

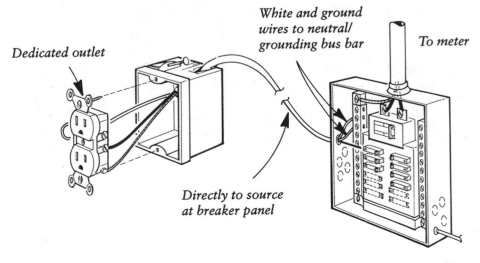

Dedicated outlet

White and ground wires to neutral/ grounding bus bar

To meter

Directly to source at breaker panel

To ground

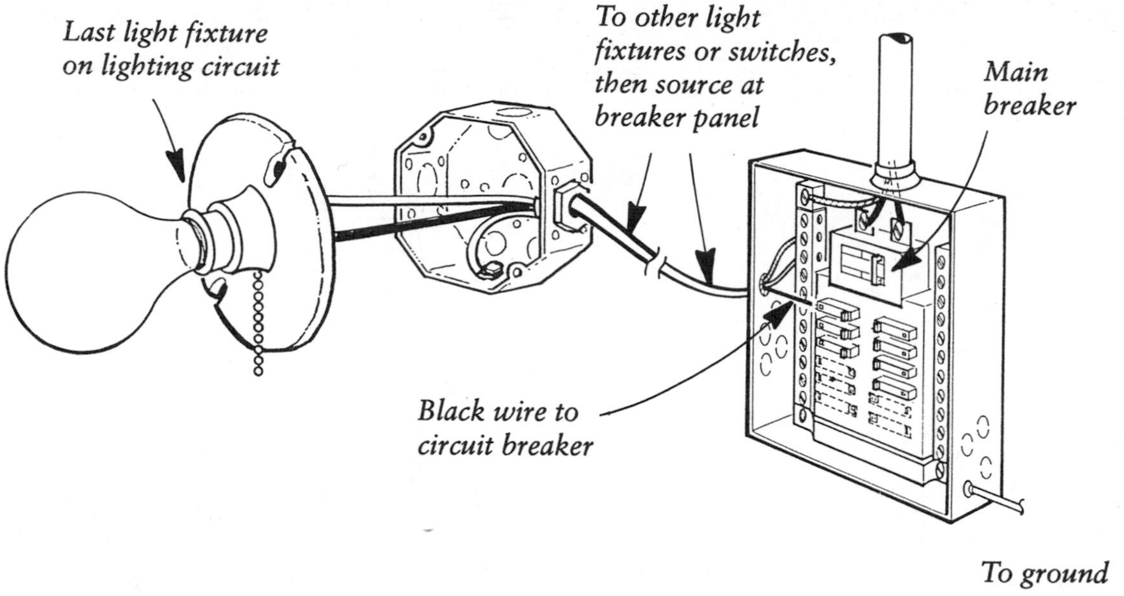
Last light fixture
on lighting circuit
To other light
fixtures or switches,
then source at
breaker panel
Main
breaker
Black wire to
circuit breaker
To ground

FIGURE 7–6

Light fixtures are wired using the same principles as outlets. Be sure the ground wire is properly attached to the metal fixture box.

circuit. Figures 7–6 and 7–7 show how a simple light fixture is wired, either with an in-line switch or a switch beyond the light. The source wire (Romex) comes from one of three places: directly from your breaker box, from another fixture box, or from a junction box (a box within which electric circuits are connected).

Figure 7–10 shows what to do with each wire. The black wire goes to the brass screw, the white wire goes to the silver screw, and the bare wire is grounded to the box by wires from the fixture's green ground screw (if it has one) and the grounding screw on the box. If you are joining two or three wires together and all of them have to connect to a single box screw, construct a pigtail. Join a number of wires in a wire nut,

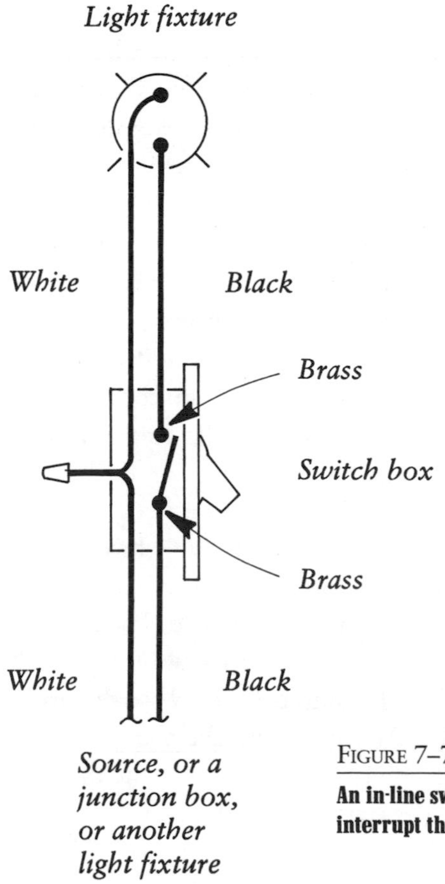
Light fixture
White
Black
Brass
Switch box
Brass
White
Black
Source, or a
junction box,
or another
light fixture

FIGURE 7–7

An in-line switch should interrupt the black wire.

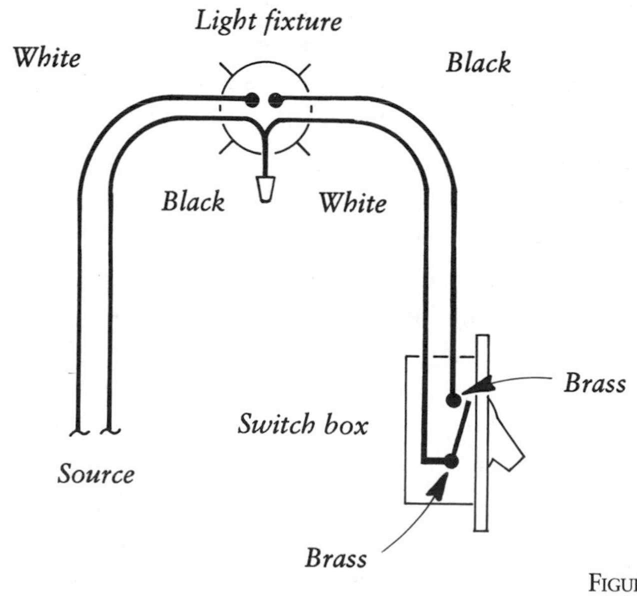
Light fixture
White
Black
Black
White
Brass
Switch box
Source
Brass

FIGURE 7–8

With a switch beyond the fixture, you still interrupt the black line, but do it with a loop consisting of black and white wires.

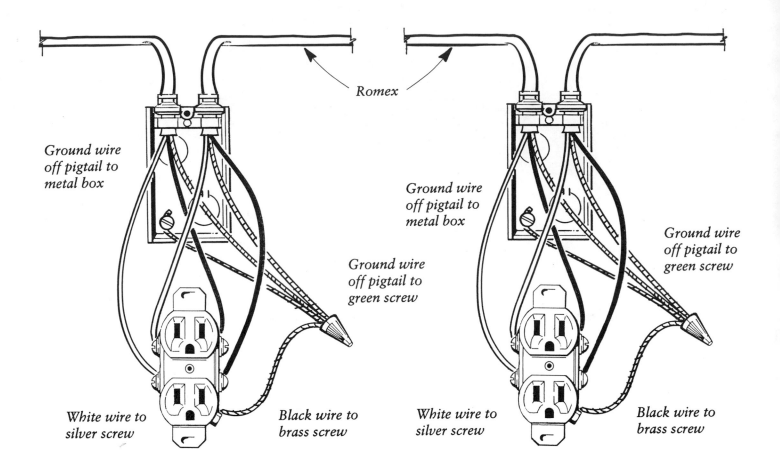

Romex

Ground wire
off pigtail to
metal box

Ground wire
off pigtail to
metal box

Ground wire
off pigtail to
green screw

Ground wire
off pigtail to
green screw

White wire to
silver screw

Black wire to
brass screw

White wire to
silver screw

Black wire to
brass screw

FIGURE 7–9

Outlets in a series can be wired on a single circuit. Be warned: Stuffing this many wires in each fixture box can be a challenge. Stuff firmly but gingerly! Avoid gouging wire insulation with sharp tools such as screwdrivers.

including a free strand that can be attached to the box's grounding screw.

Figure 7–9 shows how to wire a series of outlets. Notice that the incoming and outgoing wires of the same color are attached to the same side of the outlet. Black incoming and black outgoing should screw onto the brass screws. White incoming and white outgoing should screw onto the silver screws. The ground wire should go to the grounding screw on the box, in pigtail fashion as shown.

Figure 7–10 shows how to wire lights in a series. The principle here is the same as for outlets. The incoming and outgoing black wires attach at the brass screw and the incoming and outgoing white wires attach at the silver screw. The ground wires attach to the grounding screw on the box.

When all your circuits are wired, you can connect them via circuit breakers to your circuit breaker box. Most breakers have metal slots that allow them to be plugged onto tabs in the box, and you attach a circuit's cable to the breaker in the same way you would to an outlet or fixture: black wire to brass screw, white wire to silver screw. The ground is screwed into a grounding yoke that runs around the inner perimeter of the box. Before actually plugging a wired circuit breaker onto one of the box's prongs, shut off the power at the *box's main switch*. In addition, make sure that the breaker you choose for a given circuit is rated to handle the amperage that will run through that circuit. For example, 12-2 Romex is rated to handle up to 20 amps of electricity, while 10-3 Romex (which you would use for a dryer), is rated to handle 30 amps. By contrast, 14-2 Romex is rated to handle up to 15 amps comfortably and should therefore be fitted with a 15-amp breaker. Wire the breaker to the cable and then, with the main power switch shut off, plug the breaker into the breaker box, keeping its switch shut off, too. Once the breaker

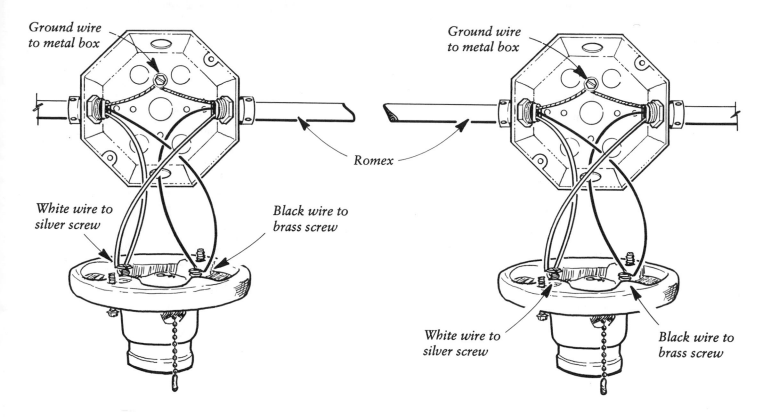

Ground wire to metal box

Ground wire to metal box

Romex

White wire to silver screw

Black wire to brass screw

White wire to silver screw

Black wire to brass screw

FIGURE 7–10

Fixtures in a series can also be wired on a single circuit. Fixtures typically sit in octagonal boxes.

is plugged in and grounded, turn on the main switch, *then* turn on the circuit-breaker switch. The moment of truth comes when you flip on a fixture switch or plug a tool into the outlet you've just connected. If you've done your wiring properly, the circuits should work and the circuit breaker switch should not shut off. If the breaker switch does trip, turn everything off and check your wiring. If you can't spot the problem, maybe it's time to call your friendly electrician.

PLUMBING

There will be two separate piping systems in your barn: one to bring clean water in and the other to take dirty water out. The clean-water system requires a source of potable water, either through a supply line from the main house, the town hookup, or a well. The easiest and cheapest of these is a line from the main house. The most difficult and costly is digging a new well because its price is unpredictable and includes the costs of a pump, casing, and pressurized tank to hold the water.

Should you do your own plumbing for your barn? Once again, your decision depends on the size of your budget and the amount of time you have available to do the job well. Modern plumbing materials make joining pipes quite easy, and really, there's never been a mystery to designing a simple system and installing tubs, sinks, and toilets. Once you master the basics, the rest should come rather quickly. You'll find that fixtures come with well-written installation instructions that are relatively simple to follow. There are wonderful full-length books on plumbing that I've listed in this book's "Resources" section. With a little study and practice you can learn plumbing basics in a few days.

If you still think you'd prefer to hire a professional plumber, fine. But do consider the costs. On average, it costs about $500 per fixture (fixture cost and labor) to have a plumber install a bathroom. That means, if you want a sink, toilet, and shower, you're looking at $1,500 for a bathroom alone, and that's if you plan on doing the tiling and other finish work yourself.

Knowing what I do about plumbing, I'd recommend, if you want to reduce your plumbing costs, that you install the potable water delivery system for all the fixtures (sinks, shower, toilets) and hire a professional plumber to do toilet installation, all fixture drainage, and all sewage system hookups. Hire the plumber to come after you've done as much as you can and arrange for him or her to inspect your work to make sure it's up to code.

Potable Water Distribution Systems

Wherever your potable water comes from—house, town, well, or spring—you should deliver it to your barn in a pipe large enough to meet your local plumbing code. (Yes, communities have plumbing codes, too!)

Your code probably calls for using a 1 1/4-inch supply-line pipe if the water travels 100 feet or more, and a 1-inch pipe for distances shorter than 100 feet. This supply pipe will be buried and brought into the barn through the slab. If you are in a frost area, you need to protect this delivery pipe against freezing by laying it below the frost line. Whether you are in a frost area or not, you should never install a supply-line pipe

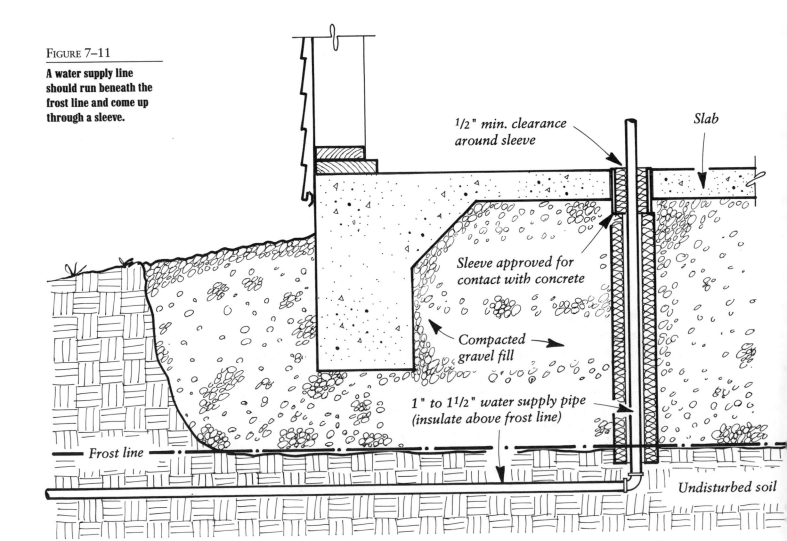

FIGURE 7–11

A water supply line should run beneath the frost line and come up through a sleeve.

1/2" min. clearance around sleeve

Slab

Sleeve approved for contact with concrete

Compacted gravel fill

1" to 1 1/2" water supply pipe (insulate above frost line)

Frost line

Undisturbed soil

where it can be heated in any way by the sun.

Local plumbing codes will tell you the materials and techniques required for running a pipe underground. Galvanized pipe is popular, but some codes allow underground-rated PVC. As you can imagine, running a rigid metal or plastic pipe under a driveway without proper protection is a recipe for breakage. If the pipe breaks, you have a real mess on your hands—especially in the winter— and lots of digging ahead of you. So, follow the code recommendations and improve on them where you can by upgrading the specs and materials. Codes provide *minimum* requirements, and if you can afford it you should probably upgrade. A good-quality supply line, for example, properly installed in a prepared bed (making sure there are no corrosives in the soil) can be buried and forgotten.

A water supply line entering the barn will probably be run through an in-slab sleeve discussed in chapter 3. You'll have prepared for this utility access during the slab's planning stages. The sleeve is typically cast iron or some other material approved for contact with concrete. No matter what it's made of, be sure that the sleeve provides at least a half-inch of clearance all the way around the water supply line. This clearance protects the pipe if the slab settles or the pipe moves (figure 7–11).

Most codes require a *shutoff valve* on the supply line before it splits into different feeds. Let's say you're running a supply line from your house, the easiest water source. You may want to put a shutoff with a drainage valve at the house and another shutoff at the barn. This is very convenient in the event you must drain the barn's entire system to fix it or if you leave the building unheated for long periods of time. If you are building an independent apartment on the barn's second floor, you'll want at least two shutoffs at the barn end of the supply line: one for the apartment and one for everything else in the barn.

Once the water supply is inside the barn, you can deliver it in any number of ways. Most people use either copper or chlorinated polyvinyl chloride, known as CPVC. Copper takes work to hook up. You must develop the skill of *sweating* (soldering) a joint which, for the first-

Before joining CPVC pipe sections with plastic "weld" glue, use light-grain sandpaper or steel wool to clean the pipe and fitting ends of burrs, dirt, and grit.

time plumber, might lead to fixing a few self-created leaks before the job is done right. The problem is, you won't know about leaks until the pipes are all hooked up and entirely charged with water. Copper's advantage: It's relatively easy to fix if there is a leak, whether it occurs right after installation or years later.

More and more these days, people are using CPVC, and CPVC is what I recommend for your barn. It's been widely approved by code for delivering both hot and cold water, and it will serve you well for your barn's water delivery system.

CPVC is remarkably easy to use, even if it is a pain to fix when there are leaks (you have to add at least two joints for each leak, as opposed to copper, where you just sweat in a joint) and its initial installation goes so quickly, it far outweighs time lost fixing any leaks. The first CPVC job I did was when I hooked up a pump to a shower and faucet at a friend's lake camp. I expected the job would take a full day. It took less than an hour. Plus, the material is so inexpensive, I didn't feel bad making mistakes. Neither will you.

CPVC pipe is available at most building-supply stores. Wherever you buy it, you'll find bins full of fixtures that will connect your CPVC pipes to any other type of fixture, from garden hose to toilet-tank supply line.

CPVC pipe is *welded* (glued) together with CPVC cement. The cement is a clear liquid you swab or brush on the pipe end and into the fitting. The procedure is extremely simple. First you cut the pipe to the desired length with a hacksaw, using a miter box to stabilize the pipe and guarantee square cuts. Then use light grain sandpaper or steel wool to clean the pipe end of burrs, dirt, and grit. For burrs on the inside, ream the pipe with a reamer or scrape it with a knife. (Some PVC cement manufacturers recommend priming the pipe with yet another of their fine products, but a good clean pipe that's been sanded and deburred is ready for gluing.)

Once the pipe is cut and cleaned, wipe the pipe and fitting with a clean rag and check how they fit together dry. The pipe should enter the fitting $1/3$ to $2/3$rd of the way. Remove the pipe and coat its end and the inside of the fitting with cement. Be sure you insert the pipe *exactly* as you want it (you may want to mark the fitting and pipe with a pencil during the dry fit so you know how they should align)—it takes just seconds for the cement to start bonding. Insert the pipe into the fitting with a slight twisting motion. Hold the pipe for about 20 seconds. Wait at least one hour or longer if you can before testing your pipes with water. See, that wasn't so bad; now you're a plumber.

Wherever you run piping in the interior of your barn, plan on supporting it with straps or hangers. Your code may ask for something special but here are the general requirements: For CPVC pipes running horizontally, add supports every 4 feet; for copper $1\,1/2$ inches diameter or smaller, use supports every 6 feet. For vertical pipe runs, CPVC should be supported at each "story height." For copper, it's every 4 feet for $1\,1/4$-inch diameters or smaller.

Typically, you can run half-inch CPVC pipes to feed your sinks, toilets, and showers, but it doesn't cost all that much more to run $3/4$-inch if you're worried about supply. In fact, you should run $3/4$-inch pipe wherever the supply line branches to serve two or more fixtures. Whatever diameter you choose, avoid running pipes in an outside wall because they may freeze. Run pipes intended for second-floor fixtures within an interior partition wall called a wet wall. If you have no interior partition wall, run the pipes on the inside of an insulated wall. If you feel exposed pipes are unsightly, enclose them in an attractive chase.

As you buy fixtures that need water delivered to them (sinks, showers, toilet tanks, water heater), the fixtures will have some kind of fittings that you have to match with your CPVC delivery line, and each hookup may be slightly different. When you purchase a fixture, unbox it and find out what type of CPVC fitting you'll need. The fixtures typically come with detailed instructions for their own installation.

Waste Water

Waste systems—the piping that takes the water and soil (human waste) away from the house—are also regulated by code. If you've ever lived in a country where there is no code for sewage, you know how blessed we are to have good sewage regulations and coding.

There are two kinds of water flowing into the waste system from any household. One is called *waste water,* also called *gray water,* which is water free of fecal material. Typically, gray water is the water draining out of your washing machine, sinks, and tubs. Next, there is *soil,* which is what drains from your toilet. This water contains human waste. Both types of water eventually meet in a single drainpipe, called the *house drain,* or *soil pipe,* that is connected to your septic system.

Some of you will be able to hire a plumber to hook up your barn's septic to the exisiting septic or sewage system that services the main house. But if you are installing a new septic system, it should be designed and installed by a professional. It's not something you want to experiment with. Usually, a septic system centers around an airtight underground tank into which all the sewage water flows. The water action in the tank separates liquids from solids. Anaerobic bacteria in the tank digest the solids, and as new sewage water flows into the tank, two things happen: Gases that accumulate from the bacterial action (methane and hydrogen sulfide) are forced up through vent pipes to exhaust above the roof of the barn, and water (called *effluent)*

TIP

ONCE YOU'VE APPLIED GLUE TO THE PIPE AND FITTING ENDS, BE SURE YOU JOIN PIPE SECTIONS *EXACTLY* AS YOU WANT THEM—IT TAKES JUST SECONDS FOR THE GLUE TO START BONDING. HINT: MARK THE FITTING AND PIPE WITH A PENCIL DURING THE DRY FIT SO YOU KNOW HOW THEY SHOULD ALIGN.

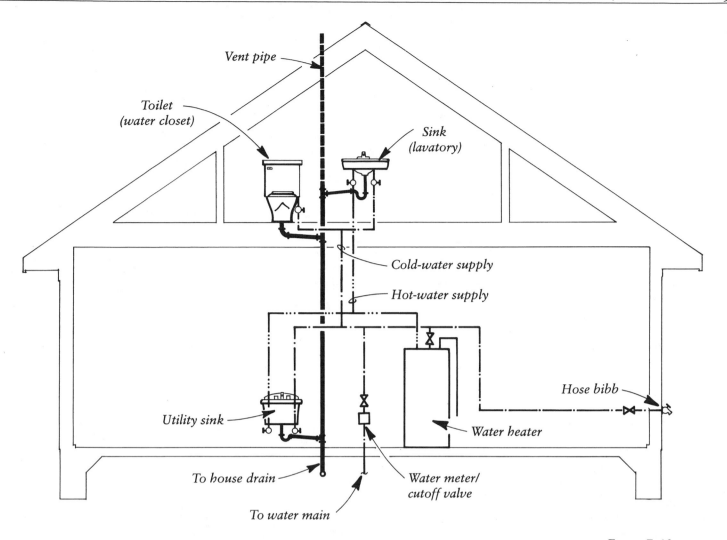

Vent pipe

Toilet (water closet)

Sink (lavatory)

Cold-water supply

Hot-water supply

Utility sink

Hose bibb

Water heater

To house drain

To water main

Water meter/ cutoff valve

FIGURE 7–12

By grouping plumbing fixtures in one area of your barn, you reduce the length of both supply and drain lines.

is forced from the tank into perforated pipes (figure 7–13). The pipes are arranged in a grid which drains into a bed of washed stone and the entire configuration is known as a leach field or *leach bed*. From the leech field the water and its contents seep into the soil, where filtration, oxidation, and evaporation occur. Meanwhile, a call to your local septic tank cleaning company can lead to your tank getting pumped out when it fills with solid waste.

Before you install the septic system, the soil that the effluent spills into through the perforated pipes must be tested to see if it will accept the water. This is called a *percolation* or *perk test*. If the soil doesn't perk properly when it is tested—that is, if the water doesn't seep into it at a rate set by your sewage authority—you may have to modify or mound the soil until it perks properly. Only then will your town or district approve the installation of the septic system.

Sizing Your Waste System

Before you can design or install your barn's waste system, you must size it, which means you must know how much wastewater will be draining from your barn. There are some standard values for the amount of water that drains from common fixtures, which are expressed in *drainage fixture units* or *DFUs*. Each "unit" is 7.5 gallons per minute. Once you know how many DFUs you have flowing into your septic system, you can size the pipe and install it. Here are some standard estimates: A washer and a bathtub each drain at 15 gallons a minute, or two DFUs. Toilets have a value of between four and six DFUs per flushing, and sinks are assigned at least one DFU, often two, depending on their size.

Before we actually size our pipes, let's look at the drainpipe's slope, which, incidentally, also affects sizing. The steeper you slope your drain-

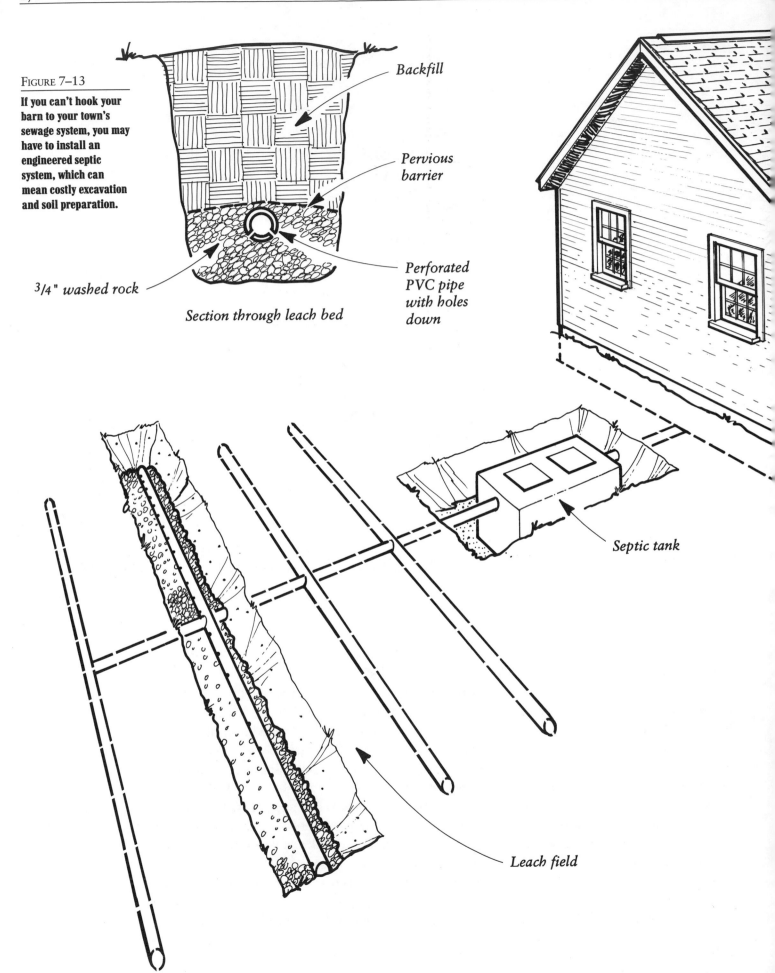

FIGURE 7–13

If you can't hook your barn to your town's sewage system, you may have to install an engineered septic system, which can mean costly excavation and soil preparation.

Backfill

Pervious barrier

Perforated PVC pipe with holes down

3/4" washed rock

Section through leach bed

Septic tank

Leach field

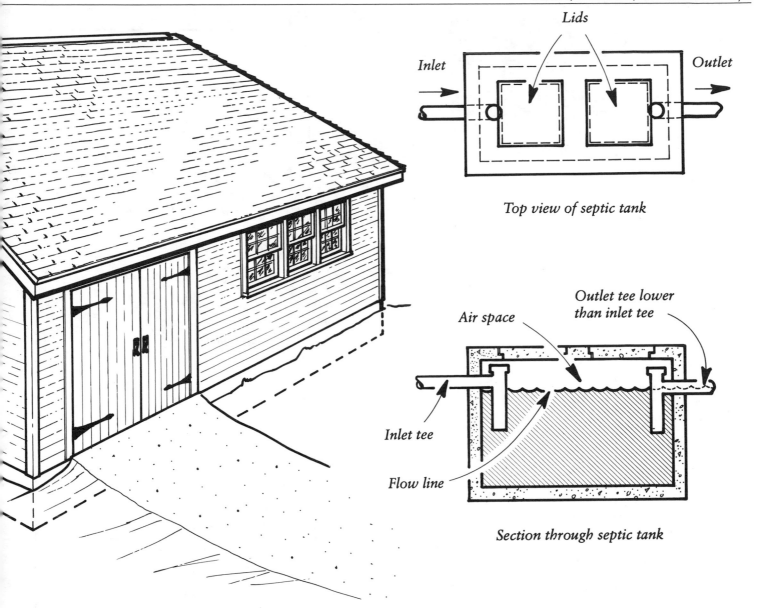

Top view of septic tank

Section through septic tank

pipe, the smaller the pipe you can use. Let's say you've determined that you have 50 DFUs draining from your barn into your house drain, which is the pipe that carries all the accumulated waste water and soil from your barn. If you slope your drainpipe at $\frac{1}{8}$ inch per foot (which is typical), you should use a 5-inch pipe, minimum. If you increase your slope to $\frac{1}{4}$ inch per foot, you can use a 4-inch pipe.

In the barn itself, the soil pipe leading to the house drain should be a minimum of 3 inches (this covers from one to 11 toilets), and the waste water pipe (for nine to 18 DFUs) that leads to your 3-inch pipe (which leads to your 5-inch

pipe!) should be 2 inches. Two general rules: As the pipes meet in junctions, no pipe downstream can be smaller than a pipe entering the system upstream. And once soil is introduced to a pipe, it's a soil pipe all the way to the house drain.

Be careful not to oversize your soil or drainpipes. Believe it or not, oversizing can lead to blockage. In a larger pipe, waterflow can slow to a trickle and become shallow. Then water can separate from the solids; the solids, no longer carried off, build up, damming the water. In extreme cases, toilets overflow when flushed and sinks fail to drain.

What happens if you get a blockage? Well,

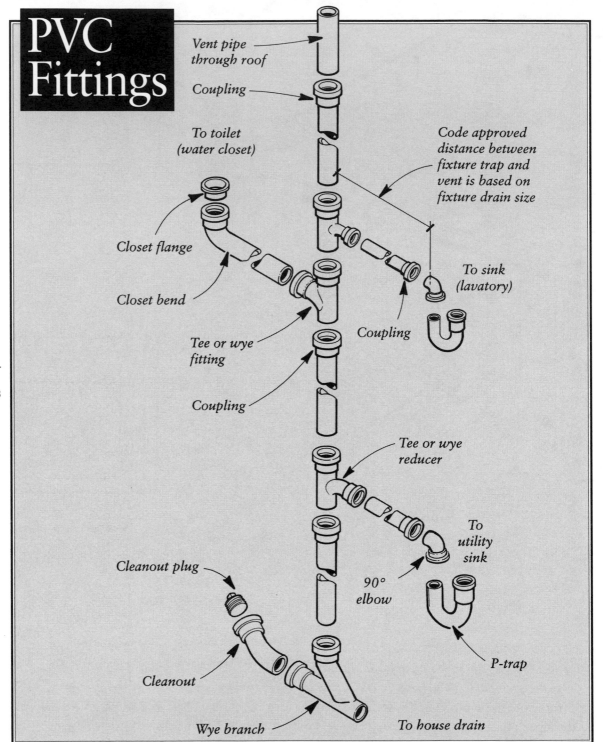

FIGURE 7–14

When ordering PVC pipe fittings, getting the names right is half the battle.

PVC Fittings

Vent pipe through roof

Coupling

To toilet (water closet)

Code approved distance between fixture trap and vent is based on fixture drain size

Closet flange

Closet bend

To sink (lavatory)

Coupling

Tee or wye fitting

Coupling

Tee or wye reducer

To utility sink

90° elbow

Cleanout plug

Cleanout

P-trap

Wye branch

To house drain

the code writers have thought of that too. Your system installation needs to include *cleanouts*—fittings with caps on them that can be unscrewed to allow access to the piping system. To unblock a line you introduce a routing cable or some other device through the cleanout. Consult your code book for cleanouts' required locations. And whatever you do, contact your code official, a good plumber, and a complete text on plumb-ing to make sure that your system specifications are adequate for your requirements.

What type of pipes should I use in the waste system I am building?

Here are a few principles concerning what type of piping to use.

Most piping used in waste systems must be code approved for *DWV*, or *drain, waste,* and *venting*. Cast iron is the old standby of waste piping, while more and more, PVC is widely used and available, though not approved by all codes. *ABS plastic* is the most widely approved modern piping for drain, waste, and venting, and like PVC plastic piping, it is "welded" using the same methods explained above (make sure you use ABS, not PVC, cement—they are different).

Any pipe that passes through a slab will do so through a sleeve poured into the slab. The sleeve should be cast iron or some other pipe approved for contact with concrete. And any drainpipe that runs beneath your slab must be cast iron as well. When cast pieces fit together, they have to be joined with oakum and molten lead. Joining and leading these pipes is a job for a professional plumber. But the rest of the system can be ABS or some other plastic piping approved for DWV that you can assemble yourself if you choose.

Figure 7–14 shows some different types of drainage fittings and what to call them by name. When you purchase your fixtures, note which pipe fittings are needed to hook up the drain and buy them. The fixtures themselves come with detailed installation instructions, including for drain hookups.

Traps.

Since your barn's DWV pipes carry water, waste, and soil to your septic tank or municipal waste system, they also provide an avenue for the return of septic gases into your barn. Figure 7–12 shows a barn schematic with a simple waste system. Notice the stack exhaust poking at least 12 inches through the barn's roof. That is where the gases escape safely into the air. But what is to stop these gases from flowing back up your drain pipes and out your sink drains into the barn itself? Answer: *Traps*. A trap—the p- or s-shaped pipe beneath your drain—remains filled with water that acts as a plug which blocks the gases from entering the room through these drains. All sinks and drains should have traps, and depending on your toilet design, the toilet should have a trap as well.

There is a phenomenon called *siphoning* where water can be sucked from the trap if the

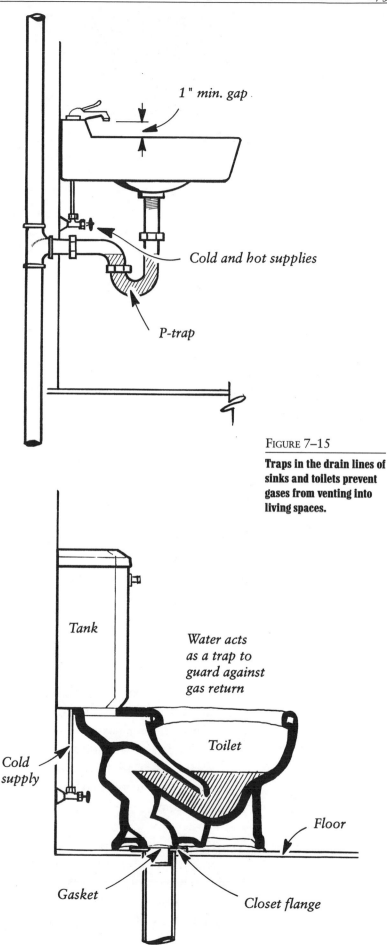

FIGURE 7–15

Traps in the drain lines of sinks and toilets prevent gases from venting into living spaces.

1 " *min. gap*

Cold and hot supplies

P-trap

Tank

Water acts as a trap to guard against gas return

Cold supply

Toilet

Floor

Gasket

Closet flange

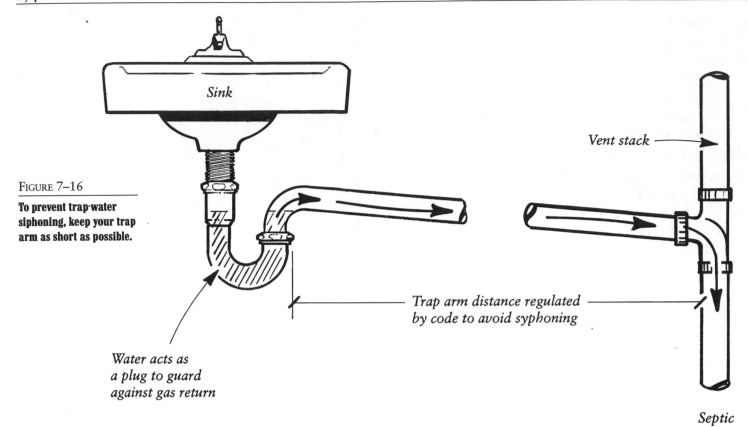

FIGURE 7–16

To prevent trap-water siphoning, keep your trap arm as short as possible.

Sink

Water acts as a plug to guard against gas return

Trap arm distance regulated by code to avoid syphoning

Vent stack

Septic

drainpipe is ever completely filled from the sink to the stack (figure 7–16). The longer the drainpipe, the greater chance there is of siphoning. To reduce that risk, the code-regulated maximum length of a trap arm section of drainpipe is usually 10 feet. Check your code to make sure your trap arm is not too long and in violation.

A note on downstairs toilet installation.

If you plan on installing a toilet on your barn's downstairs floor but are not going to finish that floor with *sleepers* (joists) and decking, you will have to prepare your slab *before you pour it* so you can hook up a toilet directly to the concrete floor. And you will have to install (or have a plumber install) DWV lines before you pour concrete for your slab. Check with a plumber to determine what you must do beforehand for such an installation.

Testing

Once you have your piping system in place, have a plumber install a temporary gauge and conduct a *pressure test* with the system charged with water. Then inspect it to see if there are any leaks. Flush the toilets and run water in the sinks to check the drainage. It's best to check thoroughly and test the system before you start finishing off the barn's overall interior (if that's your plan) because you still have easy access to the pipes that need repair.

Once the system is checked and made watertight, you can look upon your barn with some real satisfaction, not only for the money you've saved by doing some (maybe all) of the plumbing yourself, but because learning how to install the plumbing and then setting out to do the job right is no small task. Now, every time you turn on a spigot, you'll have firsthand knowledge of what it took to get water there, and firsthand knowledge of where that water goes once it drains from the tub, toilet, or sink. Yet another construction mystery revealed!

After installing all these pipes yourself, you'll also feel much more confident repairing your barn's and other plumbing systems. In fact, if word gets out that you "know plumbing," believe me, you'll find a whole new list of friends posting your number by their telephones.

HEATING YOUR BARN: WHAT ARE YOUR CHOICES?

Heating your barn can be as easy as fabricating a 55-gallon-drum wood stove, running a properly-insulated flue and chimney, and burning wood. As for wood stoves, goodness knows you can find more sophisticated models than a 55-gallon drum. In fact, you can spend oodles of money on wood stoves, and by and large get what you pay for. But as any veteran wood-stove user knows, a wood stove that is the principal (or only) source of heat requires a great deal of attention. Keeping the stove stoked with dry wood is enough of a chore, and dealing with the mess of wood chips and bark only adds to the work. Indeed, I don't know anyone who regrets leaving his or her wood stove for a good clean furnace or boiler. So, think twice before your romantic side gets the best of you and you buy a big wood stove for your barn. You might be taking on more than you bargained for.

The Wood Stove

If you do go with a wood stove, carefully plan its location, and determine its task. Will it heat just the first floor? Do you expect the heat from the first floor to rise and heat the second? Do you plan to install two stoves, one upstairs and one down? Estimate the square footage you want to heat and present that figure to a wood stove distributor or directly to the manufacturer to get an idea of what size stove you'll need. And keep these things in mind. First, note where the smoke should exhaust. You don't want smoke pouring out into prevailing winds that will take it to your main house. Situate the stove where it will do the most good in the barn but consider where the chimney and flue will lead. (A *chimney* encases a flue; a *flue* is the shaft designed to vent exhaust gases.) You can't make your chimney and flue too tall because the flue gases will cool and moisture and solids will condense along your flue's inside. Your wood stove manufacturer will be able to recommend some specs, but the rule of thumb is that a flue should be as short as possible, with a minimal number of turns.

Since you'll be hauling wood to your wood stove regularly, locate your stove near a convenient passageway where the wood can be brought in from outside. This can minimize the mess and save you lots of hauling. Also, remember that the wood stove will take up space, not just in its own volume, but in the area surrounding it. You'll be placing the wood stove on some kind of noncombustible platform such as bricks or flagstone. These platforms take up space, so avoid having the wood stove so dominate a passageway that it leads to burns or accidents caused by people brushing or falling against it.

What kind of flue liner should you install for your wood stove? Any *cementitious* liner or Type 304 stainless steel will serve you well, but tile is not generally recommended. Be sure to use an approved wall pass-through. Also, no liners have *zero-clearance,* meaning they can't come directly in contact with the chimney or chase, so properly insulate your flue liner with approved solid (not loose!) foil-faced insulation contained by a stainless steel mesh. All flue liners should be *UL (Underwriters' Laboratory)* approved. And remember that wood stove flue liners need to be cleaned often, particularly if the stoves are not burning at full efficiency all the time. (A slow fire is a dirty fire.) Creosote can accumulate and become a fire hazard (creosote buildups of more than ¼ inch are real dangers). And chimney fires are something you never want to experience, ever. They're dangerous and scary. If you have any doubts about installing a flue or chimney, hire a mason to do the job and invite your local fire marshal to inspect the finished stove installation. Play it safe with wood stoves. You don't want to destroy your handsome creation.

Oil and Gas Heat

Oil *furnaces* deliver warm air through ducts. Oil *boilers* deliver hot water through a hydronic system. A warm-air system requires a professional to size and locate the ducts, and to size, select,

FUEL VALUES OF SOME COMMON HARDWOODS

	Fuel value/cord (in millions of BTUs)
Shagbark Hickory	30.8
White Oak	30.8
Sugar Maple	29.7
American Beech	28.0
Red Oak	27.3
Yellow Birch	25.9
American Elm	23.8
Red Maple	23.8
Paper Birch	23.8
Black Cherry	23.1

Assumed efficiency of wood stove: 50 percent

and locate the thermostat, air supply, returns, and exhaust air outlets.

Since oil appliances burn fuel to heat the water or air, you need a flue to exhaust the combustion gases. You can use a Type 304 stainless steel flue (for noncondensing furnaces), or an

FIGURE 7–17

Use great care when installing a flue and chimney and follow all installation instructions exactly. Take special care to ensure proper "clearances"–the distances between the flue and anything it passes by or through.

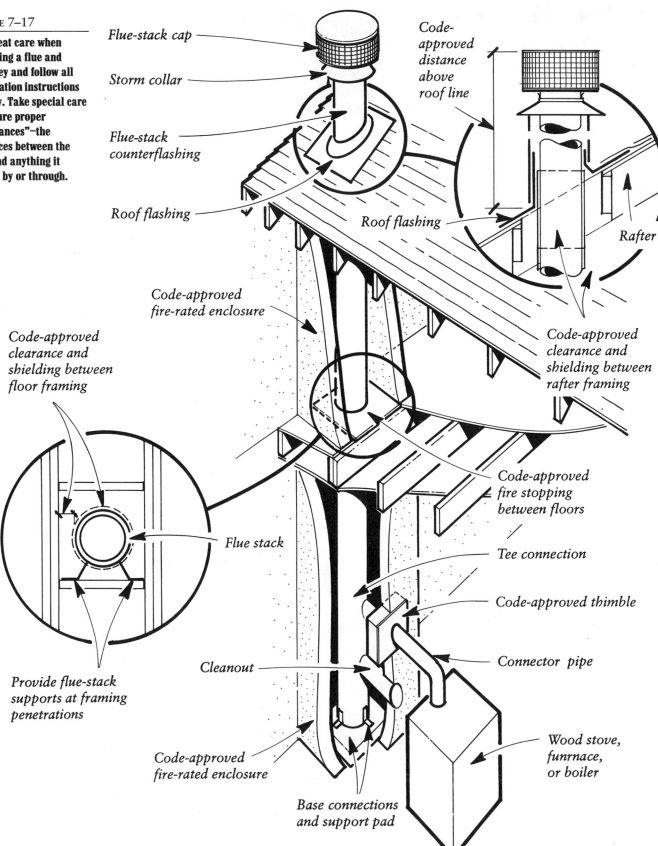

Flue-stack cap

Storm collar

Flue-stack counterflashing

Roof flashing

Code-approved distance above roof line

Roof flashing

Rafter

Code-approved fire-rated enclosure

Code-approved clearance and shielding between floor framing

Code-approved clearance and shielding between rafter framing

Code-approved fire stopping between floors

Flue stack

Tee connection

Code-approved thimble

Connector pipe

Provide flue-stack supports at framing penetrations

Cleanout

Code-approved fire-rated enclosure

Wood stove, funrnace, or boiler

Base connections and support pad

A1 20-4C stainless steel type, or a cementitious liner. The liner must be installed according to code in a chimney or chase and properly vented outside the barn.

A gas appliance can deliver either warm air or hot water, meaning you can use a gas appliance to serve a *hydronic* (hot water) system, or a warm-air, delivery-duct system.

A hot-water or hydronic system is very convenient and clean. What's best, you can split the delivery of the hot water to different *zones* through different pumps that are controlled by separate thermostats. So, for example, you could have a boiler delivering hot water heat to the upstairs apartment on a different piping system than the one serving the workshop below.

Most hydronic heating systems deliver heated water in copper pipes to baseboards. A typical baseboard contains copper pipes surrounded by aluminum fins under a sheet metal chassis.

Most heating appliances, oil or gas, are rated for their efficiency by an *AFUE rating*. AFUE stands for *Annual Fuel Utilization Efficiency*. The higher the AFUE rating, the more efficient the furnace. The more efficient the furnace, the cooler the flue gases. The cooler the flue gases, the harder it is to exhaust them without special features. For furnaces with an AFUE rating below 78 percent, the flue gases are hot enough to exhaust without their condensing in the flue. With an AFUE ranging from 78 to 83 percent, the furnace, sometimes called a condensing boiler, is designed to take some of that heat out of the exhaust gases. Cooler gases must be sucked out by a special fan. For furnaces with an AFUE over 83 percent, the flue gases must be direct-vented through special vent pipes made of high-tech plastic.

Figure 7–17 shows the basic configuration of a stainless steel liner that can vent nearly all the above mentioned sources of heat.

Electric Baseboards

Electric baseboards are inefficient and costly to run. They may be cheap to install, but when you start receiving electric bills of $250 per month in the dead of a northern winter, you'll quickly lose your installation savings. Unless you have no other alternative, or you are cheaply generating your own electrical power, use one of the other sources of heat mentioned here.

Radiant Floor Heating

Radiant floor heating is a system of whole-house heating that relies on water pumped through specially designed hoses poured into your slab. It has long been popular in Europe, and is beginning to gain attention in the United States. Some people swear by its comfort; others complain of hot feet and cold ears, though that is mainly a problem in poorly-insulated dwellings. It's worth looking into, however, as a viable heat source. The system itself is designed for installation in concrete, but it must be installed by a professional. I've often thought it would make a great added heat source, especially after I've spent three or four hours with cold feet on a cold slab while working on a project out in my shop during the winter. Radiant-floor heating is also wonderfully functional in bathrooms.

Sizing Your Heating System

Whether you install your barn's heating system or have a subcontractor do it, someone should do a *heat-loss calculation* beforehand. A heat-loss calculation (involving a very detailed and complicated formula) tells you how much heat an appliance must supply to maintain a desired temperature for your barn, even on the coldest day of the year. Without the heat-loss calculation, you risk oversizing (or undersizing) your boiler or furnace. Oversizing, which is common because it's easier to err on the side of caution, costs more at the point of purchase and in daily running expense. Rather than shrugging and paying more, why not seek out a book on heating that includes a heat-loss calculation worksheet, or ask for one from your subcontractor, and calculate your barn's heating needs. Over time, energy is only going to become more expensive, so some effort at the planning and installation stages with your heating system will likely save you real cash down the road.

WIRING, PLUMBING, & HEATING COSTS

WORKSHEET

WIRING

Romex cable #10:

_____ PER-ROLL COST X _____ TOTAL ROLLS = _____

Romex cable #12:

_____ PER-ROLL COST X _____ TOTAL ROLLS = _____

Romex cable #14:

_____ PER-ROLL COST X _____ TOTAL ROLLS = _____

Connectors for Romex:

_____ PER-BOX COST X _____ TOTAL BOXES = _____

Romex staples:

_____ PER-BOX COST X _____ TOTAL BOXES = _____

Outlet boxes (doubles) and cover plates:

_____ PER-OUTLET COST X _____ TOTAL NUMBER = _____

Outlet boxes (quads) and cover plates:

_____ PER-OUTLET COST X _____ TOTAL NUMBER = _____

Outlets (doubles):

_____ PER-OUTLET COST X _____ TOTAL NUMBER = _____

Outlets (quads):

_____ PER-OUTLET COST X _____ TOTAL NUMBER = _____

GFCI outlets:

_____ PER-OUTLET COST X _____ TOTAL NUMBER = _____

Switches and cover plates:

_____ PER-SWITCH COST X _____ TOTAL NUMBER = _____

Breakers:

_____ PER-BREAKER COST X _____ TOTAL NUMBER = _____

Breaker box and hookups:

_____ COST X _____ TOTAL UNIT COST = _____

Underground cable/conduit:

_____ PER-FOOT COST X _____ TOTAL FEET = _____

Wire shields:

_____ PER-UNIT COST X _____ TOTAL UNITS = _____

Wire nuts:

_____ PER-BOX COST X _____ TOTAL BOXES = _____

Light fixtures:

_____ PER-UNIT COST X _____ TOTAL UNITS = _____

Round boxes:

_____ PER-BOX COST X _____ TOTAL BOXES = _____

Junction boxes and covers:

_____ PER-BOX COST X _____ TOTAL BOXES = _____

NOTES:

PLUMBING

Supply line:
_____ PER-FOOT COST X _____ TOTAL FEET = _____

Supply-line fittings:
_____ PER-FITTING COST X _____ TOTAL NUMBER = _____

Supply-line insulation:
_____ COST

In-slab sleeve:
_____ PER-FOOT COST X _____ TOTAL FEET = _____

Supply-line bed:
_____ PREPARATION COST X _____ TOTAL FEET = _____

CPVC clamps:
_____ PER-CLAMP COST X _____ TOTAL NUMBER = _____

ABS clamps:
_____ PER-CLAMP COST X _____ TOTAL NUMBER = _____

Fittings:
_____ PER-FITTING COST X _____ TOTAL NUMBER = _____

2-inch DWV Coupling:
_____ PER-UNIT COST X _____ TOTAL UNITS = _____

3-inch DWV Coupling:
_____ PER-UNIT COST X _____ TOTAL UNITS = _____

5-inch DWV Coupling:
_____ PER-UNIT COST X _____ TOTAL UNITS = _____

3-inch DWV Tee/Wyes:
_____ PER-UNIT COST X _____ TOTAL UNITS = _____

3-inch DWV 90s:
_____ PER-UNIT COST X _____ TOTAL UNITS = _____

3-inch DWV 45s:
_____ PER-UNIT COST X _____ TOTAL UNITS = _____

2-inch DWV Tee/Wyes:
_____ PER-UNIT COST X _____ TOTAL UNITS = _____

2-inch DWV 90s:
_____ PER-UNIT COST X _____ TOTAL UNITS = _____

2-inch DWV 45s:
_____ PER-UNIT COST X _____ TOTAL UNITS = _____

5-inch DWV Tee/Wyes:
_____ PER-UNIT COST X _____ TOTAL UNITS = _____

5-inch DWV 90s:
_____ PER-UNIT COST X _____ TOTAL UNITS = _____

5-inch DWV 45s:
_____ PER-UNIT COST X _____ TOTAL UNITS = _____

5-inch DWV cleanouts:
_____ PER-UNIT COST X _____ TOTAL UNITS = _____

DWV traps:
_____ PER-UNIT COST X _____ TOTAL UNITS = _____

DWV couplings:
_____ PER-UNIT COST X _____ TOTAL UNITS = _____

3-inch stack pipe:
_____ PER-UNIT COST X _____ TOTAL UNITS = _____

WORKSHEET

WIRING, PLUMBING, & HEATING COSTS

WORKSHEET

WIRING, PLUMBING, & HEATING COSTS

PLUMBING (CONTINUED)

Stack roof flashing:

_____ PER-SQ.-FT. COST X _____ TOTAL SQ. FT. = _____

Closet flanges:

_____ PER-UNIT COST X _____ TOTAL NUMBER = _____

Closet-flange gaskets:

_____ PER-UNIT COST X _____ TOTAL NUMBER = _____

$3/4$-inch CPVC pipe:

_____ PER-FOOT COST X _____ TOTAL FEET = _____

$1/2$-inch CPVC pipe:

_____ PER-FOOT COST X _____ TOTAL FEET = _____

$1/2$-inch CPVC Tees/Wyes:

_____ PER-UNIT COST X _____ TOTAL UNITS = _____

$1/2$-inch CPVC 90s:

_____ PER-UNIT COST X _____ TOTAL UNITS = _____

$1/2$-inch CPVC 45s:

_____ PER-UNIT COST X _____ TOTAL UNITS = _____

$3/4$-inch CPVC Tees/Wyes:

_____ PER-UNIT COST X _____ TOTAL UNITS = _____

$3/4$-inch CPVC 90s:

_____ PER-UNIT COST X _____ TOTAL UNITS = _____

$3/4$-inch CPVC 45s:

_____ PER-UNIT COST X _____ TOTAL UNITS = _____

Shutoff valves:

_____ PER-UNIT COST X _____ TOTAL UNITS = _____

Reamer:

_____ PER-UNIT COST X _____ TOTAL UNITS = _____

Miter box:

_____ PER-BOX COST X _____ TOTAL UNITS = _____

CPVC cement:

_____ PER-CAN COST X _____ TOTAL CANS = _____

Sandpaper:

_____ PER-SHEET COST X _____ TOTAL UNITS = _____

Hacksaw blade:

_____ PER-UNIT COST X _____ TOTAL UNITS = _____

NOTES

FIXTURES

Water heater:
_____ PER-UNIT COST   X _____ TOTAL UNITS   = _____

Sinks:
_____ PER-UNIT COST   X _____ TOTAL UNITS   = _____

Toilets:
_____ PER-UNIT COST   X _____ TOTAL UNITS   = _____

Bathtub:
_____ PER-UNIT COST   X _____ TOTAL UNITS   = _____

Shower:
_____ PER-UNIT COST   X _____ TOTAL UNITS   = _____

HEATING

Furnace, wood stove, or boiler:
_____ UNIT COST

Furnace, wood stove, or boiler fittings:
_____ PER-UNIT COST   X _____ TOTAL UNITS   = _____

Baseboard units and delivery:
_____ PER-UNIT COST   X _____ TOTAL UNITS   = _____

Ducts and vents:
_____ PER-UNIT COST   X _____ TOTAL UNITS   = _____

Electrical baseboard units:
_____ PER-UNIT COST   X _____ TOTAL UNITS   = _____

Chimney and flue:
_____ PER-UNIT COST   X _____ TOTAL UNITS   = _____

Furnace flue liner tee:
_____ PER-UNIT COST   X _____ TOTAL UNITS   = _____

Flue liner:
_____ PER-UNIT COST   X _____ TOTAL UNITS   = _____

Insulation:
_____ PER-UNIT COST   X _____ TOTAL UNITS   = _____

Stainless mesh:
_____ PER-UNIT COST   X _____ TOTAL UNITS   = _____

Cleanout tee:
_____ PER-UNIT COST   X _____ TOTAL UNITS   = _____

Cap:
_____ PER-UNIT COST   X _____ TOTAL UNITS   = _____

Fuel supply tank and delivery piping:
_____ PER-UNIT COST   X _____ TOTAL UNITS   = _____

NOTES

This barn interior is being transformed into a snug, finished office space.

This barn interior is being transformed into a snug, finished office space.

8

Fitting Out the Interior

J ust as with other parts of your barn, you can vary the interior finish widely, from in-expensive, uninsulated walls with exposed stud bays, to more costly insulated walls covered with sheetrock or barn board. It all depends on your budget and how you'll use the finished barn. A finished living space or an apartment will require insulated, sheetrocked walls. Either will also probably require some kind of flooring (tile, linoleum, hardwood, carpeting). But if you intend your barn to be a utility structure for storage or a workspace, you'd be foolhardy to spend lots of time and money finishing walls and floors that will only get trashed.

What follows are some basic techniques for finishing out your barn's interior. We'll take a look at how to insulate walls properly and how to get them ready for painting, if that's your plan. We'll also look at how to build and finish interior partition walls and how to trim everything out to give it a nicely-completed look.

TIP

YOU RISK KICKBACK WHEN CUTTING SMALL PIECES OF WOOD ON A TABLE SAW. WHENEVER POSSIBLE, USE A POKER OR PUSH BOARD TO KEEP THE WOOD IN PLACE AND YOUR HANDS FREE OF THE BLADE.

WALLS

The Insulated Wall

All walls can be rated for their insulation or *R-value*. A higher R-value means a better-insulated wall. All components in a wall—sheathing, studs, fiberglass batts—add to the R-value. Even uninsulated, sheathed stud walls, with nothing but the wood between you and the cold, have an R-value, though often well under 10. By contrast, insulated stud walls can have an R-value ranging anywhere from 16 to 30, or even higher. It depends on how much insulation is used and how that insulation combines with other wall materials in different configurations.

Obviously, you want the highest R-value you can afford, because the payback comes in lower fuel bills and greater comfort. But indoor air quality is becoming more and more of a recognized problem in some buildings, and tightly-sealed, overinsulated houses that are not properly vented can pose health problems for occupants who are breathing the same air repeatedly. None of the designs represented in this chapter run the risk of choking you off with endlessly-recycled bad air. But be aware that stuffing extra thick walls with insulation and sealing up the interior with plastic, without making some accommodation for air exchanges, may affect your health.

Uninsulated Walls

Uninsulated walls are easy to deal with, and most utility-barn owners are content with them. If you have no need to insulate you can leave the walls as you framed them, with open stud bays. If you feel you want to cover the studs with *something*, go ahead and choose any wall covering that strikes your fancy. Considering money and time, I'd suggest you put on a wall covering only if you can't stand looking at exposed studs, which really aren't that ugly. (In fact, stud bays make great, natural tool-storage bins.)

If you still want a covering and don't mind the work, the simplest wall covering—which you can use over insulated or uninsulated walls—is rough-sawn pine boards, the same kind you may have used on your barn's exterior. Nail them inside any way you want. Run them diagonally, horizontally, or in fancy patterns.

The Basic Wall for a Heated Interior

A basic insulated wall usually consists of just a few components. First there are batts of fiberglass insulation in each stud bay, and second, stapled on top of the insulation, toward the barn's interior, there should be a 6-mil polyethylene *vapor barrier* (figure 8–1). Any wall covering, such as sheetrock, normally gets installed right over the vapor barrier.

The wall detail shown here is for a 2x6 wall. Sheathed properly and sealed on the outside with house wrap, insulated with 6-inch fiberglass batts and sheetrocked on the inside, it will have an R-value of about R21. By comparison, a thinner 2x4 wall, lacking as it does the extra space for a thicker insulation batt, would have an insulation value of about R15. Since you have prob-

FIGURE 8–1

A wall can be simply made of plywood and siding, or as shown here in a cross-section view from above, it can be made of layers of finish material, including sheetrock, polyethylene plastic, insulation, and house wrap.

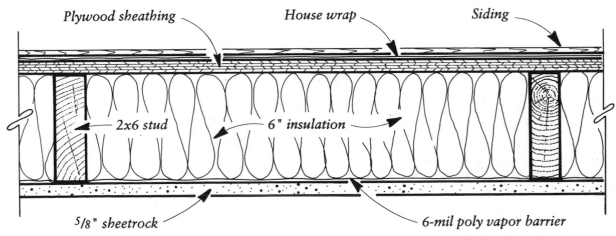

Plywood sheathing   House wrap   Siding

2x6 stud   6" insulation

5/8" sheetrock   6-mil poly vapor barrier

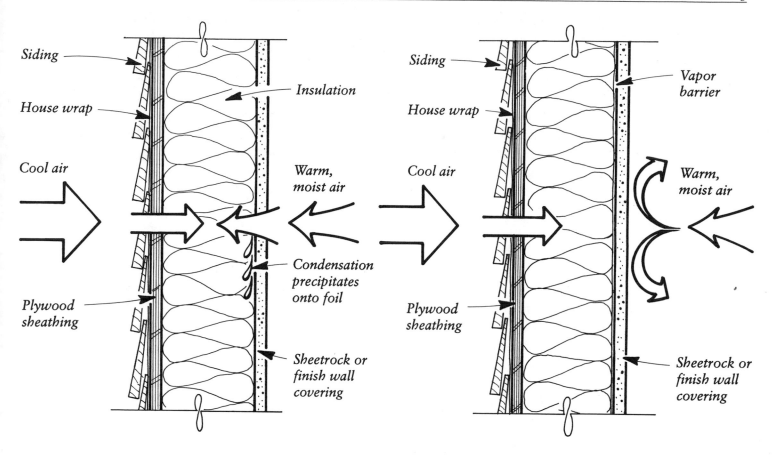

Siding

House wrap

Cool air

Insulation

Warm, moist air

Plywood sheathing

Condensation precipitates onto foil

Sheetrock or finish wall covering

Siding

House wrap

Cool air

Vapor barrier

Warm, moist air

Plywood sheathing

Sheetrock or finish wall covering

FIGURE 8–2

A vapor barrier helps stop warm, moist air from entering the wall where cooler air would otherwise condense the moisture onto the insulation.

ably built your barn with 2x6s, insulating the walls to R21 should provide a nice, cozy living space, given an adequate heat source.

Some builders modify even 2x6 walls by installing 1x3-inch strapping over the vapor barrier and screwing the sheetrock to the strapping. What for? The strapping creates a dead-air space between the sheetrock and the poly, which adds minimal insulation value (dead air is rated R1 per inch thickness). More important, this technique helps avoid penetrating the vapor barrier and allowing air to flow through the wall, while also providing a chase for electrical wires. The wires run *between* the vapor barrier and the sheetrock, and shallow electrical boxes are used that don't puncture the vapor barrier. For a conventional barn, workshop, or storage space like ours, you really don't need to go to such lengths. Even if your barn is serving as a living space, this extreme attention to maintaining the vapor barrier and sealing air might be overkill, unless you want a superinsulated living space.

Why use a vapor barrier? When warm, moist air—the kind any heated structure generates

naturally—hits cooler air, water condensation occurs. Think of warm, moist air penetrating your walls and meeting the cooler air from outside. The cool air will condense the water out of the warm air. Where will it go? On any solid surface—studs, sheetrock, foil—it can find. In short order, capillary action occurs between the moisture and your insulation, diminishing the latter's R-value. Installing a vapor barrier prevents warm, moist air from infiltrating your walls and causing problems (figure 8–2).

Installing the Insulation

There is no secret to installing insulation batts and stapling them in place. Read any instructions that come with the insulation and follow them closely. And when installing the batts, wear long sleeves! The fibers stick to your skin and can be very irritating. (Tip: To remove fibers from your skin, coat the affected area with a thin layer of water-based carpenter's glue; let it dry a little, and peel it off.)

When you install fiberglass batts, be sure to

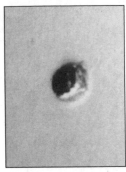

Avoid overdriving sheetrock screws (top). The resulting hole is difficult to mud properly. The head of a properly driven sheetrock screw should sit just below the sheetrock's surface (bottom).

place the foil side toward you and the heated interior, and the woolly side of the batt away from you, against the plywood sheathing. As you'll see when you start to work with it, the foil staples easily to the studs' faces. Also, be aware that the insulation offers its maximum value when it is fully extended and not crushed. Insulation squeezed into a space that is smaller than what a batt is designed for doesn't magically keep its original R-value. The R-value is mostly a factor of how much dead air the insulation is able to maintain. So, squeezing it reduces the R-value.

A common mistake is to let wiring crush insulation. As you run your Romex cables, don't let them constrict the thickness of the fiberglass batts. Make a razor cut in the batt and insert the cable in the razor cut so the batt retains its full extension.

Once you have all the batts stapled in place, staple 6-mil poly over the interior stud faces. Overlap the edges of the poly a good 6 inches. For superinsulated homes, some builders seal these seams with tape, or fold them carefully over each other so they interlock. For the conventional barn we're building, there's really no need to go to those extremes.

Staple the poly right over the window openings as if they weren't there. As you build your windows, or install prebuilts (or even if your windows are in place at the time of insulation), completely finish and trim them over the poly, as if the poly weren't there. Then, razor the poly out of the way once your trim is nailed tight.

Sheetrocking

With your walls insulated and sealed with poly, you may want to put on some sheetrock. Sheetrocking is one of those activities that you can plan out perfectly in your head, whereas actually installing the 4x8-foot panels, then taping and mudding them, can provoke vexation and gloom. Reason: Hanging sheetrock well takes real skill. Don't be discouraged if your first jobs have exposed seams, excess joint compound (mud), or overdriven screws. A little practice goes a long way, but it takes a lot of practice to be-

come an outstanding sheetrocker.

Our walls are designed for 4x8 sheets laid upright with no cutting. But before you begin installing them, you should, ideally, sheetrock the ceiling first. When it comes to installing the wall panels, you'll snug them right against the ceiling edge, and any small gaps between the wall sheetrock and the floor will be covered later with baseboard trim.

Sheetrocking the ceiling is at least a two-person job. Though one person can do it with the help of a *dead man*—a padded 2x4 stanchion that holds up one end of the sheetrock as you screw in the other end—two people and two dead men can do the job faster. For ceilings, follow the same principles I'm about to explain for sheetrocking walls.

The best and easiest way to attach sheetrock is with *sheetrock screws,* which are available at any good building-supply store. The ideal tool for driving them is a cordless drill, which spares you the bother of dealing with a power cord. Use a magnetic drill bit, so you can load the gun with a screw and still have a hand free to hold the panel in place, and consider using a drill head that regulates the depth to which you can drive the screw so that it only dimples the sheetrock.

Before you start to screw, make sure the panel is positioned exactly as you want it, flush against the studs. Don't expect the screws to "suck up" the panel, the way they might wood. If the panel is not flush against the stud, the screw will just suck itself through the sheetrock, creating an unsightly hole that will have to be filled later.

When driving the screws, you want them to go in far enough to create a dimple in the sheetrock's surface paper without puncturing it. That way, when you pass mud over the screw with your sheetrock knife, the mud will fill the dimple easily and smoothly.

Screw the sheetrock every 8 inches on every stud it hits. Don't screw closer than 3/8 inch to the edge.

You'll notice that where the panels' seams meet, the panels have a manufactured taper in them. That provides you with an ideal surface for mudding and taping—screws driven along the seam sit well below the sheetrock's surface,

Panelling Around an Electrical Box

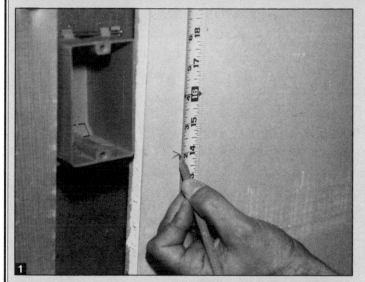

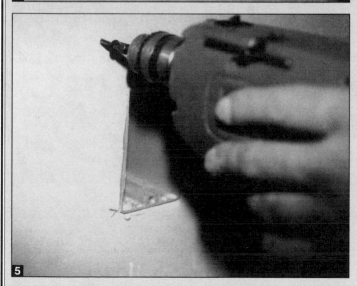

1. With the electrical box in place, mark its coordinates on the sheetrock you wish to install around it.

2. Take an identical box and trace its outline on the sheetrock at the proper coordinates.

3. With a razor knife, cut the sheetrock along the pencil lines.

4. Remove the cut-out piece of sheetrock.

5. Place the sheetrock over the electrical box. If you've marked and cut the hole properly, the electrical box should fit snugly.

and usually just a few swipes of the mud knife fill the taper.

Here's how you mud seams: Once the sheetrock is screwed in place, use a 6-inch mud knife to lay a liberal coat of fresh sheetrock mud over the seam and screws. Then, pressing on it with your mud knife, lay a length of paper or synthetic mesh *sheetrock tape* along the seam, over the coat of wet mud. Apply pressure with your knife so the excess mud under the tape is squeezed out and the tape is sealed flat against the sheetrock seam.

Bubbles under the tape should be flattened with your knife. You may have to lift the tape and insert some more mud if the area under the bubble is dry.

The next step is to use a 12-inch sheetrock knife (the one that looks like a baker's tool), and lay a coat of mud on top of the taped seam. Smooth this coat of mud out as best you can. (Later, you might have to apply yet another coat of mud on top of this one.)

You'll find that the more you work the mud (it's like kneading bread, except you do it with a tool), the easier it is to work it flat, with no tool marks. In fact, before you start mudding at all, you may want to mix the mud in the bucket by means of a mixing tool on the end of your drill. Mixed mud flows better under your knife than unmixed.

For inside corners where sheetrock panels meet, you'll see that the sheetrock tape has a fold indicator down its center. Fold the tape in half lengthwise, and mud it into place. You'll have to make two passes, one for each half of the tape or use a double-bladed mudding knife whose blades form a right angle.

For "outside" corners, where sheetrock panels on partition walls meet, you'll screw on a sheetrock *corner piece* (figure 8–9), mudding right over it and laying tape where its outer edges meet sheetrock.

For all your mudding, try your best to finish the wet mud smooth, with no tool mark. Any tool marks you leave will have to be sanded out later, after the mud dries.

For mudding over screw holes not on panel seams, put some well-worked mud on your 6-inch knife and make a pass over the screw dimple. If the dimple is deep enough (assuming your mud is going on smooth), you can cover it with one pass and just leave it. If the screw is sticking out, you either have to drive the screw in farther or build up a little mound with mud

Mudding a Sheetrock Screw

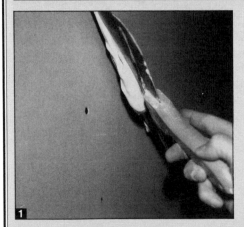

1 With sheetrock mud loaded onto your wide knife, make a downward pass over the sheetrock screw.

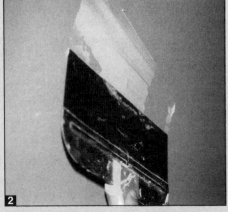

2 Coating the screw hole may require several passes. With each pass, flatten your knife to spread the mud evenly.

3 Make repeated passes to feather the sheetrock mud until the screw hole is smoothly covered.

Taping and Mudding Seams

Make a pass over the seam with a wide knife loaded with sheetrock mud. Apply a good, wide coat of wet mud.

Roll sheetrock tape over the first wet coat and follow with a wide knife loaded with wet mud. Apply firm pressure as you go and seal the tape against the wall. You may find yourself applying a third coat of mud for an absolutely smooth finish.

to cover it. (This mound *will* show up when you paint!) You may find some dimples need a second coat and sanding.

After the sheetrock mud is completely dry, sand it smooth. To sand, you have three choices. You can sand by hand with a *sanding block,* which is hard work but raises relatively little dust. You can sand with a *palm sander,* which is very fast and efficient but *very* dusty. Or, you can rub the dried mud with a damp sponge, which is a clean technique but offers a poorer finish compared to sanding.

For priming and painting, see chapter 9.

FLOORS, INTERIOR WALLS, AND TRIM

Covering the Slab

If you don't want to live on your barn's slab, you can cover it with a simple floor of pressure-treated 2x4s (called sleepers in this application) and ⁵⁄₈- or ³⁄₄-inch plywood. Over this simple floor (with the proper underlayment), you can add more elaborate covers, such as hardwood, tile, or linoleum.

Framing the understructure of this plywood decking follows the same principles we have used framing other parts of the barn, except here you *must* use pressure-treated joists because they will be in contact with the concrete and regular 2x4s would not resist the slab's moisture as effectively. In fact, you run the real risk of their rotting out. To repeat: Use pressure-treated wood for your understructure. Figure 8–3 shows a simple design, which you may want to modify. Remember, any height you add to your floor (1) needs to be compensated for in your overall design and door placement (you don't want to open an exterior door and find a 3 ¹⁄₂-inch step in front of you), and (2) reduces headroom in the first-floor living area. If you raise your floor 3 ¹⁄₂ inches, your first floor's 8-foot headroom has suddenly shrunk to 7 feet, 8 ¹⁄₂ inches. If you plan on having a floor elevated above your slab, you may want to account for its height when you are framing so that you maintain the full 8-foot ceiling height in the first floor and your doors are set at the right height.

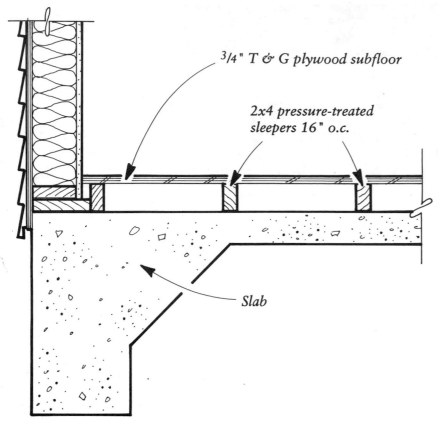

³/4" T & G plywood subfloor

2x4 pressure-treated sleepers 16" o.c.

Slab

FIGURE 8–3

A first-floor deck of ³/4-inch plywood can be installed over your slab on pressure-treated "sleepers."

WHEN PUTTING DOWN FLOORING, CUT TWO HEFTY WEDGES, OPPOSE THEM, AND NAIL ONE TEMPORARILY IN PLACE. HAMMER THE OTHER ONE SO IT SNUGS THE FLOORBOARD INTO PLACE.

If you plan on putting down a hardwood floor, check with the manufacturer to make sure that you are building your subfloor strong enough. Some wood flooring may require special joist spacing under the decking to support the floor's weight or its nailing schedule, and the same considerations may be true for any finished flooring you put on your upstairs decking—you may have to beef up the joists by adding a few or changing the on-center spacing recommended in chapter 4. One way to meet most special flooring requirements is to use 1 ¹/8-inch-thick plywood for decking and underlayment. It's expensive, but believe me, it makes for solid floors.

Tile and Linoleum

If you plan to put down tile or linoleum, you might need in advance to do these two things: First, as with hardwood flooring, you may have to fortify the floor joists beneath this section of the floor by tightening up their spacing. With the extra weight of the tile, or with a floor type like linoleum that will show up every deficiency in the underlayment beneath, you may not be

able to depend on the plywood safely spanning 24 inches. Tile, for instance, should be set on joists spaced, at most, 16 inches on center. It's a safe bet you'll have to tighten the spacing beneath linoleum as well.

Second, the underlayment beneath tile and linoleum usually requires some special attention. Don't just throw your linoleum or tile down on the ordinary CDX plywood you used to cover the joists. For linoleum, see what the manufacturer recommends, but typically you should install a second layer of plywood designed specifically as underlayment. This type of plywood is finished smooth and "plugged" so knotholes don't show where the linoleum settles. Nail the plugged plywood with 6d ring-shanked (ringlock) nails 6 inches o.c. Cover seams between the panels with *floor-patching compound* so the seams don't show through. When laying the linoleum itself, be sure to use the proper mastic or adhesive recommended by the manufacturers. Most stores that sell you the floor covering will sell you the proper adhesive.

For most types of tile (on floors or walls), the underlayment may have to be a special backer board or cement-based panel. There are a number of good products, such as Durarock®, Denshield®, and Underboard®, that will fill the bill. Using manufacturers' guidelines, match your tile (and its adhesive and grout) to the underlayment it will be set on. Be sure you take a close look at exactly what you are buying, where it is recommended for use, and how it should be set. Tile comes in a wide variety of styles and types. Be prepared to make an informed choice by knowing all you can about tile hardness, porousness, and finish. Consult the product literature. Or better yet, call manufacturers, outline your needs, and see what they recommend for tile, underlayment/backer board, adhesive, and grout.

Tiling with vinyl squares that already have the adhesive on them is an easy, economical approach to covering floors. Typically these floor tiles are for bathrooms and kitchens. To install them, you simply peel off a piece of plastic paper and lay down the tile. When you lay them, they may not seem to "take," but over the first

24 to 48 hours the mastic will really grab.

A few tips for laying these kinds of tiles: First, make sure the underlayment is clean of dust and grit. Thoroughly vacuum it. Any dust will stick to the adhesive and defeat it, similar to the way tape is defeated once it gets grit and dust on it. Also, avoid using tile cut to more than half its original width. The ratio of the tile's surface area to the amount of glue needed to hold the tile in place changes when you trim the tile. A tile two to three inches wide won't stick very well. To ensure you use tiles as large as possible, measure the floor ahead of time and divide that figure by the tile width. You may have to start each row with two $^7/_8$-size tiles to avoid ending with a $^1/_4$ tile.

Always order a few more tiles than you need. If you make a mistake (or sit on one of your tools and press it into the new tile and scuff it, as I seem to do every time I set them), peel up the tile with a flat bar and discard it. If the mastic has set, apply a little propane heat.

Scheduling

Whatever floor you put down, be sure you schedule its installation properly. You don't want to put down a hardwood floor and then start dragging sheetrock across the top of it, and you surely don't want a carpet down before you sheetrock and paint. It's best to get your floor joists and decking built, your sheetrock up and painted, your underlayment installed, and *then* bring in your flooring. After the flooring is down, trim around it with baseboards and quarter round (more on trim later).

INTERIOR PARTITION WALLS

Interior partition walls are not load bearing—they simply divide up space into rooms and hallways. Since they bear no load, they require no structural headers or diagonal bracing, though they do need single top and bottom plates. Figure 8–4 shows a simple detail that can be used for any interior walls.

Measure for the length of your interior wall and try to work in 24-inch increments if you plan on using 2x6s. If you choose to use 2x4s, fine, but frame them 16 inches on center. Note that 2x4s save money, not only in lumber, but in sheetrock; 2x6s require using $^5/_8$-inch sheetrock, while with 2x4s you can get away with using the cheaper $^3/_8$-inch stuff.

Before you build your walls, snap chalk lines inside of which the bottom plate will sit. With another wall as a reference, measure from at least two points to make sure the wall you're building is square to the existing walls.

You may find it easier to frame the interior partition walls in place. Nail the bottom plate to the plywood decking. Nail the top plate to the ceiling joists and blocking (you may have to install extra blocking so the end of the top plate breaks on blocking). Where the ceiling sheetrock butts against the top plate of the partition wall, the sheetrock should break on a ceiling joist or any other blocking you add for that purpose.

Next, install your studs between the two plates. Toenail them into your plates since you can't hammer down or up into the studs. If you want interior pass-through windows of some kind, frame for them and interior doors the same way described in chapter 4, only this time leave out the structural header.

Once the walls are in place, run your power cables and anything else you want in the wall.

If you're building the walls around a bathroom, you may want to do some simple soundproofing for privacy. You may even want to soundproof some other walls as well. One soundproofing technique is simply a matter of staggering 2x4 studs on a 2x6 plate, so that half the studs (every other one) are siding surfaces on one side of the wall, and half are siding surfaces on the other. The second technique involves running your circular saw up the center of the stud—starting about 8 inches from the bottom and ending about 8 inches from the top—to create a kerf line that frustrates noise transmittance. You can, of course, soundproof interior walls by insulating them, or insulate them in addition to doing these other things.

TIP

To lift panel material into place for nailing or screwing, make a "see-saw." Tuck one end under the panel and step on the other end with your foot.

FIGURE 8–4

Interior partition walls are often convenient passages for water pipes and electrical wiring.

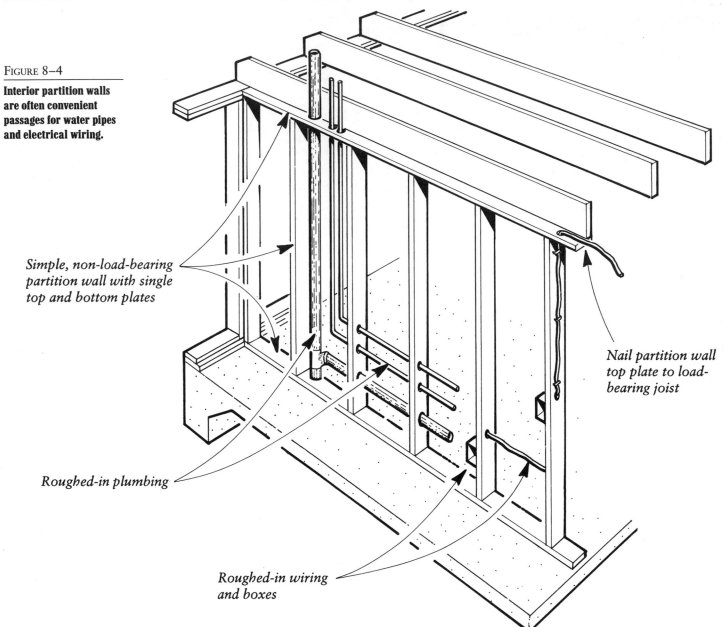

Simple, non-load-bearing partition wall with single top and bottom plates

Nail partition wall top plate to load-bearing joist

Roughed-in plumbing

Roughed-in wiring and boxes

FINISH NAILS HAMMER IN EASIER WHEN PARAFFIN LUBRICATES THEIR TIPS. DRILL OUT THE BASE OF YOUR HAMMER AND STORE PARAFFIN THERE FOR READY USE.

INTERIOR TRIM

If you have built your own windows, or salvaged windows and doors, you may end up trimming them with 1x4 pine stock. (Yes, you can use wider or narrower trim if it suits your eye.) Pine stock is a simple, inexpensive trim to work with and, painted, stained, or polyurethaned, it looks terrific.

When trimming out windows (or doors), you can either fit the trim pieces with 45-degree cuts or leave them at 90 degrees and butt them.

For baseboards, use 1x6 or 1x8 pine trim,

and once you have it nailed in place, consider trimming out the bottom of the baseboard with *quarter round* for an added touch (figure 8–5).

All trim should be cut with a hand-powered miter saw or electric chop saw to ensure clean, consistent angles. Nail trim pieces in place with finish nails, countersinking them with a nail set. If you are going to paint, fill in the countersunk holes with filler compound, then sand the compound smooth so you can't tell a nail is there after you paint. For really nice trim finishes, consider sanding the pieces before nailing them in place. And by all means, prime all trim boards before cutting and nailing them. You won't re-

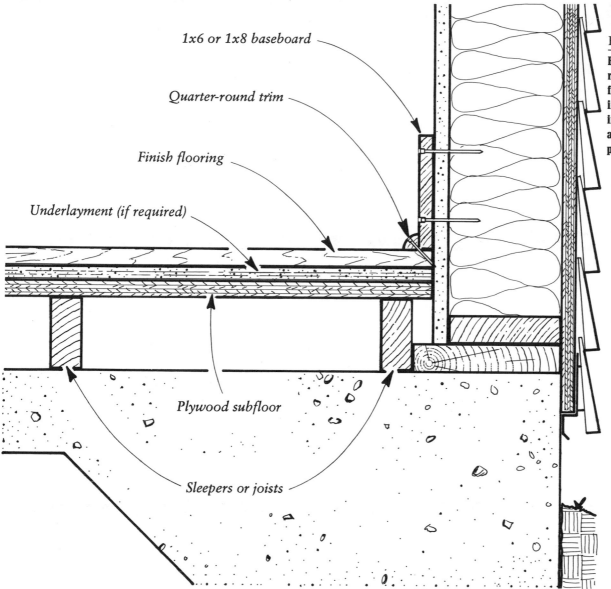

1x6 or 1x8 baseboard

Quarter-round trim

Finish flooring

Underlayment (if required)

Plywood subfloor

Sleepers or joists

FIGURE 8–5

Baseboards and quarter-round trim add a nice, finished look to any interior. They can be installed along any floor, as long as there is a proper nailing surface.

gret this timesaver, especially when your knees start to ache while you apply those coats of finish paint.

FINISHED SPACE

With your sheetrock sanded and painted, your trim in place and painted, and your tile set, you really are putting the finishing touches on your new barn. Sometimes there is a tendency to move right in and leave a few things unfinished. This is especially true if it has taken a long time to get this far. But push on through and tighten every-

thing up; buff out the little touches. It really doesn't take that much time or effort to trim out and paint your baseboards, or polyurethane your window trim with a second coat. Think of how much time it took to get this far! What's a few more days to finish out a beautiful living space?

If you've chosen the low-tech approach, you may already have your workshop or gardening center set up on the barn's main floor. Heck, you may have already used your workshop to build your first set of pine shelves or Adirondack chairs while a fellow barn builder waits for the second coat of sheetrock mud to dry.

TIP

REMOVE FINISH NAILS BY PULLING THEM *THROUGH* A BOARD. PULLING THEM OUT THE FRONT SIDE WITH A CLAW HAMMER CAN MAR THE WOOD.

INTERIOR FINISH COSTS

WORKSHEET

SHEETROCK

Sheetrock:

_____ PER-PANEL COST X _____ TOTAL PANELS = _____

Sheetrock joint compound (mud):

_____ PER-BUCKET COST X _____ TOTAL BUCKETS = _____

Sheetrock paper or synthetic mesh tape:

_____ PER-ROLL COST X _____ TOTAL ROLLS = _____

Sheetrock corner pieces:

_____ PER-FOOT COST X _____ TOTAL FEET = _____

Sheetrock screws:

_____ PER-LB. COST X _____ TOTAL LBS. = _____

Extra utility-knife blades:

_____ PER-BOX COST X _____ TOTAL BOXES = _____

BARN BOARD OPTION

Barn board interior:

_____ PER-FOOT COST X _____ TOTAL FEET = _____

Barn board nails:

_____ PER-LB. COST X _____ TOTAL LBS. = _____

Strapping or blocking:

_____ PER-FOOT COST X _____ TOTAL FEET = _____

INSULATION

Insulation:

_____ PER-BATT COST X _____ TOTAL BATTS = _____

Staples:

_____ PER-BOX COST X _____ TOTAL BOXES = _____

Vapor barrier (6-mil poly):

_____ PER-ROLL COST X _____ TOTAL ROLLS = _____

ABOVE-SLAB FLOORING

Pressure-treated joists (sleepers):

_____ PER-FOOT COST X _____ TOTAL FEET = _____

Plywood decking:

_____ PER-PANEL COST X _____ TOTAL PANELS = _____

Special underlayment:

_____ PER-PANEL COST X _____ TOTAL PANELS = _____

Finished flooring:

_____ PER-SQ. FT. COST X _____ TOTAL SQ. FEET = _____

NOTES:

WORKSHEET
INTERIOR FINISH COSTS

INTERIOR PARTITION WALLS

Studs and plates (2x6s or 2x4s):
_____ PER-FOOT COST X _____ TOTAL FEET = _____

Extra blocking:
_____ PER-FOOT COST X _____ TOTAL FEET = _____

TRIM

Baseboard trim (1x6 or 1x8):
_____ PER-FOOT COST X _____ TOTAL FEET = _____

Quarter-round trim:
_____ PER-FOOT COST X _____ TOTAL FEET = _____

Window and door trim (1x4):
_____ PER-FOOT COST X _____ TOTAL FEET = _____

Finished nails:
_____ PER-LB. COST X _____ TOTAL LBS. = _____

TILE

Tile squares:
_____ PER-BOX COST X _____ TOTAL BOXES = _____

Adhesive:
_____ PER-BUCKET COST X _____ TOTAL BUCKETS = _____

Grout:
_____ PER-BUCKET COST X _____ TOTAL BUCKETS = _____

Tile spacers:
_____ PER-BOX COST X _____ TOTAL BOXES = _____

Special underlayment:
_____ PER-PANEL COST X _____ TOTAL PANELS = _____

SHEET FLOOR COVERING

Linoleum or floor covering:
_____ PER-SHEET COST X _____ TOTAL SHEETS = _____

Special underlayment:
_____ PER-PANEL COST X _____ TOTAL PANELS = _____

Adhesive:
_____ PER-BUCKET COST X _____ TOTAL BUCKETS = _____

Seam-patching compound:
_____ PER-BUCKET COST X _____ TOTAL BUCKETS = _____

NOTES:

TIP

IF YOU DON'T HAVE THE PROPER-SIZE DRILL BIT TO PREDRILL HOLES FOR YOUR FINISH NAILS, CUT THE HEAD OFF A FINISH NAIL AND USE IT FOR THE DRILL BIT.

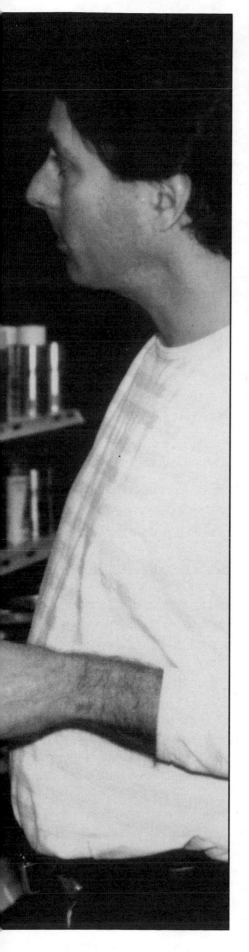

9
Painting, Staining, and Landscaping

W hether your barn's exterior siding is rough-sawn barn boards, clapboards, or plywood panels, it's essential to seal and preserve it with some kind of protective coating, either paint, stain, or oil. In this chapter, we'll look at the choices you have for protective coatings and how best to apply them. We'll cover some time-saving tips and trade secrets, and we'll learn how to properly prepare salvaged windows. First, let's discuss protective coatings.

WHAT ARE THE CHOICES?

You have three basic choices when it comes to applying a protective coat. You can paint the barn with an oil or latex paint on top of a primer. You can stain it with an oil stain (called *solid stain*). Or you can brush on a clear oil, such as linseed oil.

When choosing a paint or stain for your barn, ask the sales rep to help match your needs to a product's performance.

Paint

This popular, traditional coating looks great, comes in a wide range of colors, and is easy to obtain. Its drawback: maintenance, especially in cold weather climates. You really can't expect exterior paint (primer coat and finish coat) to last more than seven years before you are out there getting ready to put on another coat.

My advice? Only apply paint if you are trying to match the color and look of the barn with a nearby painted house, or if you love the hard work of scraping and sanding, because that's what you'll be doing in a few years when the first coat of paint wears out.

Prepping for paint.

Those of you painting clapboards may be asking, "Should I sand before painting?" The answer is, you can, but believe it or not, sanding may shorten the life of the paint. Paint adheres better to rough wood (there's more irregular surface area). If you apply paint to a very smooth, sanded surface, there's less for it to adhere to, so it may not last as long. But if you want to sand to get that really finished look, be my guest—it can make clapboards look spectacular. The best technique is to first apply the primer coat, which raises the wood texture. Then run a palm sander over the clapboard with some medium grade sandpaper. Then apply your finish coat. If you really want to go for a primo look, apply a second finish coat and sand between finished coats. (By the way, for interior trim painting, this *primer-coat, then-sand, then-finish-coat, then-sand, then-second- finish-coat* technique makes wood look great, and with no weather to tax the paint, you get more life out of the good looks!)

Should you use latex or oil? Oil-based paints will be harder and harder to find in the coming years, because many states are outlawing *VOC*, the solvent in the paint. *VOC* stands for *volatile organic compound*. Why ban them? The production of VOCs is environmentally harmful, their fumes are harmful to everyone, and their disposal presents a real problem for landfills everywhere. If you can find oil-based paint—primer and/or finish coat—it's the best thing to apply to your barn. Do your part, though, by not disposing of leftover paint improperly. And never pour extra paint down a drain or onto the ground.

If you can't get oil-based paint, latex will do just fine. The reason people prefer oil-based paint is because the VOC is a better solvent for penetrating the wood. Since latex is water-based, it doesn't penetrate as well and can actually swell the wood. Still, latex paint will protect the barn adequately, and thousands of homes—including mine—contentedly wear it.

How much should you pay for a gallon of paint? Well, with paint, you pretty much get what you pay for. If you spend eight bucks at your discount store for a gallon of Mister Outside, caveat emptor—you'll be repainting much sooner than if you spent $28 a gallon on a good name brand like Pratt Lambert or Benjamin Moore.

Priming.

Whether you are painting clapboards, barn board, cedar shakes, or plywood panels with oil-based or latex paint, you should prime the siding first. Don't just put a finish coat of paint on top of bare wood. It won't adhere as well.

Primers are usually white in color. Here's a tip: To avoid the primer lightening your finish coat or showing through in any way, have the paint store tint your primer to the color of the finished coat. It can save you lots of repainting.

Applying the paint.

Paint of the same color (yes, even factory mixed) can vary in tint from can to can. This is especially true for cans that are individually mixed at your local store with custom color. To make sure you have consistent color, *box* your paint. That is, before you start, get two 5-gallon, *very clean* sheetrock mud buckets and pour all the paint you are going to use into the buckets. Then pour the paint back and forth from bucket to bucket. Stir the paint well (a bare wire coat hanger fashioned into a paint stirrer and mounted in a drill works great). Then pour paint from these buckets into the can you'll carry up

TIP

CLEATS CAN ACT AS SAW GUIDES FOR CUTTING POSTS. TEMPORARILY NAIL THEM IN PLACE TO ENSURE A LEVEL CUT.

the ladder.

Paint can be brushed, rolled, or sprayed on a wall, but I recommend that you brush it on. Brushing works the paint into the wood. Spraying or rolling the paint simply coat the wood.

Follow the application instructions on the paint can. You don't want to apply the paint if the surface temperature of the wood is too low (usually below 50 degrees Fahrenheit) or too high (over 100 degrees). You also don't want to apply the paint if the surface of the wood is baking in sustained direct sunlight. The paint may dry too quickly, which not only compromises its bond to the wood but can also leave lines where brushstrokes from one section overlap dried brushstrokes from another.

Interior painting.

Painting sheetrock is simple. You prep by sanding the dried sheetrock mud, then applying an interior primer. When the primer dries, run your sander over it with light-grade sandpaper and apply a coat of finish paint. For interiors, using a roller to apply the paint is preferable (use a *medium-nap roller*; it holds more paint)—you aren't trying to work the paint into the sheetrock the way you are with wood.

Paint fumes can be a problem indoors; here's a tip for reducing them. When you *cut in* (when you paint with a paint brush all you can't get with the roller), cut in for the *entire* room before rolling. Then after the entire room is ready for rolling, roll on the paint. If you just cut in one wall, and then roll out that wall, you get the fumes from the paint you just rolled while you cut in the next wall. But if you wait and roll the room all at once, you suffer the fumes for a shorter period of time. Meanwhile, if the weather allows, keeping windows open while you paint is always sensible.

When painting trim, always sand between coats. (Let the paint dry thoroughly first!) This applies whether you're using paint or polyurethane. Sanding between coats gives a noticeably nicer finish because you are removing the burrs and whatever else the finish coats bring up in the wood.

As mentioned, for sheetrock walls sand

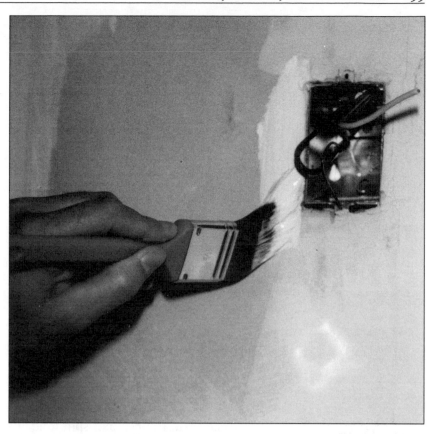

lightly between coats. Run light sandpaper over your sheetrock after you have applied your primer coat. It will take down anything you missed sanding and your second coat will be much smoother.

Budget watchers.

If you are not fussy about what color paint you use, go to your paint store and ask for *mis-mixed paint*. These are cans of paint that people had custom colored, but then returned because someone didn't like the color. (You are more likely to find mis-mixed interior paint than exterior paint.) Paint stores have these cans sitting around for the asking, and they will sell them to you very inexpensively. The paint, if fresh and not expired (check the expiration date on the top of the can), is perfectly good. If you need five gallons for your barn's siding or for the interior, gather up five gallons of mis-mixed paint. Make sure it's all the same finish and base (exterior or interior; flat, semi, or high gloss; oil or water). Then take the cans home and play mix master. Mix these paints up in sheetrock mud buckets. (You can influence the color by adding pigment, which the paint store will sell you for about $1

If you can, paint interior walls after the utilities are in place but before any finished flooring is down. Remember: "A little mud and a little paint make a carpenter what he ain't."

an ounce). See what color you get when you mix it all up (it usually tends toward light gray or light brown). If it's still too dark after adding pigment, buy a gallon of pure white and add it. Like it? No? Do you like it more knowing that you saved $15 to $20 *per can* on the cost? You do? Great....

Cleaning up.

Cleaning up with latex is easy. You hose out your brushes and use a wire brush to clean where the paint has worked its way up to the handle.

When cleaning up oil-based paint, avoid dipping your hands in paint thinner. The skin on your hands is very absorbent, and the thinner gets into your body and taxes your liver and kidneys. The best thing to do is dip your dirty brush in thinner and use a *paintbrush comb* or wire brush to remove some of the paint. With a *brush spinner,* lower your thinner-soaked dirty brush into an empty sheetrock bucket and spin it. Then, dip it in some clean thinner, and spin it again. When it is clean, stroke the bristles smooth, like feathers, before they dry.

Paint thinner can be recycled. If you leave the thinner overnight in a bucket, you will find that the solids and paints settle out of the thinner, and you can pour off clean thinner for your own reuse.

Stains.

Oil stains (called *solid stain*) are increasingly popular for good reason. They're easy to apply (they go on like water and saturate well); they come in lots of colors; they are available almost everywhere; and they protect exterior walls a lot longer than paint. Best yet, oil-stain coatings are easy to care for, because, unlike paint, you don't have to scrape and sand oil stains before you repaint years down the line. For our barn, they really are *the* choice protective covering.

You apply oil stains with a brush, just like paint, and you clean up with thinner, just as with oil-based paints.

Linseed Oil.

Linseed oil is a popular covering, especially over rough-sawn barn board. It's relatively cheap and easy to apply. Apply it to your barn and the barn will shine for a while, yet even when the oil fades, it still protects. When in doubt of its protective qualities, just put on another coat. It goes on fast. Its one major drawback: It encourages mildew. So if your barn is in shade or doesn't receive a great deal of air circulation where it's sited, you might think twice about linseed oil.

WINDOWS

Prepping Salvaged Ones

If you've salvaged windows, you may need to scrape their old paint and glaze in new window panes before you install or paint them.

The best method for removing old paint from any wood is to heat the paint with a hand-held propane torch until it bubbles, then with a paint scraper, scrape it away. For windows and doors, do this before you install them. It's a good idea to wear gloves and a carbon-activated mask when you scrape—you want to avoid touching the melted paint with your bare hands or breathing its fumes. Also, have a designated place to throw out the paint you are removing. It may contain lead, and, in any event it's bad stuff. (Consider sealing it up in an old paint can, and when your county has a household toxic-waste drop-off day, dispose of it properly.)

For removing broken glass that's locked beneath rock-hard glaze, a little torch heat on the glaze will loosen that, too.

Overheating, of course, will set the wood on fire, so start out easy and gauge how close you can get to the wood without burning it. To clean your scraper at the end of the day, heat it with the torch and scrape it clean. If paint still remains on it, sand it off.

If you decide to try this torching method to remove paint on some other project, like the clapboards of an old house, be very careful. Fire can get behind the clapboards and into the insulation without you even knowing it. It may take hours to flare up. Use extreme care.

NEED TO SET A NAIL IN A HARD-TO-REACH PLACE? LOAD THE NAIL IN THE *CLAW* OF THE HAMMER, SET THE NAIL IN PLACE, THEN TURN THE HAMMER AROUND AND DRIVE IT.

Glazing

If you have to glaze in some new panes of glass, here are a couple of tips. First, the reason glazing compound fails is that it dries out. It is manufactured to dry out slowly. Glaze that dries out too quickly is useless and must be replaced. One reason it dries out too quickly is that dry wood beneath it can suck out its solvent. To prevent

that from happening, coat the sash with primer before putting in a new pane and applying the glaze. The primer seals the wood.

The secret to good glazing itself is twofold. First, thoroughly knead the glaze (yes, barehanded; you can clean up with soap later). Work it with your hands until it is as smooth and malleable as bread dough. If it remains stiff, add a capful of thinner to the can of glaze and

Old windows can be salvaged for your barn with minimal work. A propane torch–lightly applied–and a scraper can easily remove old paint.

FIGURE 9–1

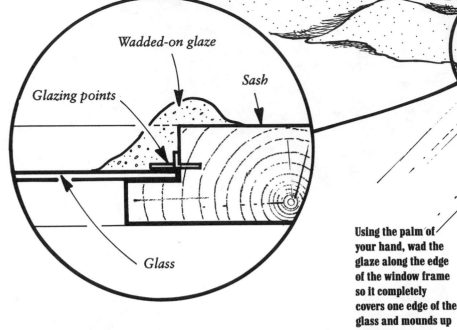

Glazing points

Wadded-on glaze

Sash

Glass

Using the palm of your hand, wad the glaze along the edge of the window frame so it completely covers one edge of the glass and mounds up onto the frame.

Knead the glaze so it is malleable and smooth, like bread dough.

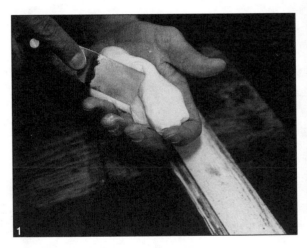

work it in with a knife.

The second secret to glazing is to apply lots of pressure with a clean glazing knife when finishing the glaze. Here's how: To apply glaze correctly, first set your glass in place with *glazing points* (triangular metal clips you press in place with your glazing knife). Be sure the glass is set snugly against the sash. Next, wad on enough glazing compound to cover the entire length of the sash section. The glaze should wad onto the glass and over the sash as far as its upper edge (figure 9–1 and photographs).

With your thumb against the corner of your knife, start in the top corner and position your knife so it forms a 45-degree angle between the glass and the sash. Press hard on the knife with the thumb of one hand and pull the knife down along the length of the sash with the other. The edge of your knife that's against the glass should cut through the glaze and leave a line along the glass. Lots of glaze will spill out beneath your knife. Let it spill as you work the knife down one length of the sash. If you find the glaze is leaving stretch marks beneath your knife, you are either not putting enough pressure on the glaze, or the glaze is too dry, or the glaze has not been worked enough.

Remove extra glaze along the glass and upper sash frame by using a ball of glaze as an eraser. Use your knife to touch up any spots that need it, but first dip the knife in thinner to melt and mold the glaze like hot butter.

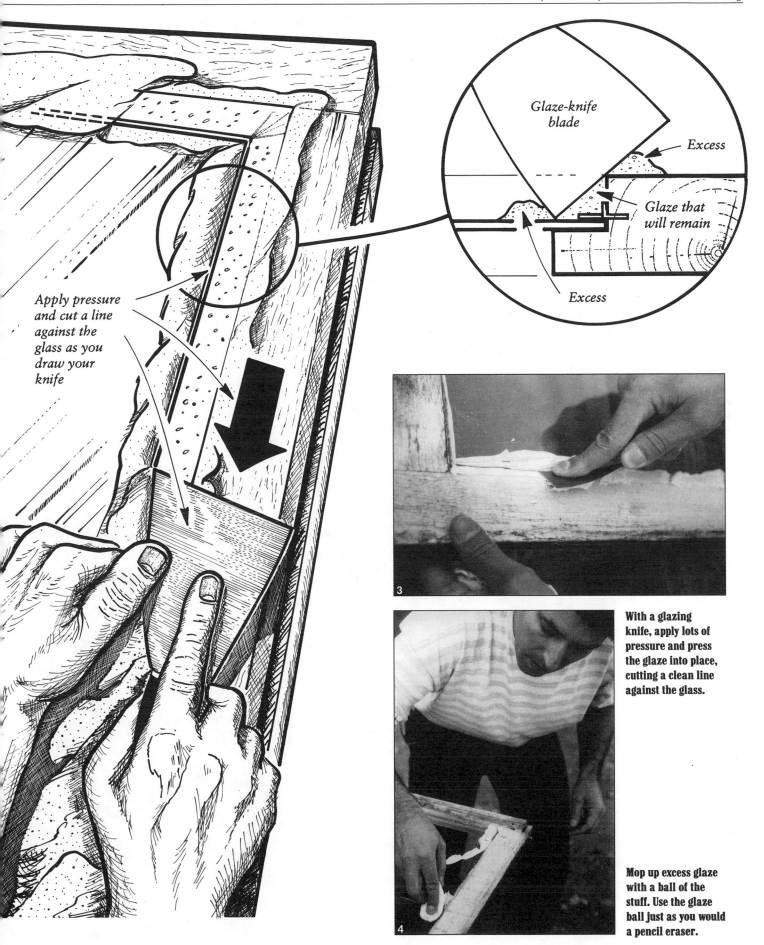

Glaze-knife blade

Excess

Glaze that will remain

Excess

Apply pressure and cut a line against the glass as you draw your knife

With a glazing knife, apply lots of pressure and press the glaze into place, cutting a clean line against the glass.

Mop up excess glaze with a ball of the stuff. Use the glaze ball just as you would a pencil eraser.

LANDSCAPING

Adding plants, shrubs, and grass around your barn not only makes it beautiful and cools it with shade, but also prevents water from splashing against the siding, minimizes erosion, and enhances the soil's ability to handle runoff.

As we saw in chapter 3 when we placed our perimeter drain, the roof is really a collector and concentrator of water (either rain or snowmelt). The water that used to fall to the ground where the barn stands now runs off the roof in concentrated amounts. Of course, the soil around the barn should taper away from the barn to carry water away. But without some vegetation nearby to protect the soil, it won't be long before you see damaging erosion.

Consult with a local nursery or landscaper to learn which plants, shrubs, and grasses are best to plant in your area. If you live in an area that doesn't receive much rainfall, you'll probably find that your municipality encourages using plants that thrive on little water.

No matter what you plant—shrubs, plants, trees—think of the consequences years down the line. You don't want to plant something that's going to grow uncontrollably and require constant trimming (like ivy). Nor do you want some plant or tree that will eventually damage your barn with a root system that upends your slab or chokes off your septic system. Instead, the object is to plant something attractive that protects your soil, protects against backsplash, doesn't cost too much or need inordinate levels of care.

Without adequate landscaping or provision for water runoff, your barn's exterior walls may become water-stained and even water-damaged.

PAINT/STAIN/OIL

Paint/stain/oil:

_____ PER-GALLON COST X _____ TOTAL GALLONS = _____

Primer (if needed):

_____ PER-GALLON COST X _____ TOTAL GALLONS = _____

Thinner:

_____ PER-GALLON COST X _____ TOTAL GALLONS = _____

MISCELLANEOUS

Sandpaper:

_____ PER-SHEET COST X _____ TOTAL SHEETS = _____

Propane:

_____ PER-TANK COST X _____ TOTAL TANKS = _____

Glaze:

_____ PER-CAN COST X _____ TOTAL CANS = _____

Glazing points:

_____ PER-BOX COST X _____ TOTAL BOXES = _____

INTERIOR PAINT

Paint:

_____ PER-GALLON COST X _____ TOTAL GALLONS = _____

Primer:

_____ PER-GALLON COST X _____ TOTAL GALLONS = _____

**Filler compound
for nail holes:**

_____ PER-QUART COST X _____ TOTAL QUARTS = _____

LANDSCAPING

Soil preparation:

_____ COST

Plants and trees:

_____ COST

Grass:

_____ COST

Other seeds:

_____ COST

Gravel or mulch:

_____ COST

NOTES:

WORKSHEET

PAINTING, STAINING, & LANDSCAPING COSTS

Resources

Here is a list of resources—periodicals, books, and trade associations—that might come in handy when you are seeking further information for building your barn.

PERIODICALS

There are two leaders in the field of hands-on, practical building magazines that supply you with drawings and clear instruction on a wide range of topics. Back issues are available from the publishers. If you are looking for something specific, call and ask for it by topic.

The Journal of Light Construction
RR2 Box 146
Richmond, VT 05477
☎ (802) 434-4747

Fine Homebuilding
The Taunton Press
63 South Main Street, Box 355
Newtown, CT 06470
☎ (203) 426-8171

BOOKS

Here is a list of good, solid reference books. I've put a check mark next to titles I consider "must haves"—books I wouldn't be without.

✔ *Advanced Framing: Techniques, Troubleshooting, and Structural Design.* Edited by John D. Wagner. Journal of Light Construction.

Bailey, Robert. *The Pocketsize Carpenter's Helper.* R.S. Wood, Box 430, Star Route 81, Liberty, ME 04949.

Byrne, Michael. *Setting Ceramic Tile.* Taunton Press.

Dries, Robert and William. *HVAC Contracting.* Craftsman.

Graff, Don. *Basic Building Data.* Van Nostrand Reinhold Company.

✔ Gross, Marshall. *Roof Framing.* Craftsman.

Hageman, Jack. *Contractor's Guide to the Building Codes.* Craftsman.

✔ Koel, Leonard. *Carpentry.* American Technical Publishers.

Koel, Leonard. *Concrete Formwork.* American Technical Publishers.

Love, T.W. *Concrete & Formwork.* Craftsman.

✔ Massey, Howard C. *Plumber's Handbook.* Craftsman.

✔ Mullin, Ray. *Electrical Wiring: Residential.*

Olin, Harold; Schmidt, John; Lewis, Walter. *Construction Principles, Materials & Methods.*

Ripka, L.V. *Plumbing: Installation and Design.* American Technical Publishers.

Schuttner, Scott. *Basic Stairbuilding.* Taunton Press.

Swenson, S. Don. *HVAC Heating, Ventilating and Air Conditioning.* American Technical Publishers.

✔ Wing, Charlie and Cole, John. *From the Ground Up.* Atlantic Little Brown.

SOURCES FOR ADDITIONAL BOOKS AND VIDEOS

There are many good books and videos on construction that I've not listed. Here are some good sources for information. Either write or call with your catalog requests, or call and ask by topic for some good book or video suggestions.

American Technical Publishers
1155 West 175th Street
Homewood, IL 60430
☎ (708) 957-1100

Builder's Booksource
1817 4th Street
Berkeley, CA 94710
☎ (510) 845-6874

Craftsman Books
6058 Corte del Cedro
P.O. Box 6500
Carlsbad, CA 92008
☎ (800) 829-8123

John Wiley and Sons
Professional Reference and Trade Group
605 Third Avenue
New York, NY 10158-0012
☎ (212) 850-6000

National Association of Home Builders Bookstore
1201 15th Street N.W.
Washington, D.C. 20005
☎ (800) 368-5242

The Taunton Press
63 South Main Street
Box 355
Newtown, CT 06470
☎ (203) 426-8171

ASSOCIATIONS

Here is a list of associations that often offer technical assistance, printed material, product information, and listings of locations that sell products or services they represent.

American Institute of Architects (AIA)
1735 New York Avenue, NW
Washington, D.C. 20006
☎ (202) 626-7300

American Institute of Steel Construction, Inc.
400 North Michigan Avenue
Chicago, IL 60611

American Institute of Timber Construction
11818 Southeast Mill Plain Boulevard, Suite 415
Vancouver, WA 98684
Thomas Williamson, Vice President, Technical Operations
☎ (800) 525-1625

American Plywood Association (APA)
P. O. Box 11700
7011 S. 19th Street
Tacoma, WA 98104
☎ (206) 565-6600

American Society of Heating, Refrigeration, and Air-Conditioning Engineers (ASHRAE)
1791 Tullie Circle, NE
Atlanta, GA 30329
☎ (404) 636-8400

American Society of Home Inspectors (ASHI)
3299 K Street, N.W.
Washington, D.C. 20007
☎ (202) 842-3096

American Wood Council
1250 Connecticut Avenue N.W., Suite 230
Washington, D.C. 20036
☎ (202) 833-1595

Architectural Woodwork Institute
2310 South Walter Reed Drive
Arlington, VA 22206
☎ (703) 671-9100

Asphalt Roofing Manufacturing Association (ARMA)
6288 Montrose Road
Rockville, MD 20852
☎ (301) 231-9050

Association of Soil and Foundation Engineers (ASFE)
8811 Colesville Road, Suite 225
Silver Springs, MD 20910
☎ (301) 565-2733

Barre Granite Association
51 Church Street
Barre, VT 05641
☎ (802) 476-4131

Cast-Iron Soil Pipe Institute
5959 Shallow Ford Road, #419
Chattanooga, TN 37421

Ceramic Tile Marketing Federation
1200 17th Street NW, Suite 400
Washington, D.C. 20036
☎ (202) 296-9200

Florida Solar Energy Center (FSEC)
300 State Road 401
Cape Canaveral, FL 32920
☎ (305) 783-0300

Hydronics Institute
P.O. Box 219
Berkeley Heights, NJ 07922
☎ (201) 464-820

Mineral Insulation Manufacturers Association (MIMA)
1420 King Street, Suite 410
Alexandria, VA 22314
☎ (703) 684-0084

National Association of Garage Door Manufacturers
655 Irving Park Road, Suite 201
Chicago, IL 60613
☎ (312) 525-2644

National Association of Plumbing, Heating and Cooling Contractors
180 S. Washington Street
P.O. Box 6808
Falls Church, VA 22046
☎ (703) 237-8100

National Center for Appropriate Technology
P.O. Box 3838
Butte, MT 59702
☎ (406) 494-4572, (800) 428-2525
(800) 428-1718 (Montana only)

National Greenhouse Manufacturing Association
8200 Greensboro Drive, #302
McLean, VA 22101
☎ (703) 442-4890

National Hardwood Lumber Association
P.O. Box 34518
Memphis, TN 38184
☎ (901) 377-1818

National Institute of Building Sciences
1015 Fifteenth Street NW
Washington, D.C. 20005

National Paint & Coatings Association
1500 Rhode Island Avenue, NW
Washington, D.C. 20005
☎ (202) 462-6272

National Particleboard Association
18928 Premier Court
Gaithersburg, MD 20879
☎ (301) 670-0604

National Wood Flooring Association
11046 Manchester Road
St. Louis, MO 63122
☎ (800) 422-4556

Occupational Safety and Health Administation (OSHA)
United States Department of Labor
200 Constitution Avenue NW
Washington, D.C. 20210
☎ (202) 523-6091

Plastic Pipe & Fittings Institute
800 Roosevelt Road, Building C, Suite 20
Glen Ellyn, IL 60137
☎ (312) 858-6540

Portland Cement Association (PCA)
5420 Old Orchard Road
Skokie, IL 60077
☎ (312) 965-7500

Red Cedar & Handsplit Shake Bureau
515 116th Avenue NE, Suite 275
Bellevue, WA 98004
☎ (206) 453-1323

Solar Energy Industries Association
1730 N. Lynn Street, Suite 610
Arlington, VA 22209
☎ (703) 524-6100

Southface Energy Institute
P.O. Box 5506
Atlanta, GA 30307
Dennis Creech, Executive Director
☎ (404) 525-7657

Timber Framers Guild of North America
P. O. Box 1046
Keene, NH 03431

Underwriters' Laboratories (UL)
333 Pfingsten Road
Northbrook, IL 60062
☎ (312) 272-8800

USDA Forest Products Laboratory
1 Gifford Pinchot Drive
Madison, WI 53705
☎ (608) 231-9200

Vinyl Siding Institute
Vinyl Window and Door Institute
355 Lexington Avenue
New York, NY 10017
☎ (212) 503-0600

Western Wood Products Association
Western Red Cedar Lumber Association
1500 Yeon Building
Portland, OR 97204
☎ (503) 224-3930

Wood Heating Alliance
1101 Connecticut Avenue
Washington, D.C. 23036
☎ (202) 857-1181

BUILDING CODE ORGANIZATIONS

Here is a list of the four main building code organizations. At least one of these groups likely covers the region in which you are building. Write or call them to obtain code books or general information.

Building Officials & Code Administrators International (BOCA)
4051 W. Flossmoor Road
Country Club Hills, IL 60477
☎ (708) 799-2300

Council of American Building Officials (CABO)
5203 Leesburg Pike
Falls Church, VA 22041
☎ (703) 931-4533

International Conference of Building Officials (ICBO)
5360 South Workman Mill Road
Whittier, CA 90601
☎ (310) 699-0541

Southern Building Code Congress International (SBCCI)
900 Montclair Road
Birmingham, AL 35213
☎ (205) 591-1853

Notes

Fasteners

Shown here are a variety of fasteners and fastening techniques you will likely use in constructing your barn.

Frequently-used nail sizes

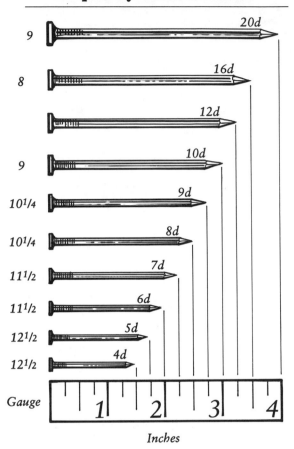

Gauge		
9	20d	
8	16d	
	12d	
9	10d	
10¼	9d	
10¼	8d	
11½	7d	
11½	6d	
12½	5d	
12½	4d	

Inches

Types of nails

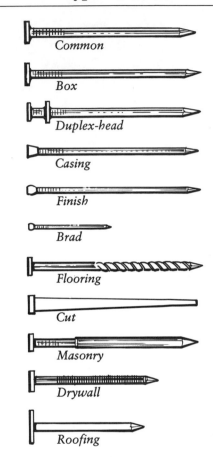

Common

Box

Duplex-head

Casing

Finish

Brad

Flooring

Cut

Masonry

Drywall

Roofing

Nailing techniques

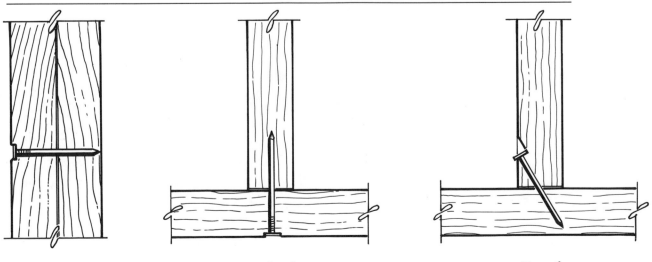

Face nail   *End nail*   *Toenail*

Types of screws

Flathead (slotted or phillips)

Roundhead (slotted or phillips)

Drywall

Self-tapping screw *Self-tapping screw with gasket*

Types of bolts

J-bolt

Lag

Roundhead

Carriage

Screw expansion

Anchor

Types of staples

Heavy-duty *Medium-duty* *Electrical*

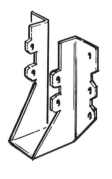 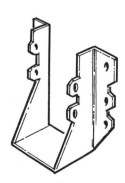

Joist hangers

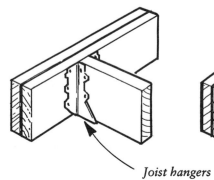 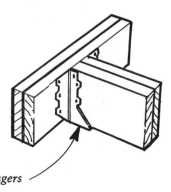

Joist hangers

Index

• *Italicized page numbers indicate supporting illustrations*

• Italicized page numbers indicate supporting illustrations

• *Italicized page numbers indicate supporting illustrations*

• *Italicized page numbers indicate supporting illustrations*

More good books from
WILLIAMSON PUBLISHING

To order additional copies of **BUILDING A MULTI-USE BARN,** please enclose $14.95 per copy plus $2.50 for shipping and handling. Follow "To Order" instructions on the last page. Thank you.

PRACTICAL POLE BUILDING CONSTRUCTION
by Leigh Seddon

Saves money, time, labor; no excavation. Complete how-to-build information with original architectural plans and specs for small barn, horse barn, shed, animal shelter, cabins and more.
176 pages, 8 ½ x 11, over 100 architectural renderings, tables
Quality paperback, $10.95

BUILDING FENCES OF WOOD, STONE, METAL & PLANTS
by John Vivian

Complete how-to on wood fence, stone fence, block, brick and mud fence, living fence and hedgerows, primitive fence, wire livestock fence, electric barrier fence, and classic horse fence. Next best thing to having a teacher by your side!
224 pages, 8 ½ x 11, hundreds of drawings, photos, tables, charts
Quality paperback, $13.95

THE SHEEP RAISER'S MANUAL
by William Kruesi

With a unique approach, William Kruesi takes you one step further than the basics with an in-depth look at business management practices so that your flock can be profitable as well as productive. Presents all the options to make a practical pasture management choice regardless of the size of the operation.
288 pages, 6 x 9, illustrations, photos, charts, tables
Quality paperback, $13.95

RAISING PIGS SUCCESSFULLY
by Kathy and Bob Kellogg

This book is written for the small, hobby hog farmer who strives for self-sufficiency. Everything you need to know for the perfect low-cost, low-work pig raising operation. Choosing piglets, to housing, feeds, care, breeding, slaughtering, packaging, and even cooking your own grown pork.
192 pages, 6 x 9, illustrations and photographs
Quality paperback, $9.95

RAISING POULTRY SUCCESSFULLY

by Will Graves

An expert small-scale farmer, Will Graves shows how to have quality meat and/or quality eggs in the most cost-efficient and time-efficient manner possible. Loads of information on incubation andrearing chicks, keeping a flock healthy, housing, watering, fencing, and much more.
192 pages, 6 x 9, illustrations and photographs
Quality paperback, $9.95

RAISING RABBITS SUCCESSFULLY

by Bob Bennett

Written by one of the foremost rabbit authorities, this book is ideal for the beginning rabbit raiser. Considerable information on raising for food, fun, shows, and profit.
192 pages, 6 x 9, illustrations and photographs
Quality paperback, $9.95

RAISING MILK GOATS SUCCESSFULLY

by Gail Luttman

Gail Luttman, an experienced writer as well as an expert in the field of milk goats, has written the leading book on this popular subject. All you need to know on selecting milk goats, feeding, housing and equipment, milk and cheese, breeding, and health care.
176 pages, 6 x 9, illustrations and charts
Quality paperback, $9.95

KEEPING BEES

by John Vivian

Whether you are an experienced beekeeper or just plain curious about these fascinating creatures, beekeepers and readers agree that this manual should be on every beekeeper's bookshelf. Noted homesteader John Vivian packs his book with everything the beekeeper needs to know. Plenty of how-to including building your own hives, stands, and feeders.
240 pages, 6 x 9, illustrations and photographs
Quality paperback, $10.95

HOME TANNING & LEATHERCRAFT SIMPLIFIED

by Kathy Kellogg

Leather was man's first clothing material and can still be used to create beautiful, useful garments, footwear, and crafts. Kathy Kellogg explains the easier, faster, less expensive, new home tanning methods for the beginner. Also covers more traditional, labor-intensive tanning methods.
192 pages, 6 x 9, illustrations and photographs
Quality paperback, $9.95

COUNTRY SUPPERS From Uphill Farm
by Carol Lowe-Clay

Gather around the kitchen table, the fireplace, or your favorite picnic spot and enjoy the simple pleasures of the evening meal. With Carol Lowe-Clay's newest collection of country recipes, you'll experience authentic farmhouse cooking that will nourish the body and the spirit. For years, the welcoming aromas of wholesome suppers and pungent, spiced cobblers and pies filled the kitchen at Uphill Farm. Now you can enjoy the warmth and flavors of these exceptionally delicious foods.
160 pages, 8 x 10, illustrations and photographs
Quality paperback, $10.95

SUMMER IN A JAR: Making Pickles, Jams & More
by Andrea Chesman

Here are tantalizing condiments made in quantities as small as a single quart or even a single pint. Pickles, relishes, chutneys, plus low-sugar jams, jellies, and marmalades that taste like summer-fresh fruit...not like sugar. Includes canning basics and helpful hints.
160 pages, 8 1/4 x 7 1/4, illustrations
Quality paperback, $8.95

THE BROWN BAG COOKBOOK: Nutritious Portable Lunches for Kids and Grown-Ups
by Sara Sloan

Now in its ninth printing this popular book has more than 1,000 brown bag lunch ideas with 150 recipes for simple, quick, nutritious lunches that kids will love. Breakfast ideas, too! The more people care what they eat, the more popular this book becomes.
192 pages, 8 1/4 x 7 1/4, illustrations
Quality paperback, $9.95

GOLDE'S HOMEMADE COOKIES
by Golde Soloway

Over 50,000 copies of this marvelous cookbook have been sold. Now it's in its second edition with 135 of the most delicious cookie recipes imaginable. *Publishers Weekly* says, "Cookies are her chosen realm and how sweet a world it is to visit." You're sure to agree!
176 pages, 8 1/4 x 7 1/4, illustrations
Quality paperback, $8.95